Raising an Empire

 Other titles on Latin America available from the
University of New Mexico Press:

Independence in Spanish America: Civil Wars, Revolutions,
and Underdevelopment (revised edition)
—Jay Kinsbruner

Heroes on Horseback: A Life and Times of the Last Gaucho Caudillos
—John Charles Chasteen

The Life and Death of Carolina Maria de Jesus
—Robert M. Levine and José Carlos Sebe Bom Meihy

¡Que vivan los tamales! Food and the Making of Mexican Identity
—Jeffrey M. Pilcher

The Faces of Honor: Sex, Shame, and Violence in Colonial Latin America
—Edited by Lyman L. Johnson and Sonya Lipsett-Rivera

The Century of U.S. Capitalism in Latin America
—Thomas F. O'Brien

Tangled Destinies: Latin America and the United States
—Don Coerver and Linda Hall

Everyday Life and Politics in Nineteenth Century Mexico: Men, Women, and War
—Mark Wasserman

Lives of the Bigamists: Marriage, Family, and Community in Colonial Mexico
—Richard Boyer

Andean Worlds: Indigenous History, Culture,
and Consciousness Under Spanish Rule, 1532–1825
—Kenneth J. Andrien

The Mexican Revolution, 1910–1940
—Michael J. Gonzales

Quito 1599: City and Colony in Transition
—Kris Lane

Argentina on the Couch: Psychiatry, State, and Society, 1880 to the Present
—Edited by Mariano Plotkin

A Pest in the Land: New World Epidemics in a Global Perspective
—Suzanne Austin Alchon

The Silver King: The Remarkable Life of the Count of Regla in Colonial Mexico
—Edith Boorstein Couturier

National Rhythms, African Roots:
The Deep History of Latin American Popular Dance
—John Charles Chasteen

Series advisory editor: Lyman L. Johnson,
University of North Carolina at Charlotte

Raising an Empire

Children in Early Modern Iberia and Colonial Latin America

Edited by
ONDINA E. GONZÁLEZ
and
BIANCA PREMO

University of New Mexico Press ⚜ Albuquerque

12 11 10 09 08 07   1 2 3 4 5 6 7

LIBRARY OF CONGRESS CATALOGING-IN-PUBLICATION DATA

Raising an empire : children in early modern Iberia and colonial Latin America /
[edited by] Ondina E. González and Bianca Premo.
p. cm. — (Diálogos)
Includes bibliographical references and index.
ISBN 978-0-8263-3441-1 (pbk. : alk. paper)
1. Children—Iberian Peninsula—History.
2. Children—Latin America—History.
3. Iberian Peninsula—Social conditions.
4. Portugal—Colonies—America—Social conditions.
5. Spain—Colonies—America—Social conditions.
I. González, Ondina E., 1958–
II. Premo, Bianca.
HQ792.I24R35 2007
305.230946—dc22
2007014102

DESIGN AND LAYOUT: MELISSA TANDYSH

To Susan Migden Socolow, mentor and friend

and to

Blanche Premo-Hopkins, mother and friend

❧

Contents

∾

List of Illustrations

∞

Introduction

Children of the Empire

Ondina E. González

∾

❖ URSULA SUÁREZ DE ESCOBAR, BORN INTO AN ELITE FAMILY IN COLONIAL Santiago, Chile, in 1666, described herself as a lazy child who was prone to sleep in late, causing her mother no end of consternation. Yet that sleep was often filled with nightmares and horrifying dreams of witches and demons. In fact, Ursula's mother became so alarmed by the frequency and ferocity of her daughter's dreams that she turned to other family members for help. More than a century later, in Seville, Spain, another mother also sought help for her child. María González's extreme poverty meant that she could not properly care for her son. The demands of her various jobs made it impossible for her to supervise and educate him. Instead of turning to family, María looked to San Telmo, an orphanage whose purpose was to train boys for maritime service in the Spanish fleet. She was sure that her son's future would be more promising if he were in the care of the orphanage rather than at home with her.

Both women—more than a century and an ocean apart—wanted what was best for their children. Both sought help from other adults when the situations they confronted were beyond their control, never questioning whether society believed children to be worthy of care, nor, for that matter, wondering what defined "childhood." Yet, as we will find in the pages that follow, the ideas that the inhabitants of early modern Iberia and colonial Latin America held about children and childhood, while varying according to time and place, did have tremendous impact on these two mothers.

It is clear that the Spanish and Portuguese who settled in the Americas wanted to reproduce their Old World ways of nurturing children. But that simply was not possible for a variety of reasons. First, child-rearing practices across the Iberian Peninsula itself were not monolithic; thus, the customs that came with the colonists were already extremely diverse. Second, the very reality of the Indies meant that whatever crossed the Atlantic did not long resemble what had left the European continent. This should come as no surprise to us, especially when we consider the racial dynamics, cultural encounters, and economic exploitations that defined life in the colonies. Third, colonialism itself altered patterns from the Old World. The act of colonizing the Americas meant that what was seemingly benign in Iberia became highly politicized in the colonies. For example, in Iberia, although race was important, it did not carry the same significance it did in the Americas. In the Indies the multitude of "races" meant that one's phenotype, comportment, and reputation largely determined one's social standing. In the end, the act of growing up or raising children in colonial Latin America involved confronting the politics of colonialism.

Who Is a Child?

When we ask ourselves, "Who is a child?" or "What is childhood?" we often think the answer is self-evident. On reflection, however, we quickly realize that there is no single correct answer. Instead we come to understand that what we might view as immutable—the definitions of children and childhood—are, in fact, rich and complex ideas that go beyond simple reductions. The textured quality of such concepts becomes all the more evident when we recognize that ideas about childhood and children are bound by culture and time, with each culture deciding when infancy ends, when adolescence begins, and when adulthood is reached.

What makes the study of children and childhood so appealing for historians is its multivalent nature. As Asunción Lavrin tells us, "The historical subject 'child' cannot be defined in and of itself. It depends upon the conceptualization that other social actors give it, until such time as the 'child's' physical development is such that it allows him [or her] to separate from the nuclear family and assume his [or her] own destiny."[1] Cultures in different places and times have provided boundaries for each life stage that, in part, help to define childhood and who is a child. For example, in the pre-Columbian Andes the first of two naming ceremonies took place at the time of an individual's first haircut, around the age of four or five.[2] Still today the Roman Catholic Church uses first confession and first communion, when a child is around seven years old, to signify that an individual has moved from infancy and early childhood to the age of moral accountability. In eighteenth-century England, embarking on the Grand Tour was often the symbol that the eldest son of an elite family was moving into manhood.[3] And in some West African cultures, a father's recognition of his infant child after an eight- or nine-day waiting period symbolized that the infant was now "regarded as part of this world."[4]

Historians, by scrutinizing the definitions of childhood and the history of children, also gain unique perspectives into the social norms of the past. For example, adults naturally absorb the prevailing definitions of childhood and the "best practices" on how to raise children. Then, more often than not, they apply those standards to their own interactions with the youngest of their society. By examining patterns of interactions between adults and children, historians can comprehend some of the fundamental assumptions upon which a society is built.

Raising an Empire takes the reader on a journey into the world of children and childhood within the early modern Portuguese and Spanish Atlantic empires, a journey where seemingly simple concepts like definitions of childhood become complex issues deeply tied to the massive colonial project in the New World. The Portuguese and Spanish conquerors and settlers of Latin America, and the officials who oversaw their ventures, assumed that their theoretical and theological concepts of children would naturally follow them wherever they transplanted the institutions needed for children's nurture, education, and care. Yet, their attempts at cultural replication failed, sometimes miserably. The very encounter of a multiplicity of cultures—the varied and vibrant ones of the pre-Columbian peoples, of Africans forcibly brought to the Americas, and of Europeans who, for the most part, came willingly—ensured that nothing would be exactly the same as it was in the metropolises.

The Study of Childhood

Although using the array of ideas surrounding children and childhood to
understand the colonial process may be new, certainly the study of children and childhood is not. There is a rich historiography that provides
the foundation for *Raising an Empire*. Much of the early work is by and/
or about Europe and North America, particularly the United States. But
although scholars of Latin America have only recently begun to study
children, they too have produced compelling and provocative works from
which many of the authors in this volume draw.

Certainly the seminal study in the history of childhood is Philippe
Ariès's *Centuries of Childhood*, first published in English in 1962. Ariès was
not, of course, the first scholar to be concerned with children. Historians
and other researchers examining geographic regions throughout the world
have long studied children as part of larger social groupings. Likewise, the
statistics that outline the basic composition of a society (for example, birth
rates, death rates, family size) are, in part, drawn from vital information
about children and have been and continue to be of interest to historians
and demographers alike. In the end, however, it is difficult to overestimate
Ariès's impact on the study of children and childhood. Simply stated, he
opened a new area for inquiry and debate and presented a new way of
viewing society.

Ariès's work represented a departure from the collection and analysis
of statistics. He examined childhood in its own right, declaring that by the
sixteenth century the concept of childhood as a distinct stage of life "had
made its appearance in the family circle," initially in the form of "cod-
dling."[5] Prior to children being the focus of the family, he argued, they
were relegated to minor roles, dressed as miniature adults, and largely
inconsequential. What Ariès believed he had found in identifying the
beginnings of the child-centered family was a marker for modernity, a
point at which attitudes—in this case toward children—shifted to what we
could call "modern."

Furthermore Ariès also argued that the concept of childhood "sprang
from a source outside the family: churchmen or gentlemen of the
robe, . . . eager to ensure disciplined, rational manners[,] . . . saw [chil-
dren] as fragile creatures of God who needed to be both safeguarded
and reformed."[6] In other words, Ariès viewed the ideas associated with
childhood as not simply confined to the family. Rather, he saw them as
part of much larger social and religious phenomena. These ideas, he

argued, shaped society as much as they were shaped by society. It is in this conviction—that ideas of childhood influenced society—that we most visibly see Ariès's imprint in this volume.

Only a few years after Ariès's work first appeared in English, other scholars elaborated on the theme of modernity through the lens of childhood. Those historians who followed in Ariès's footsteps further developed his theories and claimed that before the eighteenth century children were both physically and emotionally distant from and routinely abused by their parents. These scholars also maintained that one of the hallmarks of modernity was precisely the closing "affection" gap between adults and children.[7] They argued that by the eighteenth century offspring occupied an all important place in their parents' lives, and a new concept of the family with the child in the center became commonplace.

Other historians who disagreed with Ariès and his disciples argued for a continuity of parental affection and devotion over the ages, challenging the notion of a shift over time to a "modern" attitude toward children. Rather, Ariès's revisionists claimed, children "were loved by their parents and teachers, their nurture the highest of human vocations, their proper moral and vocational training humankind's best hope" long before the modern period.[8] For this group of historians, markers of modernity did not include changing attitudes toward children.

Search for the Children

In spite of their apparent differences, Ariès and his followers shared a common element with their revisionists: they all focused on adult attitudes toward and about children, making their studies about adults. That would begin to change in the 1990s. Increasingly, studies concerning children would be about children, not primarily adults' concepts of childhood. Historians endeavoring to write children's stories, however, faced a problem. Where could they retrieve the children's voices and lived experiences seemingly lost to time and indifference? After all, children did not often leave written sources to which historians could turn.

Occasionally the historian's search for a child subject was easy, as in the case of Ursula, the sixteenth-century upper-class girl from Santiago, Chile, mentioned at the beginning of this essay. Her religious autobiography (*vida*) is examined for this volume by Jorge Rojas Flores. The very nature of a vida, an autobiography commissioned by a confessor to ensure the religious and doctrinal purity of its author, has led many historians to discount the historical value of such work as overly imprinted with religious formula. But, as Rojas Flores proves, these autobiographies can, in fact, bring the reality of one child's life into relief, giving us that elusive glimpse into the daily experiences of a child.

Unfortunately, most individuals did not write autobiographies, spiritual or otherwise. Nor did they, like the famous Nazi victim Anne Frank, leave diaries giving details of their childhood for subsequent generations to explore. Thus, the answer to the question of where can we hear children's voices from the past is often less direct than we might want. Nevertheless, we can hear their echoes. Historians of childhood have been able to detect those most clearly in institutional sources, such as records from foundling homes, apprenticeship contracts, and Christian education manuals.

Although these sources are one step removed from the children themselves and tended to reflect an urban perspective (largely because of the absence of similar sources from a rural context), they do present us with a picture of the lived experiences of *some* children, albeit as a group rather than as individuals. Even with their inherent limitations, institutional sources revealed what past societies believed was acceptable for children and how these accepted norms had an impact on children. By combing through such documents, historians discovered a means to examine the lives of children as laborers, paupers, students, foundlings, orphans, and witnesses to or victims and perpetrators of crimes.[9] Children within the home, within religion, and even at the point of death were soon engaged by historians as well.[10]

From these studies we learned of the seemingly desperate lives of many children as well as about the hopes, expectations, and responsibilities borne by the adults who surrounded them. And, if we were very lucky with institutional records, we occasionally caught a momentary glimpse into the intimate lives of children. The manner in which apparently mundane records can generate intimate portraits of children is evidenced in the chapter by Teresa Vergara included in this volume. Among other sources, Vergara examines apprenticeship records to understand Indian youth migration in seventeenth-century Lima. She tells the story of Andrés, whose mother placed him as an apprentice to a carpenter in 1601. Andrés's contract stipulated that his master was to teach the boy the trade, provide room and board, and educate him in Catholic doctrine. As Vergara suggests, by assuring her son had ties within the Spanish community, Andrés's mother was undoubtedly trying to position her child more securely within the colonial world, where Indian communities already familiar with the advantages of social linkages took old patterns of patronage and kinship and melded them into Spanish patterns, often for the benefit of their children.

Political Implications of Rearing Children

It was precisely the amalgamation of the "Old World" and the "New World" that altered existing social realities in the Americas and created totally new practices associated with childhood. These colonial mixtures, however, were steeped in new political meanings that did not exist in either the European countries that conquered Latin America or the various indigenous cultures that predated the Iberians' arrival. In terms of child rearing and childhood itself, stages of life became more than steps in growing up. Child rearing moved beyond simple cultural replication in which adults taught children the essentials of existence in Spain or Portugal, in myriad pre-Conquest cultures of the Americas, or in various African cultures. Unlike in the mother countries, childhood experiences in the American colonies included significant encounters with others of different races. In the Iberian American colonies, child-rearing practices and childhood itself became part of the very process of creating an empire, of establishing the cultural and social boundaries of life in the Indies, as well as the racial and political domination of Europeans over others.

Additionally, what was taught to children in the colonies was crucial to the maintenance of the colonial order. As such, child-rearing practice and childhood were highly politically charged. It *mattered* how one raised children. For, as adults, these children would have to accept a world in which they were subjects of distant political powers that knew little of the realities of the colonies and focused largely on extractive policies that brought the crowns wealth. These children, most of whom would have been born in the colonies, would have to function within a public culture that proclaimed Catholicism the one true faith, yet they would be raised, for the most part, by women of indigenous and African origins who held fast to traditional religions. And these same colonial children would have to navigate a world of multiple castes, where race and social position carried an importance they did not have in the Old World.[11]

Ann Twinam's work on the juncture of race and legitimacy status in the lives of Havana's late eighteenth-century *expósitos* (abandoned children) makes the meaning of race in the Americas abundantly clear. She examines the promulgation of the Royal Pragmatic of 1794 that granted legitimate status to all expósitos in the Spanish empire. Such a decree did not pose a great threat to the upper classes in Spain where there was limited racial diversity. But in Spanish America the reaction to the Pragmatic was strong indeed. In the colonies, not surprisingly, many of the abandoned children were not white. Thus the king's pronouncement meant that expósitos also received "the racial benefit of the doubt." In the colonies, where whiteness was often equated with elevated social status, the race-conscious elite simply could not accept a decree they found so intolerable, one that would render equal children of questionable racial origins with the elite's own children. For the elite, it was imperative that their offspring understand that they would need to exert every effort to maintain social, political, and economic structures that kept them at the top tier of society. The entire existence of the colonial enterprise, from the adults' perspective, depended on children learning their lessons well.

Beyond Questions of Modernity

It is precisely work such as Twinam's that allows the study of children and childhood in colonial Latin America to move away from questions about modernity and instead focus on a different issue: what, precisely, was "colonial" in colonial society. In particular, examining themes in the history of childhood on both sides of the Atlantic permits a deeper understanding of the process of building an empire. How did growing up in the colonies differ from growing up in Iberia?

Several themes in *Raising an Empire* provide points of comparison between the Iberian Peninsula and the American colonies: child circulation (being raised away from one's natal home), abandonment, illegitimacy, labor. Valentina Tikoff studies orphanages in Seville that were established in order to educate and train fatherless children, both male and female, for their gender-specific adult roles. Recall María, the woman whose story opened this Introduction. Just as she did for her son, many Sevillian families chose to seek admittance for their offspring into the orphanages in hopes of bettering the children's prospects. These families, often too poor to provide any education to their progeny, opted to remove the children from their homes in exchange for a brighter future. But the orphanages had their say in who was accepted. In determining who could have the coveted spaces, the administration of the charity homes specified selection based on social standing—as determined by the strata of society into which one was born not by one's wealth. Only the "better" classes of children were to be admitted.

My own study of another charity institution designed to provide succor to children—this time a home for foundlings in Havana—highlights once again the politically charged nature of issues concerning children in the colonies. Much like the families in Seville who turned to the orphanages for help, parents in Havana left their children at the foundling home, choosing the possibility of a positive future for their offspring. And, just like the Sevillian homes, Cuba's foundling home limited those to whom it would offer help: admittance to Casa Joseph was race-based. In fact, the bishop who founded the home in the early eighteenth century specifically sought royal permission to limit those accepted into the foundling home to whites, a request that was granted. The bishop knew it was important that the home reflect the racial divisions present on the island if he were to have any chance of finding patrons among the island elite.

Yet, despite their similarities, a comparison of the orphanages in Seville and the foundling home in Havana shows how charitable institutions were transformed as they were transplanted in the Americas. While the goal of providing assistance to children in need was the same, the underlying presuppositions concerning who was worthy of that help was different in the colonies. In Seville, assistance was given only to the "deserving" poor, defined as those from the upper echelons of society who had fallen on hard times. In Havana, if an abandoned child was white—of any class— that child was given a home and taken for legitimate. If the child happened to be mulatto, black, mestizo, or Indian, there was no help to be found at Casa Joseph.

Certainly leaving children at foundling homes or orphanages constituted one of the many ways in which children were passed from the care of one adult to another. Child circulation—moving a child from one caregiver to another—was a commonplace reality both in Iberia and in the colonies. But did the process differ from one side of the Atlantic to the other? The contributions of Isabel dos Guimarães Sá on Portugal, Laura Selton on northern Mexico, and Elizabeth Kuznesof on Brazil reveal that not only was circulation present in the colonies as well as in the metropolis, but that it existed in both rural and urban settings and was often the result of labor needs. As Guimarães Sá tells us, children in cities might be raised outside of their natal homes for a variety of reasons: abandonment, apprenticeships, opportunity for education. She also finds that children in rural Portugal moved with the harvest of crops, much like migrant workers. And as we might expect, the children captured within such circulation tended to be males. Yet she also finds that females were removed from families largely for economic reasons: to improve a family's prospects through a daughter's marriage, to rid itself of one more mouth to feed, or to send her into domestic service.

Shelton's study reveals that in Sonora (in northern Mexico) child-custody cases often arose because there was increased demand for child labor during the early nineteenth century. The courts in the region heard arguments about the rights of parents who had left their children in the care of others and then tried to reclaim those same offspring once they reached an economically productive age. The masters and patrons who employed these children certainly did not think parents had those rights. And increasingly courts did not think so either, favoring "economic" patriarchy over "biological" patriarchy, especially as demands for labor increased during the early republic period. The judicial attitudes that privileged masters over parents, argues Shelton, reflected the advent of liberalism, yet they were filtered through the age-old process of child circulation and the need for workers that characterized the Sonora region. The efforts at cultural replication of West African traditions by Brazilian slaves that Kuznesof explores also reveal another element of the colonial process: the struggles by oppressed peoples to maintain unique cultural identities. Kuznesof suggests that in rural settings slave family units were more likely to remain intact, making it possible for parents to pass traditional cultural patterns to children, and, ultimately, making remaining "African" easier. In Iberia, the very survival of oppressed groups—namely Jews and Muslims—relied on individuals' ability to blend as seamlessly as possible into the social fabric. In contrast, the survival of the enslaved communities, particularly in rural areas, in the Indies tended to be corporate in nature and depended on each group remaining as distinct as possible from the European culture. The study of slave children not only highlights the efforts by the slaves themselves to pass along African customs to children but also brings into relief the difference between the rural and urban worlds.

Our hope in presenting these essays is to stimulate broad questions by scholars and students alike about children and childhood in the early modern Iberoamerican world. But more than that, we hope to demonstrate that our inquires about children and childhood lead us far beyond consideration of the lives of the young in a society, and even beyond the question of the advent of modern ideas about childhood, which once dominated the field. Instead, understanding childhood in the history of Spain, Portugal, and their American possessions can provide a key to understanding the entire colonial process and a means to explore the web that linked one social group to another in a complex and evolving "new world" that drew from old precedents.

So, who is a child, or what is childhood? After reading these essays, readers will encounter the ongoing challenge in forming a convincing answer. And, if in presenting these essays we reach our intended goal, readers will also see how the establishment of Iberian institutions for children fostered dynamic and often unexpected change as indigenous and African peoples, geographic isolation, and shifting economic interests in the Americas altered the cultural inheritance from Iberia. Perhaps it should be obvious that each new generation must grapple with what it receives from the one that precedes it, and that in so doing, it reproduces cultural norms as well as creates something unique. As historians of the Iberian world, our initial step then is to know these people of the past as children. In doing so, we will better understand the world they first inherited and subsequently created.

✤ NOTES ✤

1. Asunción Lavrin, "La niñez en México e Hispanoamerica: Rutas de exploración," in *La familia en le mundo iberoamericano*, ed. Pilar Gonzalbo Aizpuru and Cecilia Rabell (Mexico City: Universidad Nacional Autónoma de México, 1994), 43.

2. Manuel M. Marzal, "Andean Religion at the Time of the Conquest," in *South and Meso-American Native Spirituality: From the Cult of the Feathered Serpent to the Theology of Liberation*, ed. Gary H. Gossen (New York: The Crossroad Publishing Company, 1993), 102.

3. Michèle Cohen, "The Grand Tour: Constructing the English Gentleman in Eighteenth-Century France," *History of Education* (Great Britain) 21, no. 3 (1992): 241–57.

4. Barbara Bush, *Slave Women in Caribbean Society, 1650–1838* (Bloomington: Indiana University Press, 1990), 146.

5. Philippe Ariès, *Centuries of Childhood: A Social History of Family Life*, trans. Robert Baldick (New York: Vintage Books, 1962), 132.

6. Ibid., 132–33.

7. See, for example, Lawrence Stone, *The Family, Sex, and Marriage in England, 1500–1800* (New York: Harper and Row, 1977); or Elisabeth Badinter, *Mother Love: Myth and Reality: Motherhood in Modern Times* (New York: Macmillan, 1981); or Lloyd de Mause, ed., *The History of Childhood* (New York: Psychohistoric Press, 1974), for work that builds on Ariès's.

8. Steven Ozment, *When Father Ruled: Family Life in Reformation Europe* (Cambridge, MA: Harvard University Press, 1983), 177. For examples of work that challenge Ariès's hypotheses, see Linda A. Pollock, *Forgotten Children: Parent-Child Relations from 1500 to 1900* (Cambridge: Cambridge University Press, 1983); or Alan Macfarlane, *Marriage and Love in England: Modes of Reproduction, 1300–1840* (New York: Blackwell, 1985). For a sweeping history of children, covering five thousand years and having as a recurring theme the unchanging nature of childhood, see A. R. Colón and P. A. Colón, *A History of Children: A Socio-Cultural Survey Across Millennia* (Westport, CT: Greenwood Press, 2001).

9. See Anthony Fletcher and Stephen Hussey, eds., *Childhood in Question: Children, Parents and the State* (Manchester, England: Manchester University Press, 1999) for information, drawn largely from legal and welfare records,

on children as victims and witnesses to violence, as perpetrators of crime, and as recipients of welfare in Britain. See Hector Ricardo Cicerchia, "Minors, Gender, and the Family: The Discourses in the Court System of Traditional Buenos Aires," *The History of the Family: An International Quarterly* 2, no. 3 (1997): 331–46; and Bianca Premo, "Pena y protección: Delincuencia juvenil y minoridad legal en Lima virrenal, siglo XVIII," *Histórica* (Peru) 24, no. 11 (2000): 85–120; or Premo's *Children of the Father King: Youth, Authority, and Legal Minority in Colonial Lima* (Chapel Hill: University of North Carolina Press, 2005), for information on children of colonial Latin American and the court systems.

For a study of children and their mothers as victims of poverty, see John Henderson and Richard Wall, eds., *Poor Women and Children in the European Past* (London: Routledge, 1994). Children as laborers are examined by Isabelle Robin, "Orphans, Apprenticeships, and the World of Work: The Trinite and Saint-Esprit Hospitals in Paris in the Seventeenth Century," *History of the Family* 6, no. 3 (2001): 439–53; and by Margaret Pelling, "Apprenticeship, Health and Social Cohesion in Early Modern London," *History Workshop Journal* 37 (1994): 33–56. For information on child labor, see, for example, Jorge Rojas Flores, "Trabajo infantil en la minería: Apuntes históricos," *História* (Chile) 32 (1999): 367–441; and Horacio Gutierrez and Ida Lewkowicz, "Trabalho infantil em Minas Gerais no primeira metade do seculo XIX," *Locus: Revista de Historia* (Brazil) 5, no. 2 (1999): 9–21. Orphans and the state response to them is studied by Antoinette Fauve-Chamoux, "Beyond Adoption: Orphans and Family Strategies in Pre-industrial France," *History of the Family* 1, no. 1 (1996): 1–13; Anne E. C. McCants, *Civic Charity in a Golden Age: Orphan Care in Early Modern Amsterdam* (Urbana: University of Illinois Press, 1997); Charles Carlton, "Changing Jurisdictions in Sixteenth and Seventeenth Century England: The Relationship Between the Courts of Orphans and Chancery," *American Journal of Legal History* 18, no. 2 (1974): 124–36; and Timothy Joel Coates, "Exiles and Orphans: Forced and State-Sponsored Colonizers in the Portuguese Empire, 1550–1720" (PhD diss., University of Minnesota, 1993). Also see Kathryn Sather, "Sixteenth and Seventeenth Century Child-Rearing: A Matter of Discipline," *Journal of Social History* 22, no. 4 (1989): 735–43.

For information on the school for young Indian nobles, see W. Michael Mathes, *The America's First Academic Library: Santa Cruz de Tlatelolco* (Sacramento: California State Library Foundation, 1985). For information about schools for girls in Guatemala, see María Milagors Ciudad Suárez, "El Colegio de Doncellas: Una institución femenina para criollas, siglo XVI," *Mesoamérica* 17, no. 32 (1996): 299–314. For information about education in Mexico, see Edmundo O'Gorman, "La enseñanza primaria en la Nueva España," *Boletín del Archivo General de la Nación* 11, no. 2 (1940): 247–302; Pilar Gonzalbo Aizpuru, *Historia de la educación en la época colonial: La educación de los criollos y la vida urbana* (Mexico City: El Colegio de México, 1990); and *Historia de la educación en el mundo indígena* (Mexico City: El Colegio de México, 1990); Rosalina Ríos Zuñiga, *La educación de la colonia a la república: El Colegio de San Luis Gonzaga y el Instituto Literario de Zacatecas* (Mexico: Universidad Nacional Autónoma de México, 2002); and Silvia Arrom, *Containing the Poor: The Mexico City Poor House, 1774–1871* (Durham, NC: Duke University Press, 2000). For information particularly on education of young girls in Peru, see Luis Martín, *Daughters of the Conquistadores: Women of the Viceroyalty of Peru* (Dallas: Southern Methodist University Press, 1983); Purificación Gato Castano, "La promoción social en el alto Perú: El colegio para huérfanas de Charcas a finales del siglo XVIII," *Revista de Indias* (Spain) 48, no. 184 (1988): 735–63; and Kathryn Burns, *Colonial Habits: Convents and the Spiritual Economy of Cuzco, Peru* (Durham, NC: Duke University Press, 1999). For information on education in Cuba, see John James Clune, "Redefining the Role of Convents in Late Eighteenth-Century Havana," *Colonial Latin American Historical Review* 10, no. 1 (winter 2002): 127–45; and Angel Huerta Martínez, "El clero cubano y su participación en la enseñanza primaria (1800–1868)," *Anuario de Estudios Americanos* XLVIII (1991): 479–556. See Elizabeth Kuznesof, "The Puzzling Contradictions of Child Labor, Unemployment, and Education in Brazil," *Journal of Family History* 23, no. 3 (July 1998): 225–39, for information about Brazil. For general information on education in colonial Latin America, see Angeles Galino Carrillo, *Textos pedagógicos hispanoamericanos* (Madrid: Narces, S. A., 1974); John Tate Lanning, *Academic Culture in the Spanish Colonies* (London: Oxford University Press, 1940); and Luis Resines Llorente, *Catecismos americanos del siglo XVI*, 2 vols. (Salamanca: Junta de Castilla y León, Consejería de Cultura y Turismo, 1992).

Perhaps the best-known study on child abandonment is by John Boswell, *The Kindness of Strangers: The Abandonment of Children in Western Europe from Late Antiquity to the Renaissance* (New York: Pantheon Books, 1988). For a succinct overview of the response of Western European countries to abandonment, see David Ransel's introduction to his study of abandonment in Russia (David L. Ransel, *Mothers of Misery: Child Abandonment in Russia* [Princeton, NJ: Princeton University Press, 1988], 3–7). Other works in English that focus on Western Europe and their institutional responses to abandonment include Jean Meyer, "Illegitimates and Foundlings in Pre-industrial France," in *Bastardy and its Comparative History: Studies in the History of Illegitimacy and Marital Nonconformism in Britain, France, Germany, Sweden, North America, Jamaica, and Japan*, ed. Peter Laslett, Karla Oosterveen, and

Richard M. Smith (Cambridge, MA: Harvard University Press, 1980): 249–63; Rachel Fuchs, *Abandoned Children: Foundlings and Child Welfare in Nineteenth-Century France* (Albany: State University of New York Press, 1984); Joan Sherwood, *Poverty in Eighteenth-Century Spain: The Women and Children of the Inclusa* (Toronto: University of Toronto Press, 1988); Isabel dos Guimarães Sá, "The Circulation of Children in Eighteenth Century Southern Europe: The Case of the Foundling Hospital of Porto" (PhD diss., European University Institute, 1992); and Otto Ulbricht, "The Debate About Foundling Hospitals in Enlightenment Germany: Infanticide, Illegitimacy, and Infant Mortality Rates," *Central European History* XVIII, nos. 3/4 (September/December 1985): 211–56. Some works on Spain place foundling homes within the context of social welfare. See, for example, Linda Martz, *Poverty and Welfare in Habsburg Spain: The Example of Toledo* (Cambridge: Cambridge University Press, 1983), especially pages 224–36, or Alberto Marcos Martín, *Economía, sociedad, pobreza en Castilla: Palencia, 1500–1814* (Palencia: Diputación Provincial, 1985).

Certainly a parallel area of study to that of abandonment is the work on illegitimacy. Rates of illegitimacy and the consequences of illegitimate birth have been the focus of many Latin American historians. Among such works are those of Guiomar Duenas-Vargas (for example, *Los hijos del pecado: Ilegitimidad y vida familiar en la Santa Fe de Bogotá colonial* [Bogotá: Editorial Universidad Nacional, 1997]); Pilar Gonzalbo Aizpuru (for example, "La familia novohispana y la ruptura de los modelos," *Colonial Latin American Review* 9, no. 1 [June 2000]: 7–19); Elizabeth Kuznesof (for example, "Who Were the Families of 'Natural' Children in Nineteenth-Century Rio de Janeiro, Brazil? A Comparison of Baptismal and Census Records," *History of the Family* 2, no. 2 [1997]: 171–82); Linda Lewin (for example, *Surprise Heirs* [Stanford: Stanford University Press, 2003]); María Emma Mannarelli (for example, *Pecados públicos: La ilegitimidad en Lima, siglo XVII* [Lima: Ediciones Flora Tristán, 1993]), and Ann Twinam (for example, *Public Lives, Private Secrets: Gender, Honor, Sexuality, and Illegitimacy in Colonial Spanish America* [Stanford: Stanford University Press, 1999]).

For responses to abandoned children in Mexico, see José Luis Aranda Romero and Agustín Grajales Porras, "Niños expósitos de la parroquia del Sagrario de la ciudad de Puebla, México, a mediados del siglo XVIII," *Anuario del Instituto de Esudios Histórico-sociales* VI (1991): 171–80; Felipe Arturo Avila Espinosa, "Los niños abandonados de la Casa de Niños Expósitos de la ciudad de México: 1767–1821," in *La familia en el mundo iberoamerican*, ed. Pilar Gonzalbo Aizpuru and Cecilia Rablee (Mexico City: Instituto de Investigaciones Sociales, 1994), 265–310; Sara Bialostosky de Chazán, "Estuatuto jurídico de los niños ilegítimos, huérfanos y abandonados desde el México prehispánico hasta el siglo XX," *Revista de la Facultad de Derecho de México* 23, nos. 91–92 (1973): 313–45; and Elsa Malvido, "El abandono de los hijos—una forma de control del tamaño de la familia y del trabajo indígena—Tula (1683–1730)," *Historia Mexicana* 29, no. 4 (1980): 521–61. For Chile, see René Salinas Meza, "Orphans and Family Disintegration in Chile: The Mortality of Abandoned Children, 1750–1930," *Journal of Family History* 16, no. 3 (1991): 315–29. For Peru, see Mary A. Y. Gallagher, "Aristocratic Opposition to the Establishment of a Foundling Home in Arequipa, Peru," *Studies in Eighteenth-Century Culture* 9 (1970): 45–58. For Argentina see José Luis Moreno, "El delgado hilo de la vida: Los niños expósitos de Buenos Aires, 1779–1823," *Revista de Indias* (Spain) 60, no. 220 (2000): 663–85; Vicente G. Quesada, "Fundación de la casa de niños Expósitos en Buenos Aires," *La Revista de Buenos Aires* 1 (1863): 339–49; and María Isabel Seoane, "La guarda de los huérfanos en el siglo XVIII (Aspectos de un estudio general de la institución en el actual territoria argentino)," *Anuario Histórico Jurídico Ecuatoriano* VI (1980): 407–38. For Cuba, see César A. Mena and Armando F. Cobelo, *Historia de la medicina en Cuba*, vol. 1 (Miami: Ediciones Universal, 1992); and Evaristo Zenea, *Historia de La Real Casa de Maternidad de esta ciudad, en la cual se comprende la antigua casa cuna, refiriéndose sus fundaciones, deplorable estado y felices progresos que después ha tenido hasta el presente* (Havana: D José Severino Boloña, Impresor de la Real Marina, 1838). For Brazil, see Renato Pinto Venâncio, "O abandono de crianças no Brasil antigo: Miseria, ilegitimidade e orfandade," *História* (Brazil) 14 (1995): 153–71; and "Infancia e pobreza no Rio de Janeiro, 1750–1808," *História: Questões & Debates* (Brazil) 19, no. 36 (2002): 129–59.

10. Marcia J. Bunge, ed., *The Child in Christian Thought* (Grand Rapids, MI: William B. Eerdmans Publishing, 2001) is a collection of essays on the views toward children presented in the writings of Christian church thinkers. For an examination of children in death, see Avery Gillian and Kimberley Reynolds, eds., *Representations of Childhood Death* (New York: St. Martin's Press, 2000); and Ralph Houlbrook, "Death in Childhood: The Practices of 'Good Death' in James Janeway's *A Token for Children*," in *Childhood in Question: Children, Parents and the State*, ed. Anthony Fletcher and Stephen Hussey (Manchester, England: Manchester University Press, 1999), 37–55.

11. Of course in Iberia race mattered, as is evident in the importance of *limpieza de sangre* (purity of blood), but there it was far more muted than in the Indies and did not carry the same political overtones it did in the colonies.

CHAPTER ONE

Up and Out

Children in Portugal and the Empire
(1500–1800)

Isabel dos Guimarães Sá

❧ ONE OF THE FEW REPRESENTATIONS OF CHILDREN IN PORTUGUESE
art of the sixteenth century is seen in the work of Gregório Lopes. In
his painting of Salomé presenting the head of John the Baptist to Herod
and his wife, the artist depicts four children in the foreground. Three of
the boys are colorfully dressed, and at least two of them wear daggers.
They are playing together on the floor, and one of them spins a top while
another adolescent dressed in black stands in attendance. It is likely that
this group at play depicts the prince and some of the youths with whom
he was educated and raised. The standing boy, perhaps a page, is clearly
not part of this select group.

This painting tells us a great deal about childhood and social status in
early modern Portugal. One of the first things we notice about the painting is that it reflects the "childhood" of only a select group of youths.
There are no girls playing with the boys. We also notice that most of the
boys are roughly the same age and size and therefore probably not members of the same family. Most of the boys are portrayed at play rather than
at work, indicating that they could be noble children sent to court to be

1.1. Gregório Lopes, *Apresentação da Cabeça de S. João Baptista*
(The presentation of the head of St. John the Baptist), Igreja de S. João Baptista,
Tomar (1539–41[?]). Source: Photo by José Pessoa in *Gregório Lopes*, comp.
José Alberto Seabra Carvalho (Lisbon: Círculo de Leitores, 1999), 69.

educated. The presence of the boy who is attending the table and does not belong among the prince's companions only further underscores the manner in which childhood experience might vary by social status. Yet these court children most likely also shared experiences that, broadly speaking, were similar. Like other early modern Portuguese children, they often moved among different households and into the care of adults to whom they were not related by blood. The servant as well as the noble child could leave their natal homes at young ages—the objects of what historians call "child circulation."

Child circulation took many forms. Irrespective of class or gender, children frequently were placed with wet nurses, entrusted to other households, or sent to institutions at very early ages. Boys could be shipped off to become sailors, soldiers, or missionaries to the colonies at the beginning of their adolescence; they might be apprenticed to a master artisan's household in another town; or they might be sent to boarding school. The lives of poor or marginalized children, especially foundlings, were often dark caricatures of this seemingly benign circulation system. Unless they were very lucky, foundlings would be brought up by a succession of wet nurses and passed on to several employers during their adolescence.

There were several reasons for the high prevalence of child circulation in early modern Portugal. First, there were no serious nutritional alternatives to breast milk for infants, and physical conditions or social conventions prevented many mothers from nursing their own children, so they hired other women to perform the task. In addition, family poverty often dictated that parents place their children on the labor market to ease the economic pressure experienced by the household group, or in some cases to place a child in a foundling home. If a child was to learn a work skill, this often meant he had to be professionally trained away from a parent's home, as learning a skill often required that he move into the artisan's home. Receiving an education, too, might imply migration to larger towns where boarding schools were located. Last but not least, the search for new opportunities in distant colonies in America, Africa, or Asia often started at early ages and led children to faraway lands.

In a world in which labor was not yet confined to adults and societal definitions of appropriate separation between parent and child were fairly broad, life on one's own (away from one's natal home) could start early. Social mobility or mere survival often depended on the ability to move children to foster families or to travel to other regions with better prospects for making a living. Although in early modern Portugal the experience of childhood varied according to social class and gender, children from a broad spectrum of social classes and both genders shared one common experience: they frequently grew up around adults who were not their parents. Whether the children were prosperous or poor, male or female, urban or rural, their parents or other adults responsible for them frequently chose to send them to be reared, trained, or supervised by others.

My conclusions are based, in part, on the existing state of knowledge on children and childhood in early modern Portugal, but I also hope to do more than simply review current scholarship, especially given that knowledge of the history of childhood in Portugal is still fragmentary and incomplete. Instead, I revisit old sources, examining in particular texts from the era such as iconography, the chronicles of Portuguese kings, and laws. These sources have been well used in other fields of Portuguese history, but here I examine them with the intention of studying childhood.

Before proceeding to my analysis, it may be fruitful to explore the limitations of the sources—in other words, to acknowledge what we do not or cannot know. Chronicles, synod constitutions, confraternity regulations, and canon and civil law are the kinds of historical records that historians have turned to since Ariès first pioneered this field, and these sources can teach us a great deal about the ways in which adults dealt with children in Portugal's past. Nevertheless, we must bear in mind that, with the exception of chronicles, most of this material is prescriptive in nature; these texts are normative literature that might not correspond to the actual practices of either parents or children. Although prescriptive sources abound, more intimate glimpses into children's lives are rare. Diaries detailing a specific individual's childhood years or descriptions that directly address Portuguese attitudes toward children remain difficult to find. Further complicating matters, childhood games and play, which must have occupied the thoughts if not the time of youngsters, are difficult to analyze since thus far most of what we know was gathered as part of ethnographic studies in the nineteenth and twentieth centuries.[1]

It will also be difficult to trace change over time, particularly before the eighteenth century. For a long time, Portugese laws concerning children remained relatively static, with most following the tradition of Roman law. Likewise, other sixteenth- and seventeenth-century sources pertaining to children, such as chronicles or manuals for children's education, indicate a relative level of stability that would only begin to shift in the eighteenth century, at which point we can observe undeniable change in a variety of areas. It was in this century that child abandonment rose to a massive scale, serious medical concern for children emerged, and programs for basic schooling were implemented.

Finally, within these centuries-long patterns, the civic, natal status (legitimate or illegitimate), and religious boundaries that set the parameters of childhood were fluid even while the laws or prescriptions that set these boundaries were not. I have tried to remain faithful to my sources' fluid notions of what constituted the different stages of childhood, as there is little point in tracing boundaries between phases such as infancy, childhood, adolescence, and young adulthood when no such sharp demarcations were made in everyday practice.

What can be known about childhood and what is detailed in this chapter concern two seemingly contradictory phenomena. On the one hand, we learn something expected from the printed sources of early modern Portugal: not all children were viewed in the same way or were afforded the same experiences. Indeed, the life of a child was marked by strong distinctions based on age, natal status, social class status, and gender. Thus the essay begins with an examination of the vertical hierarchies into which children were born—the "up" in the title of this essay. But focusing on hierarchies and distinctions within definitions of childhood alone would mask the common, "horizontal" experiences that many youths shared during the era. Compared to modern children, early modern Portuguese children often were raised out of their natal homes and even moved around a great deal during their early years to work, to be trained, to be schooled, or due to abandonment. Therefore, after exploring the effects of age, natal status, gender, and social class on childhood as a category and as a lived experience, the essay turns to the topics of education, child circulation, and labor—the "out" in the title.

Up: The Hierarchies of Childhood

In early modern Portugal, age and social position—most notably class and gender—together created cleavages among children. These divisions provided the structures that affected childhood experiences as well as the lives of adults. As Gregório Lopes's painting reminds us, although most children could spin tops, not all of them sat on Oriental rugs while they played.

One source for the creation of these hierarchies, and particularly for circumscribing individuals' actions according to age, was the law. From a legal point of view, children became adults in their early twenties: males at twenty-five and females at twenty. Prior to reaching adulthood, children were subject to all manner of control by the *paterfamilias*, or male head of household, who had the legal right (*patria potestad*) to constrain and punish members of his household, including children, wife, and servants. Upon reaching majority age, individuals were guaranteed a level of personal freedom that allowed them to marry without paternal consent, and, in the case of male children, to assume an administrative post or to be ordained a priest.[2] Once orphans reached adulthood, they became legally entitled to take full control of any wealth they might have inherited. But prior to gaining such liberties, an individual—still in his or her legal minority—had to go through many stages of childhood, from infancy to adolescence.

As with civil law, synod constitutions are also a rich source of information about the various stages of childhood. These written texts articulated religious legislation, such as the definition of the moments at which children could receive the sacraments and the ages at which children would be held responsible for their actions.[3] For instance, baptism was to be administered within eight days of birth. The sacrament of confirmation could take place anytime after baptism. After the Council of Trent (1545–63), however, seven was set as the age of confirmation, although some synod constitutions prescribed the age of five.[4] At seven, children were considered old enough to lie and thus could sin, and, as a result, they were deemed to be of an appropriate age to confess and perform penitence.

Adolescence was believed to begin between twelve and fourteen. By age fourteen, children were required to take the Eucharist at least once a year and were deemed capable of marrying "by words in the present," although many synod constitutions still differentiated between the age of marriage for boys and girls (ages fourteen and twelve, respectively).[5] Adolescents were also free to take vows of chastity—but not final ones— or undertake religious pilgrimages.[6] Furthermore, the Catholic Church deemed individuals who were at least fourteen years old to be of sufficient maturity to assume the responsibilities associated with godparentage.[7]

Funeral rites are also sound indicators of the boundaries between childhood and adolescence. For example, the 1639 synod constitutions of Braga, in northwestern Portugal, stated that any person could choose his or her burial site after the ages of fourteen (for boys) and twelve (for girls), without the permission of their fathers.[8] Furthermore, the manner in which religious brotherhoods (confraternities) regulated the rites surrounding the deaths of their members and families clearly indicate that there was an age-related complexity to the ritual. For instance, in some artisan guild confraternities of the city of Porto, the number of candles lit in a child's funeral increased from eight to twelve if the child was older than twelve.[9]

During the period 1500–1800 there were no significant changes in the legal ramifications of natal status (meaning whether an individual was considered legitimate or illegitimate). The label "legitimate" was reserved for the offspring of married parents or, in other words, when the father of the child was the mother's husband at the time of the birth. Illegitimacy was divided into a variety of different categories determined by the degree of sin attached to children's conception. Children could be "natural" (when their parents were legally and canonically able to marry each other but had not), or "spurious" (born of damned coitus, in other words, born to parents could not marry each other). Among the latter category of offspring were incestuous, adulterous, and sacrilegious children (children born to a parent who had a religious vocation). These latter categories were considered so heinous that only the king had the power to legitimize anyone born with such a "stain."

Although historians have still not uncovered the extent to which illegitimate children were subject to discrimination by their contemporaries in Portugal, some signs do indicate that they were held in disrepute. For example, after the Council of Trent the marital and sexual relationships of priests were more severely punished; therefore, they were less likely to acknowledge their children and did not publicly assume their paternity as had been common in the late Middle Ages.[10] Additionally, by the time of the Council of Trent there were several discriminative devices used to distinguish legitimate children from illegitimate ones. Illegitimate children could not be registered in baptismal records in the same manner as legitimate children; that is, the name of the father could not be mentioned. In situations in which the social standing of the mother required secrecy, her identity could also be withheld from the baptismal record.[11] Such discriminatory efforts did not, however, result in a decrease in the number of illegitimate births. In fact, the high volume of illegitimate births in urban northwestern Portugal indicates that it must have been an accepted fact of life for many of the country's inhabitants. In areas such as northwestern

Portugal, illegitimate births could represent between 10 and 15 percent of the total birth registers in a given parish.[12]

In addition to age and natal status, gender exerted an influence on most of the issues related to children: it dictated play and social life, education, occupation, and life expectations. Although we know little about children's play, it is likely that the popular games that anthropologists and other academics observed in the nineteenth and twentieth centuries existed well before they were cataloged.[13] In rural areas, climbing trees, picking fruit, or stealing birds' nests were common activities among boys. There also were collective games played outside of churches on Sundays and feast days in which young men also participated.

The fact that these games were practiced in the open air may have discouraged girls from taking part since social rules favored their domestic seclusion. One of the first Portuguese books dedicated to the education of children, authored by Alexandre de Gusmão, advised that girls should not leave the house after being weaned and also advised parents to keep an eye on visitors to their homes since the actions of these men might damage their daughters' honor.[14] Instead of the open-air pastimes of boys, girls' play included an array of toys and games that were gender-specific, encouraging them to imitate feminine domestic life (small kitchen tools), to mimic motherhood tasks (dolls), or to dress as a woman (flower necklaces). There were also collective games normally enjoyed exclusively by girls, such as skipping rope or playing hopscotch.[15] However, in spite of all the precautions prescribed in parental literature, we can hardly imagine that girls actually lived such highly gender-segregated childhoods, especially in rural areas, where even girls must have played outside the perimeters of houses and gardens.

Life in the royal court was highly segregated by sex, as is evident in the spatial layout of the palace, where women were kept completely separate from men. A foreign visitor to the Portuguese court remarked that men could only present themselves at the threshold of the women's apartments in which daughters of the royal family were expected to keep to the company of their mothers and sisters, as well as their very young brothers.[16] As we might assume had already occurred in the life of the young prince in our painting, there was a moment in a prince's life when he was expected to depart from the company of women. This ideally would take place anywhere from the age of twelve to sixteen when his staff and attendants would form a new household.[17] But this was an expensive undertaking, and thus the establishment of a princely house-hold often was delayed.

For a prince, the act of establishing a separate residence represented a coming of age and the possibility of exerting authority over his own servants. For a princess, the crucial moment of separation from her family was marriage, which generally meant leaving Portugal for another European court accompanied by her own set of courtiers and with her dowry.[18] Although puberty, or the onset of menstruation, was considered a clear sign that girls were ready for marriage, most of the Portuguese princesses did not marry until their late teens or early twenties.[19] For example, Isabel (1503–39) married emperor Charles V at the age of twenty-two, and Catherine of Braganza (1638–1706) married Charles II of England at twenty-three.

In the sixteenth century, royal children, especially male, lived and were brought up in the company of other children who resided in court. These boys even slept in the prince's quarters, where their social status was measured by their proximity to the prince's own bed.[20] Some of the prince's companions slept in contiguous rooms, but others slept on the prince's bedroom floor. These children were often also educated alongside the prince. By the eighteenth century, however, formal princely education seems to have been more secluded. Young Dom João III (1502–57) shared a teacher with court children other than his own brothers and sisters. Yet by 1768, an essay on the education of the heir to the throne advised the prince not to engage in conversations with servants and workers who entered in the palace and to restrict verbal contact to court gentlemen.[21]

It is worth noting that the sisters of Dom João III received their elementary education together with the heir to the throne. Much as with play, education among girls of the upper classes reflected idealized gender roles. Instruction in reading and writing for girls of high social status was generally limited to those lessons deemed necessary for a solid domestic and devotional life.[22] Nonetheless, many, especially of the highest class, learned enough reading and writing to be able to send and receive letters. In fact, it was rare to find total illiteracy among the women of the high nobility.

Most ordinary girls were taught skills associated with home management and their role as future mothers.[23] Literacy and basic counting were only minor parts of their education, and they learned to count just enough to avoid wasteful spending. No schools for lower-ranking girls existed until the second half of the eighteenth century; before then, only a minority of girls received education, and that was either at home or in Portugal's convents and *recolhimentos* (lay religious houses). Although the latter were designed for boarding orphaned girls, they admitted other girls upon payment. The paying students could attend the school either on a daily basis or as boarding students, an arrangement that was more convenient for girls living in distant rural areas.[24]

Since learning religious doctrine and maintaining a devotional life were seen as the goals of female education, most girls were taught the rudiments of reading alone, and writing was considered an unnecessary skill. The early modern Portuguese also considered imparting some manual skills to girls as essential to maintaining the household economy. These abilities included sewing and knitting, particularly for making socks. Girls were also taught some "refined" skills such as embroidery, tatting, and other crafts in order to make sophisticated textiles and objects.

Until at least the early eighteenth century, the primary purpose of literacy for the majority of children in the lower strata of Portuguese society was instruction in basic religious precepts. Most synod constitutions focused on the need to give religious education to children and make them good observant Catholics. At the end of the sixteenth century, a well-known Portuguese catechism, addressed to all parents, stated that their obligation toward their children was not only to support their physical growth but also to educate them in the love and fear of God. Although this catechism made no reference to teaching children how to read and write, becoming literate was inseparable from the teaching of religious doctrine.[25]

The first known printed alphabets were included in catechisms published in the first quarter of the sixteenth century.[26] Such catechisms, some of which included the rudiments of reading music, were designed for children who sang in the choir and who might follow an ecclesiastical career. Later, catechisms became one of the most frequent works printed for the use of missionaries. In Brazil and in the Portuguese colonies in Asia, they would be published in Portuguese as well as in local languages, and most of them were designed for children, who were viewed as the ideal subjects of indoctrination and missionary efforts.[27] It appears, however, that nonclerical teachers did not have primers or materials specifically designed to teach children to read; rather, they used manuscripts and sometimes transcriptions of judicial documents as teaching tools.[28]

Out: Schools, Circulation, and Work

The circulation of children crossed many of the hierarchical statuses of children that we have explored so far. Poverty, illegitimacy, breast-feeding, education, or work could take children away from their natal home, either temporarily or for long periods of time, and thus the practice affected individuals from a broad array of social groups. As is obvious from the discussion of the hierarchies of education in early modern Portugal, for some youths, instruction meant leaving home for the royal court or religious institutions. And, of course, many male youths went to school or entered training in crafts and trades. Boys' secondary education in *colégios*, institutions between elementary school and the university, was entrusted primarily to the Jesuits, and youths were expected to be able to read and write before they were admitted into a colégio. At the time that the Jesuits were expelled from the kingdom in 1759, they were running the University of Évora and twenty colégios dedicated to secondary studies—which required prior knowledge of reading and writing—in addition to a handful of other educational institutions. Yet the number of schools dedicated to the teaching of rudimentary academic skills totaled only twelve in the entire kingdom, which raises questions about where children were receiving their basic education.[29] The absence of information about elementary schools suggests that boys were educated at home, entrusted to freelance teachers dwelling in the cities, or instructed by priests in cathedral chapters as the use of catechisms suggests.

Ironically, it was when the Jesuits were expelled from Portugal and its colonies and the empire's inhabitants were left without teaching institutions that royal officials began to emphasize the importance of primary education. Elementary and middle-level education was reorganized under the direct supervision of the state in 1772—one of the first attempts to organize an official elementary educational system in Europe. The newly created schools taught students reading, writing, and counting, together with religious doctrine and rules of civility.[30]

As part of the post-Jesuit reforms, the state invested in the public schooling of the court aristocracy through the creation of the Colégio dos Nobres (College of the Nobility), which operated between 1766 and 1838. The school was designed to control and discipline the children of the court nobility while preparing them for their future roles in leading positions in the administration and the army. The Colégio was planned as a boarding high school for boys, admitted between the ages of seven and thirteen, who already knew how to read and write. Its curriculum included literary studies (Latin, Greek, history, languages), scientific fields (mathematics, physics, architecture), and physical development (horseback riding, fencing). Good pupils were ready to move on to the university when they finished this curriculum. The aristocracy, however, showed little interest in the college, which indicates that domestic education continued to predominate in this powerful class.

Who among the nobility went to school and where they went were influenced by birth order and inheritance practices. The oldest son inherited the title of the family and the family's main estate, which was indivisible. The practice of entailment, therefore, meant that the destiny of second-born sons was radically different from that of the main heir; usually it was the younger sons who went on to colleges or to the university.[31] The significance of birth order was even evident in the regulations of the Colégio dos Nobres, which prescribed different dress codes for first-born and second-born sons.[32]

Ultimately the Colégio dos Nobres was rather unsuccessful. The enrollment of few students (only twenty-four pupils to begin with), the low investment of the aristocracy in the college, and a chronic lack of discipline and bad management forced the state to reduce the scientific studies offered in the school to basic arithmetic and geometry. The college lingered on the verge of collapse until the 1830s, when it was absorbed into the Colégio Militar, which was the main educating facility for careers in the military.[33]

Who were the children who went to school, then, since the nobility did not seem interested in the Colégio dos Nobres, a school designed with them in mind? It is possible that the middle strata of society became the main clientele of public schools. There is also reason to believe that in some areas many boys attended colleges that had been originally founded for orphaned males. A scarcity of other schools might explain why the orphanage schools became popular and accepted nonorphaned boys on a fee-paying basis. For families living in isolated rural areas, such colleges might have been the only opportunity to give a middle-level education to their sons without having them pursue an ecclesiastical career.

Often, being educated outside of the home conferred on a child the status of *criado*, a term that literally means "brought up." Criado was applied to all children—male or female—who were either entrusted to the courts or to masters. (In fact, the term ultimately became a synonym of "servant.") The name implied that children who were criados were not simply lodged, fed, and dressed, but also received training of some sort and, in the meantime, performed various duties and tasks. For a young page at court, these duties included helping the master to mount a horse or mule, waiting on him, accompanying him on his sojourns, joining him during hunting, and other such activities. Damião de Góis, the famous humanist, and his brother Frutos grew up in the royal court. Born in the same year as the Prince João, Damião was sent to court at the age of eleven after the death of his father in 1513. There he and his brother were educated alongside the prince, much as the boys in Lopes's painting might have been.[34] The brothers continued to serve the royal court as adults, and Damião eventually wrote the chronicle of King Dom Manuel in the 1560s.

But not all criados were placed with such illustrious patrons. When Lazarillo de Tormes, one of the most important fictive characters in picaresque literature, was eight years old, his father left home after being accused of fraud and eventually died in a war. After being widowed, Lazarillo's mother moved with her son to town. There she had another son by a man who, unfortunately, proved to be a thief. As a result, he was convicted and Lazarillo's mother was punished along with her lover. At this point, the mother entrusted Lazarillo, who must have been younger than twelve, to a blind beggar. He claimed to be taking Lazarillo as a son, not as a servant.

Like Damião, Lazarillo would have occupied a precarious status in the household, which points to the ambiguity of criados. For Lazarillo, his "adoption" by the beggar began a life in which he lived with six other masters before marrying and settling in Toledo.[35] Other youths grew up as criados of peasants, and their tasks could consist of feeding domestic animals, looking after cattle, or simply joining workers in the fields. Apprenticed boys living in the cities often ran errands for adults or performed menial tasks that were deemed suitable for their age and status. Many of the criados experienced total separation from their birth homes, though not all children who were circulated lost touch with their biological families. Lazarillo never saw his mother again, but Damião stayed in touch with various relatives who also resided in court, including his brother.

Circulation could, however, start long before adolescence, even in infancy. Royal or aristocratic families could afford wet nurses who resided with them while other families often sent their children to rural areas to be breast-fed. In fact, officials in many countries throughout Europe even monitored this common practice. In France, for instance, the Bureau des Nourrices (Board of Wet Nurses) exerted control over parents and wet nurses.[36] Since there was no such agency in early modern Portugal, institutional sources are silent about wet nursing except when it comes to foundlings. In their case, information is overwhelming in hospital records, often enabling the historian to map the geography of breast-feeding, which could extend in a perimeter as far as forty miles around large cities such as Lisbon and Porto.[37]

Beyond the records of foundling hospitals, there is a wealth of information that attests to the prevalence of wet nursing throughout Portugal. Literature written in French as well as in other European languages concerning how to choose a good wet nurse was translated into Portuguese. Portuguese doctors themselves authored several texts on what to look for and what to avoid when selecting a woman to nurse one's child.[38] The widespread presence of such literature indicates that wet nursing crossed all social strata, and that children—even those from the "best" homes—routinely were raised away from their parents at least until weaning, which could take place from twelve months to two years of age.

Some children abandoned by their parents tended to experience what we might call "extreme circulation." These children were often passed from one family or household to another several times during their childhood—and probably eventually from employer to employer—until we lose track of them in the sources. Other foundlings would be cared for by a wet nurse hired by the institution; she might then continue to rear the child after weaning and might even incorporate him or her into her household after the child was no longer under the care of the foundling hospital.

It must be noted that, even in the case of foundlings, members of biological families could find ways to track down the whereabouts of circulated children and might even keep some contact with them. Occasionally, birth mothers hid the fact that they were the mothers of abandoned children and managed to get themselves hired by the foundling homes as wet nurses to their own children. In doing so, they saved themselves the public disrepute of having an illegitimate child or simply found a creative way to get paid for breast-feeding their own offspring.

Within the upper echelons of society, noble children could be entrusted to other noble households whose social ranking was even higher. Of these, the highest household was, of course, the king's court. At the beginning of the seventeenth century, an author commented that "the custom of the kings of Portugal is not only to support their criados, but to take their [the criados'] children as servants as soon as they are twelve years old." Later in the same text the author asserted that this habit of taking subsequent generations of criados from the same families was extensive among the nobility. In fact, it was considered an offense if a man ceased giving his sons to the same family in which he and his ancestors had been criados.[39] Simply stated, circulation was a device to ensure upward social mobility or social reproduction of status for the upper tiers of society. For those at the bottom, circulation of children was a matter of basic survival.

Some historians have argued that few European children were workers during the early modern period.[40] In Portugal, however, there is a great deal of evidence to suggest that children in the lower classes were put to work as soon as they were able to make a contribution, direct or indirect, to the household economy. Although not strictly wageworkers, children could tend to their younger siblings, run errands, or take care of domestic tasks, thus leaving their parents free to work outside of the house.

Although urban children most certainly worked in early modern Portugal, it appears that child workers were more commonly found in rural areas, where the obligation to perform agricultural tasks (shepherding, herding, feeding cattle, and so on) was universal among children. Sixteenth-century records attest to the presence of children and adolescents among seasonal workers. For example, records from the general hospital in Évora in southwestern Portugal reveal that young adolescents emigrated from the northwest in seasonal harvest journeys in the late sixteenth century, although it is impossible to know if children and young adolescents worked in the fields together with their parents or alone.[41]

What is more, the calendar of schooling adapted to the rhythm of agricultural work. In the minds of both educators and parents, it was clear that children should use their time outside school to participate in the family economy. Many testimonies refer to the reluctance of parents to let their children go to school because their work was required at home. Some parents also thought that literacy was useless to the future of their children, because as peasants, fishermen, or shepherds they would not need it.[42]

Until the nineteenth century, long-distance emigration began in early adolescence, and it was even common for some youths to depart for Brazil or other parts of the empire at twelve or thirteen years of age. This was the case among the first Jesuits sent to Brazil: nine orphans from Lisbon went to Bahia in 1550 with the friars. Five years later, another eighteen arrived in the colony to work with the Jesuits. These children helped the missionaries who taught Catholic doctrine; they also sang during and assisted with mass.[43] Emigration to the colonies during early age could even result in financial success: João Pais, born in Viana in northern Portugal to a family of the local nobility, was one of the many second sons for whom the Iberian practice of entailing property for first-born sons meant being left without inheritance. He went to Pernambuco, Brazil, when he was only thirteen and eventually became the owner of several sugar mills.[44] His case was not unique. Until the nineteenth century it was not uncommon for Portuguese boys to leave for Brazil at age seven, often serving as cabin boys aboard ship. Likewise, young boys also worked on ships sailing for India. Most of the young male emigrants—either to Brazil or to India—were between twelve and seventeen years of age.[45]

Within Portugal, child labor before adolescence tends to be invisible in historical sources due to its informal and nonremunerated nature. In fact, by law no wages were due before fourteen years of age for boys, and no labor contracts could be signed before that age. Yet, in the royal household, children of court nobles were listed in the king's payrolls at age twelve.[46] Child labor patterns become only slightly more visible when boys at age fourteen could be apprenticed to master craftsmen, but only for cases in which formal contracts were drawn up by notaries. While apprenticeship contracts from the region of Coimbra, for instance, represent only 1 percent of all existing notary records, they do suggest that the most common age at which boys began learning a craft was fourteen years old.[47]

The evidence that does exist for child labor, other than apprenticeship, suggests that children worked well before the age at which they would have formalized their working status or received wages. Orphans and foundlings often worked for their foster families—who were also their overseers—long before the age at which they could sign formal contracts. By law children younger than seven were not to receive wages since their upbringing was deemed sufficient payment for whatever service they might render.[48] It seems that any economically useful activity performed before adolescence was viewed as a type of *antidora* (counterdonation; that is, the reciprocation of a gift) on the part of the child, akin to a repayment for child support and upbringing.[49]

Conclusions

A review of "traditional" sources in the history of childhood for the case
of early modern Portugal reveals that children grew up in a society replete
with hierarchies based on birth status, gender, and social and economic
position. In the higher ranks of society, unequal ranking within the family
created an important divide between sons according to birth order. High-
status girls, deprived of such careers, were raised for marriage or convent
life, in either case developing the skills to survive in the feminine world.

Any history of childhood in early modern Portugal must take into
account not only the differences between childhood experiences but also
the mobility of children and the fact that few of them remained with their
birth parents from infancy to adulthood. Some were left with foster parents or charitable institutions such as foundling homes or orphanages.
Many children were given to wet nurses, and formal education often meant
boarding at schools far from home. Being entrusted to master craftsmen
implied moving from the village to the city, while working as domestic
servants conferred parental rights on the children's patrons, thus severing
legal control by parents over children. Learning to be a missionary often
meant a one-way trip at an early age to a distant land such as Portuguese
America or Asia; emigrating overseas or even enrolling in the army was a
fact of early adolescence for many male youths.

While the specific circumstances that led to child circulation may
have varied from family to family, there are some basic underlying causes.
For children from families without significant property, the struggle for
survival dominated life, which sometimes led to drastic actions on the part
of the parents. In families where there was something to inherit, sons who
were not the first to be born had to strive for a career outside the family's
home, and thus they too tended to be displaced. Circulation of children
was mainly masculine. Many girls had to wait until marriage to leave their
parents' homes. If there was not a possibility for a suitable match, these
girls entered convents. Only when the family was too poor to ensure a
daughter a dowry would she enter the labor market as a worker in the
fields or as a domestic servant.

The world of children changed gradually in the time period 1500–
1800. Not until the second half of the eighteenth century would medical scientists and government officials turn their attention to the unique
problems of childhood and adolescence. Then, an enlightened royal state,
having expelled the Jesuits from the empire, set an official public school

system in motion from the 1760s onward. Yet, even with this increased pace of change, much remained the same, particularly in education: girls continued to be instructed separately, and their education was still directed to expectations of marriage and domestic management. Children of the lower classes were seldom educated, even in fundamentals. And only religious indoctrination was considered necessary for all children, regardless of gender, social status, or wealth.

What remains clear is that children of early modern Portugal were affected by many of the same divisions that formed their parents' world, divisions caused not so much by the individuals but rather by the circumstances of their birth. Nevertheless, even while the experiences of childhood in early modern Portugal may have varied, many infants and young people performed an act that, to them, must have been commonplace—leaving home.

✦ NOTES ✦

1. The intention of the surveys of games was to record behavior that the authors very rightly perceived were at risk of disappearing. Many of them did, especially in the second half of the twentieth century with the urbanization of the country and an increase in consumer society, which resulted in toys being industrially produced rather than handcrafted. The main ethnographers associated with this tradition are Adolfo Coelho (1847–1919) and J. Leite de Vasconcellos (1858–1941). The former compiled traditional games and nursery rhymes (*Jogos e rimas infantis*, 1883) and popular tales (*Contos populares portugueses*, 1879). Vasconcellos is the compiler of *Etnografia portuguesa*, a corpus of ethnographic notes that were later organized by his students.

2. Isabel dos Guimarães Sá, "Child Abandonment in Portugal: Legislation and Institutional Care," *Continuity and Change* 9, no. 1 (1994): 72.

3. I surveyed a number of synod constitutions and list them here in chronological order in order to avoid repetition. Future references will only mention "S. C." (Synod Constitution) followed by the name of the diocese and date: Valença (1444); Braga (1477); Valença (1486); Porto (1496); Guarda (1500); Braga (1505) published in Garcia y Garcia, *Synodicon Hispanum II. Portugal*, (Madrid: Biblioteca de Autores Cristianos, 1982). Lisbon (1537): *Constituições do Arcebispado de Lixboa* (Lisbon: Germão Galharde, 1537). Porto (1541): *Cõnstituições Sinodaes do Bispado do Porto ordenadas pelo muito Reverendo e magnifico Senhor dom Baltasar Limpo bispo do dicto bispado* (Porto: Vasco Diaz Tanquo do Frexenal, 1541). Coimbra (1548): *Constituições Synodaes do Bispado de Coimbra* (Coimbra, 1548). Algarve (1554): *Constituições do Bispado do Algarve* (Lisbon: Germão Galharde, 1554). Viseu (1556): *Constituições Synodaes do Bispado de Viseu* (Coimbra: Ioam Alvares, 1556). Angra (1560): *Constituições Sinodaes do Bispado d'Angra* (Lisbon: João Blavio de Colonia, 1560). Lamego (1563): *Constituições Synodaes do Bispado de Lamego* (Coimbra: Ioam de Barreyra, 1563). Miranda (1565): *Constituições Synodaes do Bispado de Miranda* (Lisbon: em casa de Francisco Correa impressor do Cardeal Iffante, 1565). Portalegre (1589): *Constituições Sinodaes de D. Frei Amador Arrais bispo de Portalegre (1589)*, ed. Tarcisio Fernandes Alves (Portalegre: Cabido da Sé de Portalegre, 1999). Viseu (1617): *Constituições sinodaes do bispado de Viseu feitas, e ordenadas em Synodo pelo illustrissimo, e reverendíssimo Senhor Dom João Manuel* (Coimbra: Nicolau Carvalho, 1617). Braga (1639): *Constituições synodaes do Arcebispado de Braga ordenadas no anno de 1639. pelo . . . Arcebispo D. Sebastião de Matos e Noronha, e mandadas imprimir a primeira vez pelo . . . Senhor D. João de Sousa*

... (Lisbon: Oficina de Miguel Deslandes, 1697). Porto (1687): *Constituições synodaes do bispado do Porto, novamente feitas, e ordenadas pelo illustrissimo, e reverendissimo senhor Dom João de Sousa, bispo do dito bispado [?] propostas e aceitas em o synodo Diocesano que o ditto Senhor celebrou em 18 de Mayo de Anno de 1687* (Coimbra: No Real Colégio das Artes da Companhia de Jesu, 1735).

4. Among them, the synod constitutions of Lisbon (1537), Coimbra (1548), Lamego (1563), Miranda (1565), Braga (1639), and Lisbon (1640). On Trent and the age for confirmation, see Matheus Soares, *Pratica e ordem para os visitadores dos bispados* (1569; reprint, Lisbon: Jorge Rodriguez, 1602), 6.

5. The expression *por palavras de presente* was used to distinguish from the promises of marriage (*por palavras de futuro*) that could take place at age seven. The marriages of twelve- and fourteen-year-old children were a matter of some friction between the Catholic Church and the laity, especially in aristocratic families and civil law, which considered the father's consent desirable to protect the family's interests, while the church favored the complete freedom of the betrothed. See António Manuel Hespanha, "A Família," in *História de Portugal*, ed. José Mattoso, vol. 4, 275–76; and António Manuel Hespanha, "Carne de uma só carne: Para uma compreensão dos fundamentos antropológicos da família na época moderna," *Análise Social* XXVIII, nos. 123–24 (1993): 951–73.

6. Martim de Azpilcueta Navarro, *Manual de confessores e penitentes*... (Coimbra, 1552), 90–91.

7. Synod constitutions were unanimous on the age of godparents. As to court testimonies, there was no differentiation between boys and girls, who could both testify at age fourteen. See *Ordenações manuelinas*, bk. 3, tít. XLII, §15; *Ordenações filipinas*, bk. 3, tít. LVI, §6.

8. S. C., Braga (1639), 295.

9. "Estatutos da Confraria de Nossa Senhora da Silva e Compromisso dos Ofícios de Ferreiro, Serralheiro e Anzoleiro—1593" and "Estatutos da Irmandade e Confraria do Bem-aventurado Santo António e do Ofício dos Tanoeiros—1621," in Ana Ladeira Simão, *Introdução ao estudo das confrarias corporativas do Porto (Época Moderna)*, vol. 2 (master's thesis, University of Porto, 1996), 26, 95.

10. S. C., Porto (1687), 522–23.

11. S. C., Porto (1687), 36. On mothers' rights over illegitimate children, also see *Tratado de confissom, chaves 1489*, ed. José V. de Pina Martins (Lisbon: Imprensa Nacional, 1973), 233. As to lifelong discrimination, persons of illegitimate birth could not legally accede to public office, be priests, or become members of high-status confraternities. The logic behind these discriminative devices

is the same that was practiced against New Christians, people of African descent, or the children of criminals (namely, those charged with *lese-majesty*), because they all had "tainted" blood.

12. Maria Norberta Amorim, "A diversidade de comportamentos demográficos no Portugal de Antigo Regime," *População e Sociedade*, no. 3 (1997): 146–47; António Augusto Amaro das Neves, *A ilegitimidade no norte de Guimarães (séculos XVI–XVIII)* (master's thesis, Braga, Universidade do Minho, 1996), 118–24.

13. See Adolfo Coelho, *Jogos e rimas infantis* (1st ed., 1883; reprint, Lisbon: Edições Asa, 1994); António Cabral, *Jogos populares portugueses* (Porto: Editorial Domingos Barreira, 1985); Manuela Hasse and João da Silva Amado, *Jogos e brinquedos tradicionais* (Lisbon: Instituto de Apoio à Criança, 1993); and J. Leite de Vasconcellos, *Etnografia portuguesa*, vol. V (Lisbon: Imprensa Nacional, 1967), 99–107. It bears noting, however, that these works do not consider the history of games.

14. Alexandre de Gusmão, *Arte de crear bem os filhos na idade da puericia* (Lisbon: Oficina de Miguel Deslandes, 1685), 377ff.

15. J. Leite de Vasconcellos, *Etnografia portuguesa*, vol. V (Lisbon: Imprensa Nacional, 1967), 100.

16. Giuseppe Bertini, "The Marriage of Alessandro Farnese and D. Maria of Portugal in 1565: Court Life in Lisbon and Parma," in *Cultural Links Between Portugal and Italy in the Renaissance*, ed. K. J. Lowe (Oxford: Oxford University Press, 2000), 56.

17. By the age of twelve, João III's son, also named João, was taken from the company of women, and a separate household was formed for him (Andrada, *Crónica de D. João III*, 987–88, 1102).

18. Andrada, *Crónica de D. João III*, 7–8.

19. The upper nobility modeled its practices on those of the court. But the average age of marriage for common girls was very low (younger than eighteen). In addition, like women in the royal family, noble mothers did not breast-feed but entrusted their children to wet nurses. See Nuno Gonçalo Monteiro, "Seventeenth- and Eighteenth-Century Portuguese Nobilities in the European Context: A Historiographical Overview," *E-Journal of Portuguese History* 1, no. 1 (summer 2003).

20. Andrada, *Crónica de D. João III*, 1102.

21. Maria Beatriz Nizza da Silva, "A educação de um príncipe no período pombalino," *Revista de História das Ideias* IV, vol. I (1982–83): 377–83.

22. Rogério Fernandes, "Ensino elementar e suas técnicas no Portugal de quinhentos," in *A abertura do mundo. Estudos de história dos descobrimentos europeus. Em homenagem a Luís de Albuquerque*, ed. Francisco Contente Domingues and Luís Filipe Barreto, orgs., vol. I (Lisbon: Editorial Presença, 1986), 57.

23. Francisco Ribeiro Sanches, "Educação de hua menina até à idade de tomar estado, no reyno de Portugal. Escrita a meu amigo o Dr. Barbosa a Elvas (1754)," in Luís de Pina, "Plano para a educação de uma menina portuguesa no século XVIII (no II centenário da publicação do Método de Ribeiro Sanches), *Revista da Faculdade de Letras do Porto* 1 (1966): 9–50.

24. One of these institutions, the Recolhimento de Nossa Senhora da Esperança in Oporto, opened in 1734. Its statutes of 24 May 1725 document the existence of one female teacher who taught everything from religious doctrine to crafts (in J. A. Pinto Ferreira, *Recolhimento de Órfãs de Nossa Senhora da Esperança: Fundado na cidade do Porto no século XVIII* [Porto: Câmara Municipal, n.d.]).

25. D. Frei Bartolomeu dos Mártires, *Cathecismo ou doutrina christam, e practicas spirituaes* (Lisbon: António Alvarez, 1594), 67; Fernando Castelo-Branco, "Cartilhas quinhentistas para ensinar a ler," *Boletim Bibliográfico e Informativo* 14 (1971): 109–52; Rogério Fernandes, "Ensino elementar e suas técnicas no Portugal de quinhentos," in *A abertura do mundo. Estudos de história dos descobrimentos europeus. Em homenagem a Luís de Albuquerque*, org., Francisco Contente Domingues and Luís Filipe Barreto, vol. I (Lisbon: Editorial Presença, 1986), 53–67.

26. Francisco da Silva Cristóvão, "Catequese e catecismos," in *Dicionário de história religiosa de Portugal*, ed. Carlos Moreira Azevedo (Lisbon: Círculo de Leitores, 2000), 304–5.

27. See, for instance, *Cartilha em tamul e português impressa em 1554 por ordem do Rei* (Lisbon: ed. facsimile of Museu Nacional de Arqueologia e Etnologia, 1970); António de Araújo, S.J., *Catecismo brasilico da doutrina Christãa, com o ceremonial dos sacramentos, & mais actos paroquiais. Composto por Padres Doutos da Companhia de Jesus, aperfeiçoado, & dado à lus pelo padre . . . da mesma companhia. Emendado nesta segunda impressão pelo padre Bertholameu de Leam, da mesma companhia* (1st ed., 1618; reprint, Lisbon: Oficina de Miguel Deslandes, 1686); Luís Vicencio Mamiani, *Catecismo da doutrina Christãa na lingua brasilica composto pelo . . . , da Companhia de Jesus, Missionario da Provincia do Brasil* (Lisbon: Oficina de Miguel Deslandes, 1698).

28. Áurea Adão, *Estado absoluto e ensino das primeiras letras. As escolas régias (1772–1794)* (Lisbon: Fundação Calouste Gulbenkian, 1997), 227.

29. Adão, *Estado absoluto e ensino*, 20.

30. Ibid., 50–51. See also Rogério Fernandes, *Os caminhos do ABC. Sociedade portuguesa e ensino das primeiras letras* (Porto: Porto Editora, 1994), 68–76.

31. Monteiro, *O crepúsculo dos grandes*, 141–53 and 521–22. Ecclesiastic careers were an option for the second-born son, and daughters entered convents if unmarried. Only in the second half of the eighteenth century was there a decrease in the number of sons and daughters of the nobility who took holy vows. On entailment and the Portuguese aristocratic family, see Monteiro, "Seventeenth and Eighteenth-Century Portuguese."

32. *Estatutos do Collegio Real dos Nobres da Corte, e Cidade de Lisboa* (Lisbon: Oficina de Miguel Rodrigues, 1761), 11–12.

33. Rómulo de Carvalho, *História da fundação do Colégio Real dos Nobres de Lisboa, 1761–1792* (Coimbra: Atlântida, 1959).

34. On the childhood and education of the prince and his mates, see Ana Isabel Buescu, *D. João III* (Lisbon: Círculo de Leitores, 2005), 23–61, especially 48.

35. Anónimo, *Lazarillo de Tormes* (Madrid: Castalia, 1984).

36. George D. Sussman, *Selling Mothers' Milk: The Wet-Nursing Business in France, 1715–1914* (Urbana: University of Illinois Press, 1982).

37. Maria Teresa Ferreira da Costa, *O abandono e a roda—A Real Casa dos Expostos de Lisboa—1780–84* (postgraduation course monograph, Lisbon, University of Lisbon, 1998), 63; Isabel dos Guimarães Sá, *The Circulation of Children in Eighteenth-Century Southern Europe: The Case of the Foundling Hospital of Porto* (PhD diss., European University Institute, 1992), 302–13.

38. Among others, see the international best seller of self-help medicine by Madame Fouquet, originally published in Lyon in 1674, with six Portuguese editions until 1749 (*Recopilaçam de remedios escolhidos de Madame Fouquet, faceis, domesticos, experimentados, e aprovados para toda a sorte de males internos, e externos, inveterados, e dificeis de curar, para alivio dos pobres, sexta impressam augmentada* [Lisbon: Oficina de Domingos Gonsalves, 1749]); Francisco Morato Roma, *Luz da medicina, pratica racional, e methodica, guia de enfermeyros. Directorio de principiantes, e sumario de remedios para poder acodir, e remediar os achaques do corpo humano, começando no mais alto da cabeça, e descento athe o mais baixo das plantas dos pés; obra muito util, e necessaria, não só para os professores da arte de medicina, e cirurgia, mas também para todo o pay de familias; de que se poderão aproveitar pobres, e ricos na falta de medicos doutos. Composto pelo Doutor Francisco Morato Roma, medico da Camara de Sua Magestade, e do Santo Officio da Inquisição, Cavaleiro Professor da Ordem de Cristo: Acrescentado nesta ultima impressão com o tractado unico das tersans perniciozas e malignas, e compendio de varios remedios de cirurgia* (recopilado do Thesouro de Pobres, e outros autores, por Gonçalo Rodrigues de Cabreyra, Coimbra, na Oficina de Francisco de

Oliveira, Impressor da Universidade, e do Santo Oficio, Anno de 1753). This work had at least five editions between 1664 and 1753.

39. Duarte Nunes de Leão, *Descripção do reino de Portugal* (Lisbon: Jorge Rodriguez, 1610), 304–10.

40. Hugh Cunningham, "The Employment and Unemployment of Children in England c. 1680–1851," *Past and Present* 126 (1990): 115–50.

41. Arquivo Distrital de Évora, *Fundo da Misericórdia*, Hospital do Espírito Santo, books 276 and 277.

42. Joaquim Ferreira Gomes, *Para a história da educação em Portugal* (Porto: Porto Editora, 1995), 79–80.

43. *La mission jésuite du Brésil. Lettres et autres documents (1549–1570)*, ed. Jean-Claude Laborie and Anne Lima (Paris: Chandeigne, 1998), 110, 189–90, 223.

44. Evaldo Cabral de Mello, *O nome e o sangue. Uma parábola familiar no Pernambuco colonial* (Rio de Janeiro: Topbooks, 2000), 23.

45. Henrique Rodrigues, *Emigração e alfabetização. O alto minho e a miragem do Brasil* (Viana do Castelo: Governo Civil, 1995), 59–60. Francisco Contente Domingues and Inácio Guerreiro, "A vida a bordo na Carreira da Índia (século XVI)," *Revista da Universidade de Coimbra* XXXIV (1988): 201.

46. See Note 29 above.

47. Vítor Fernando da Silva Simões Alves, "Os contratos de aprendizagem e a regulamentação do artesanato em Coimbra e sua região de 1560 a 1670," *Munda* 10 (1985): 61–63; António de Oliveira, *A vida económica e social de Coimbra de 1537 a 1640*, vol. 1 (1971): 443–48. Even though the modal age for beginning an apprenticeship was fourteen, the records also reveal that some apprentices were as old as eighteen when they began learning their craft.

48. *Ordenações filipinas*, bk. IV, tít. 31, §8.

49. On the concept of antidora, see Bartolomé Clavero, *La grâce du don. Anthropologie catholique de l'économie moderne* (Paris: Albin Michel, 1996), 79.

CHAPTER TWO

"Not All the Orphans Really Are"

The Diversity of Seville's Juvenile Charity Wards
during the Long Eighteenth Century

VALENTINA TIKOFF

∞

⊹ LITERAL AND FIGURATIVE "ORPHANS"—CHILDREN SEEMINGLY BEREFT
of parents' love and supervision—have a special place in early modern
Spanish culture, reflected in the picaresque youngsters of Seville who
populate the pages of Cervantes's "Rinconete y Cortadillo" and Murillo's
baroque canvases of the city's beggar boys.[1] Such juveniles also were a
chronic concern for some of the most prominent social critics and reformers of Hapsburg and Bourbon Spain, who often likened them to "tender
plants" that needed to be nurtured and cultivated so they would develop
into productive maturity rather than grow wild and unruly.[2] Yet neither
artistic images nor prescriptive treatises reveal as much about children
and charity in early modern Spain as do the lives of the young people who
entered orphanages. And perhaps no city provides a better look at this
population for those interested in the histories of Iberia and colonial Latin
America than Seville, the Spanish city most closely identified with Spain's
transatlantic empire.

2.1. Bartolomé Esteban Murillo, *Three Boys Playing Dice*, c. 1670.
Source: Xanthe Brooke and Peter Cherry, *Murillo:*
Scenes of Childhood (London: Merrell, 2001), 122.

Early modern Seville had earned considerable renown for its many charitable institutions. By the mid-eighteenth century, these included a variety of specifically juvenile institutions, several of which also became well known far beyond this city on the Guadalquivir River. Through the records of these juvenile institutions, we learn much about how individuals in this society both defined and made provisions for needy children, and also about the identities of the young people and families who had recourse to them. As Kathryn Lynch has pointed out, for too long historians of the family and historians of charity and philanthropy have worked in separate spheres, as if their respective subjects had little to do with one another.[3] This case study of Seville spans that breach in one respect, exploring children's entrance into orphanages as an important, concrete moment when these two historical fields intersect and one that moreover illuminates the broader cultural context.

Like other contributions to this volume, this chapter explores the history of children and childhood, but it does so specifically through records generated by orphanages. Although based on institutional records, this study is not strictly speaking an institutional history; rather than chronicling the origins and development of a city's orphanages, it instead seeks to rethink the identities of the children who resided in them and how they came to be there. Even though individual children's voices are often difficult to detect at this juncture, their backgrounds and experiences— and their diversity—are evident and often differ from what we might infer from orphanage founders' stated intentions and prescriptive policies. Thus, this study demonstrates that even when we do not have direct access to children's voices, we need not rely solely on adults' statements about how children should be treated, nor should we despair of learning anything more about actual children. For additional insight, we can also fruitfully look at children's *identities* and *experiences*, even when gleaned through words penned by others—in this case, by public officials, institutional administrators, and relatives. This approach illuminates not only young people's history but also the important roles that adults in various positions played in shaping their experiences, both during children's own lifetimes and in the historical record.

This study therefore complements other approaches to children's history, such as legal studies, examinations of philosophical and pedagogical thought, and even more traditional institutional histories, all of which improve our understanding of the intellectual and social structures related to children and childhood but which generally pay less attention to specific children's lives. Though neither a quantitative analysis nor a detailed microhistory of a particular case, the approach employed in this chapter in many ways resembles scholarship that has approached the history of children and youth through police and legal records—other archival sources that likewise capture the reality of individual children's experiences within the social and cultural contexts in which they lived.

This chapter contends that orphanage populations hold important potential for understanding the history of childhood not only because they existed in many communities but also because they reveal connections between children and the social and cultural settings in which they were enmeshed. In Seville, at least, orphanage populations were less marginalized than is often presumed. This chapter especially challenges two perceptions about orphans: first, the common but often erroneous conflation of orphans and foundlings as children without families; and second, the common perception that orphanages served only the "children of marginals."[4] In reality, Seville's orphanages accommodated a diverse population of young people. This diversity was not represented in every institution, however, as children from different family backgrounds entered different rungs within a hierarchy of institutions. The diversity and social segregation of Seville's orphanage population resulted in part from institutional founders' and administrators' divergent objectives and the different populations that they targeted. But children's families also shaped orphanage populations. Although Seville's orphanages had originally been established for destitute and parentless children, it was very common for relatives—including parents—to tap the resources of these institutions, with the result that orphanages accommodated large numbers of children who were only half-orphans (children with one deceased parent), and some who were not orphans at all. Thus, it was both the family *identity* of orphans and also often the active *intervention* of family members that strongly influenced whether and where a particular child was institutionalized.

Since the diversity of orphanage populations resulted from both compliance with and violations of prescriptive institutional policies, it is important to examine both the institutional policies regarding the admission of children and the ways that families worked within and around these guidelines. The discussion below, therefore, begins with a brief overview of the different institutions in Seville and their official admission policies, followed by an examination of the ways that families interacted with institutions to secure places for children. It concludes with an assessment of how these findings compare to other scholarship on orphanages and the social and cultural history of early modern Spain. Ultimately, this case study of the children and families who used Seville's orphanages not only furthers our understanding of children, families, and charity but also sheds light on issues of gender and social stratification. Finally, it underscores the importance of age as a category of analysis informing all these issues. The scope of this study—encompassing not just one institution but all the orphanages in Seville—is crucial in illuminating the diversity of the city's orphanages and the wards they accommodated. However, examining multiple institutions also complicates attempts at quantification. Many of the institutions discussed here left inconsistent and sporadic records, which are difficult to combine and summarize in reliable statistics. Indeed, extant records at some institutions do not permit reliable quantification over time at all, and the problem is only compounded when one attempts to aggregate statistics from multiple institutions. The extant documentation is rich, though, in noting contemporaries' policies, observations, and actions. Although these cannot be easily summed up mathematically, they do illustrate clear patterns in orphanage operations and thus figure prominently in the analysis provided here. This qualitative evidence also provides rare insight into the lives of the children and adults who lived in, worked at, and interacted with Seville's orphanages.

The chronological focus is the "long eighteenth century," here defined as the years 1681 to 1831. The year 1681 marks the establishment of the first of the four "new" orphanages founded in the late seventeenth and early eighteenth centuries; the end date marks the year of the long-awaited opening of Seville's general poorhouse (*hospicio general*), which thereafter absorbed many of the functions of orphanages and fundamentally changed the ways in which charity was organized and distributed in Seville.[5] This chronological scope also corresponds roughly with the last century and a half of both Spain's "Old Regime" social welfare system—largely dismantled during the *desamortización* (nationalization of church property) in the 1830s—and Spain's role as an imperial power in the continental Americas.[6]

Seville's Orphanages: History and Hierarchy

Although the literature on charity children in preindustrial Europe commonly lumps together foundlings and orphans, contemporaries viewed these children as very different populations and generally treated them as such. As Brian Pullan has noted, "Although distinctions were sometimes obscured by phrases such as the English 'fatherless children,' the abandoned were in principle different from orphans; for orphans had been separated from known and lawfully married parents by the death of a father or mother or both." Foundlings, by contrast, "lacked the identity and the minimal security afforded by known and honest parents, by stable residence, by a good reputation among neighbours."[7] As a result, foundlings and orphans were often housed in separate institutions. Pullan might have referred to eighteenth-century Seville as a case in point, for in this city there was one foundling home and six different orphanages.

Seville's foundling home took in babies and quickly dispatched them to wet nurses.[8] In contrast, orphanages housed children who were much older than foundlings when they entered institutional care (typically between the ages of six and fourteen) and retained them in-house and under the direct tutelage of institutional officials considerably longer than foundlings were: most orphans were not expected to leave institutional care until their late teens or early twenties. Moreover, whereas the foundling home and its administrators assumed responsibility for nearly all infants deposited to their care (most of whom had been anonymously abandoned), orphanages did not automatically accommodate all the poor or orphaned children of the city. In fact, they did not even accept all those children for whom admission was sought, who themselves made up only a subset of Seville's children in need. The demand for orphanage spaces consistently outstripped the supply, and administrators could choose which children to admit and which to exclude. Since institutional policies consistently stated a preference for orphans, I refer to the institutions as "orphanages," though contemporaries more commonly used a bevy of other terms: *hospicio* (poorhouse), *colegio* (school), *casa* (house).

Foundlings did occasionally enter Seville's orphanages, but they did so in relatively small numbers. Like the foundlings of other preindustrial cities, Seville's foundlings experienced horrific mortality rates, and the vast majority died well before they reached the ages of six to eight, at which time they would have been eligible to enter the city's orphanages. Yet so many babies were abandoned to the care of Seville's foundling home—they represented between 20 and 40 percent of all births in Seville for years between 1800 and 1830—that there was undoubtedly still a sizable population of foundlings who reached the ages at which they might have entered Seville's orphanages.[9] Unlike its counterparts in some other Spanish cities, though, Seville's foundling home had no standard practice, nor even a prescriptive policy, for channeling its older wards into orphanages.[10] Domestic employment was the likely fate of many of Seville's foundlings who survived the perilous initial years, and even formal adoptions from the city's foundling home likely masked arrangements in which young people served as cheap labor.[11] Generally assumed to be illegitimate and the responsibility of another institution, foundlings never were the population that Seville's orphanages chiefly targeted or accommodated.

Yet orphanages also differed from one another in terms of the children they accommodated. Thus, although orphanage residents in many respects had more in common with each other than with foundlings, they did not constitute a homogenous group. The diversity of orphanage wards stems in part from the variety of institutions in eighteenth-century Seville. Contrary to common assumptions that poor relief was the exclusive preserve of the church, we find in Seville a patchwork of orphanages under royal, municipal, secular, and religious authority. Oldest were the municipal boys' and girls' homes, established in the fifteenth and sixteenth centuries, respectively.[12] By the late seventeenth century, however, both the municipal School of Christian Doctrine for Boys (Colegio de Niños de la Doctrina, as municipal orphanages throughout the kingdom of Castile were called) and it sister institution, the municipal Orphaned Girls' Home (Casa de Niñas Huérfanas), had become impoverished and housed only a handful of residents.[13] Throughout most of the eighteenth century, they operated on a very small scale, barely surviving for many years before the city council finally closed them in 1828 and 1795, respectively.

Four new institutions established in Seville between 1681 and 1725— two for boys, two for girls—increasingly provided residential charity for juveniles in Seville. The one most closely linked to Seville's role in the transatlantic empire was the Royal School of San Telmo (Real Colegio Seminario de San Telmo), where poor and orphaned boys were taken in and prepared for maritime careers in the Spanish fleets. Orphans and foundlings were common in early modern European maritime fleets, ubiquitous on Venetian, Dutch, British, and Spanish ships alike, and frequently recruited from charitable institutions.[14] Since the sixteenth century, officials in Spain had discussed proposals to create an orphanage expressly dedicated to the navigational training of its wards, and there were several attempts to establish such institutions in the seventeenth century.[15]

These efforts were short-lived, however, until Seville's Seafarers' Guild (Universidad de Mareantes) established the Royal School of San Telmo in Seville in 1681 with the support of King Charles II. In light of this institution's mission, it is no surprise that the guildsmen and crown named it after a favorite patron saint of sailors (in English, Saint Elmo). The Seafarers' Guild administered the orphanage in coordination with royal officials until the 1780s, when naval authorities assumed direct supervision. After several decades of financial distress in the first half of the nineteenth century, this orphanage for training sailors finally closed its doors in 1847.

The other principal male orphanage in Seville was known most often simply as "The Toribios" after founder Toribio de Velasco, a tertiary (lay) member of the Order of Saint Francis. In his will of 1730, Velasco named a variety of secular and religious authorities in Seville as the "protectors" of this institution.[16] Accordingly, the city council, *asistente* (Seville's chief royally appointed municipal officer, the equivalent of the *corregidor* in other Spanish cities), archbishop, and members of the cathedral chapter all continued to have roles in the administration of this institution until it was absorbed into the general poorhouse in the 1830s.[17]

The two newest orphanages for girls in eighteenth-century Seville were both run by religious women, but otherwise they had very different origins and missions. Archbishop Manuel Arias established one at Seville's Espíritu Santo Convent in 1711, mandating that its wards be drawn exclusively from among the city's noble but poor girls.[18] Though he gave them the name "Girls of the Holy Spirit" (Niñas del Espíritu Santo), the institution became better known as the "Noble Girls' School" (Colegio de Niñas Nobles), as I also refer to it, until the archbishop of Seville finally overturned its founding bylaws in 1969 during the Franco years.

The Beaterio of the Most Holy Trinity (Beaterio de la Santísima Trinidad) was the other female orphanage in the city. Isabel Moreno Caballero and two female followers founded it in 1720. As *beatas*, these women were not formally nuns, but they wore garb resembling habits and lived together in communities known as *beaterios*. By the eighteenth century, there already was a rich history of these devout female laywomen in Seville, often linked to charitable work on behalf of orphans and other young girls in danger. Beginning in the Counter-Reformation, these women and the communities in which they lived increasingly fell under the supervision of the secular clergy.[19] While for most of the eighteenth century the Beaterio of the Most Holy Trinity housed only a handful of girls at a time, it grew dramatically in scale to accommodate over a hundred girls in the 1790s, and it would grow even further in the nineteenth century.

These brief sketches of Seville's eighteenth-century orphanages reveal that these institutions differed from each other not only in terms of administration and funding sources but also in terms of their populations. The variety of institutional structures and purposes helps explain the diversity of Seville's orphanages and the broad array of children whom they served. We see this most directly in orphanage bylaws pertaining to children's eligibility, which reflect founders' and administrators' attempts to target specific populations of young people. Although orphanages consistently mandated that orphans be the preferred candidates for admission, they differed strikingly in other admission criteria. Especially significant were those regarding the family backgrounds of prospective wards. Administrators' different attitudes and policies concerning admission resulted in the segregation of young people into different institutions according to their family backgrounds. Children of legitimate birth from higher-status families went to more selective institutions, where they were prepared for adult roles befitting their respectable family backgrounds, whereas young people of illegitimate birth or unknown or undistinguished families attended less selective institutions where they were prepared for more humble roles.

Both male and female orphanages were socially tiered, but the hierarchies were gendered, and thus somewhat different. Administrators of the female institutions restricted enrollment to more privileged sectors of society: natives of Seville and the daughters of legitimate marriages. Moreover, the female institutions in particular explicitly sought to ensure the respectability of wards by capping the age of admission. For example, Seville's city councilmen adopted bylaws for the municipal girls' orphanage that stated:

> Because the principal business and vocation of the said house is the asylum and internment of lost orphaned girls[,] the administrator is ordered and charged that no one exceeding age fourteen be taken in, since older girls might be dangerous people and improper for the bad examples that they might give to the other girls, and also because, being older than the said age, they have the freedom to run away and to disturb the rest, as has been experienced, and many of them have been dismissed from homes

where they have been serving for their bad examples and theft, and it is just to avoid this harm.[20]

Echoing such concerns, administrators at the Beaterio de la Santísima Trinidad similarly stipulated that the girls entering their institution must do so "between the ages of seven and ten, since this is a house of education, not correction."[21] Even the nun who served as the girls' teacher at the Noble Girls' School advised the archbishop not to accede to requests to admit girls older than ten, arguing that "the earlier they are removed from the world, the fewer bad traits they bring, which are difficult or perhaps even impossible to shed."[22] And, of course, the Noble Girls' School furthermore required that its wards be from Seville's noble families.

Although none of the male orphanages restricted entry to sons of the nobility, there also was a clear hierarchy for boys that became more pronounced over time. Both the orphanage of San Telmo and the orphanage-cum-reformatory known as the Toribios were originally established to take in the ubiquitous poor and apparently parentless boys who seemed to overrun Seville's streets, as the municipal School of Christian Doctrine had been established to do in the sixteenth century. Administrators of the Toribios always targeted this population, admitting boys with little regard for lineage, sometimes even forcibly rounding up and interning them. In contrast, the administrators of San Telmo became more discriminating in their admission policies, increasingly demanding proof of age, legitimacy, and other requirements. This process had begun already in the late seventeenth century and would continue, despite arguments by some members of the Seafarers' Guild that these tighter admission guidelines were at odds with the goal of serving the neediest boys.[23] Most dramatically, in 1721 administrators began requiring all prospective applicants to submit documentation attesting to their "blood purity" (*limpieza de sangre*), barring the descendants of Jews, Muslims (Moros), mulattoes, gypsies, individuals punished by the Spanish Inquisition, and those who had practiced any of a long list of "unrespectable" (*desestimados*) or "vile" (*viles*) trades, which included butchers, muleteers, and actors, among others.[24] Although they granted some exceptions, San Telmo administrators were generally vigilant about ensuring that these admission criteria regarding age and family backgrounds were met by requiring documentation, including paperwork, concerning an applicant's identity and proof of orphanage, legitimacy, and affirmation of his own and his family's good character.[25]

In contrast, the Toribios continued to serve boys of diverse backgrounds, who were admitted with little regard given to their personal or parental background. We see this clearly in a note written by Toribios administrator José María Rodríguez in 1833 to accompany a requested roster of Toribios residents and their parents. He remarked, "[The names of] some of the parents do not appear here because they [the boys] do not know them, nor does this institution have it on record since they were admitted on orders that only stated the child's name. . . . It will take time to verify the relatives of those who have them, while there are others who know no family at all."[26] Clearly, Rodríguez had not been too meticulous in demanding extensive information about the background of the children he took in nor had his predecessors, mindful of their mission to take in children who appeared to live in the streets, seemingly abandoned by parents and other adult caretakers. Whereas San Telmo became more selective and elitist over the course of the eighteenth and early nineteenth centuries, the Toribios expanded to accommodate boys and men who had committed crimes or who were sent there for other punitive reasons.

The disparities in admission criteria at both male and female institutions certainly help explain the diversity of Seville's orphanage population, as well as its distribution across institutions. But the range of children actually resident in Seville's orphanages was even greater than might be inferred from looking solely at prescriptive documents, since children also entered these institutions at the margins—or even in flagrant violation—of prescriptive admission criteria. Relatives, including parents, were often responsible for encouraging administrators to waive admission requirements. It was thus not just institutional founders and administrators who shaped the identities of the clienteles they served but also family members and other adults who did so by advocating and arranging the entry of particular young people into Seville's orphanages.

Families' Roles in Securing Places for Children

Relatives often made the requests for children's admission to orphanages. Aunts, uncles, and grandparents were common advocates for their young family members, entirely in keeping with orphanage policies. The founders and supporting patrons of these institutions consistently mandated that orphans be the preferred or, as was the case for San Telmo, even exclusive candidates for admission. The Spanish term "orphan" (*huérfano, huérfana*) applied to any child survivor of a deceased parent, though adjectival clauses commonly differentiated different kinds of orphans: those whose mothers had died (*huérfanos de madre*), those whose fathers had died (*huérfanos de padre*), and those who had no surviving parent (*huérfanos de padre y madre*; in English, "full orphans").[27] Generally, children with no surviving parents were to be given highest priority in admission decisions, and among children that had been orphaned by one parent ("half-orphans") those whose fathers had died were generally preferred to those whose mothers had died.

Despite these requirements and the demographic profile of Seville that must have resulted in far more full orphans than the total capacity of Seville's orphanages, children with one or both parents living abounded at these orphanages.[28] This is because parents joined other relatives and adult advocates in seeking children's placement into these institutions. They did so at least at the four principal institutions of Seville in this period. (Parents may also have placed children at the smaller municipal orphanages, though the admissions and matriculation records for these institutions are scant and preclude firm conclusions on this point.[29]) Administrators of the girls' home at the Beaterio de la Santísima Trinidad, for example, noted in the 1790s that "experience shows that many girls enter at the request of their mothers,"[30] a trend that continued into the nineteenth century.[31] A few neighborhoods away at the Noble Girls' School, when Valentina Veles y Mondragón sought to enroll her daughter María de la Concepción, she reminded the archbishop that there had been precedents for admitting noble girls with surviving parents.[32] Parents also sent their sons to orphanages. A Toribios administrator noted in 1792 that the "helpless boys" (*niños desamparados*) served by his institution included those admitted "on the request of their poor fathers, or widowed mothers, who cannot maintain them, educate them, nor provide for them any way of learning an honest trade."[33] Likewise, one observer of the San Telmo maritime orphanage remarked in 1746, "Not all of the [orphans] really are, since through the work or inclinations of the administrators this particular [admission] criterion is waived."[34]

In their efforts to tap the charitable benefits originally intended for orphans, parents frequently argued that their children were de facto orphans due to poverty or other disadvantages. It was especially common for widowed mothers to make such pleas. María González used some familiar rhetorical strategies when she sought a space at San Telmo for her son in 1788. Addressing orphanage officials, she described herself as a "poor widow" with "no help except that of God and you" and mentioned employment requirements (as a wet nurse and domestic servant) that reflected the precariousness of her economic situation and prevented her from raising a child. She also was typical in highlighting specific circumstances that she hoped would merit favorable attention and a special claim on charity dispensed by the institution, in this case the fact that her son's grandfather had been a master shoemaker for the orphanage. (Other applicants cited physical handicaps, a large number of other children, or—at the maritime orphanage of San Telmo—the nautical service of a boy's deceased father or another family member.) María González also resembled other mothers in expressing fears over the fate of a child who she otherwise could not properly supervise and educate, a tack that relatives and guardians would employ even more emphatically when they explicitly expressed interest in the educational opportunities that orphanages offered. Finally, like many other applicants, María González included in her petition to orphanage officials external corroboration of the family's good character and legitimate poverty, signaled by the official designation as a member of the "solemn poor" (*pobre de solemnidad*).[35]

Through such efforts by parents—generally tenacious widows—sometimes half-orphaned children were admitted even when there were full orphans awaiting slots. For example, when administrators at the maritime orphanage of San Telmo decided to enforce more vigorously the policy of preferential admission for complete orphans, widows adjusted their strategies, now circumventing the regular admission process at the orphanage by appealing directly to royal officials who could effectively override official admission guidelines. San Telmo administrators might even have encouraged this approach. When the widow María Seco sought to have her eight-year-old son, Josef Muñoz, admitted to San Telmo in 1783, administrators told her that, since there were full orphans awaiting spaces at San Telmo, Josef could not be admitted without a special dispensation from royal authorities. She took the hint and wrote directly to José de Gálvez, a high-ranking official in the Spanish royal government who interceded on her behalf. The ploy worked, and her son Josef Muñoz was admitted.[36]

Cases such as this demonstrate how widows with children had indeed "learned to use the paternalism of a social order that considered them most needful of protection," as Mary Elizabeth Perry has contended poor

women did in sixteenth- and seventeenth-century Seville. But widows'
interactions with orphanages in the eighteenth century also show that
they balanced the strategies of "obedient submission"—which Perry
also has found—with vocal claims for themselves and their children.[37]
Far from being silent and ignored or shunning institutional relief, when
it came to securing an orphanage slot for their children, these widows
could clamor loudly and insist on being heard, often quite effectively.
In response to a steady stream of requests by widows, some orphanage
administrators even began to argue that by admitting the half-orphaned
sons of widows, they could actually best practice charity, since they would
thereby help both a child and his widowed mother.[38]

Although widows were most prominent among the parents seeking
their children's admission to orphanages, fathers also sought places at
orphanages for their children. This was especially common at the elite
Noble Girls' School, where we also observe the admission of girls who
were not even half-orphans. Keenly aware of the requirement of nobility,
fathers (both widowers and not) highlighted their families' reputations
in correspondence to the archbishop seeking places for their daughters.
Ygnacio Chacón y Rivera, for example, pointed out that his daughter
"met all the qualifications of well known and accomplished [executoriada]
purity and nobility of blood and poverty."[39] Relying on their reputations, others referred simply to their family's "known nobility" (conocida
nobleza). They also frequently remarked on military leadership positions
and other service rendered to the crown as proof of their family's social
status and sometimes submitted elaborate proofs of lineage to bolster
their claims.[40]

Yet the families of prospective Noble Girls' School wards also argued
that they needed the assistance that this institution provided. The poverty
claimed by these families was not, however, the same indigence claimed
by applicants to other institutions; instead, it was a need measured relative to their social status and obligations. Indeed, one reason that noble
families were especially interested in placing daughters at this institution was the promise of a future dowry that would enable wards to take
the black veil at one of the city's elite convents. Pedro Ortiz de Escobar
y Abet, for example, implicitly conveyed his interest in the dowry benefit when he sought to guarantee a place for his daughter, Felisiana, at
the Noble Girls' School. In his petition, he described three-year-old
Felisiana as

showing signs even at such a tender age of following the religious
life, this being the only life to which she can aspire since God has
given her a father and grandparents who are of noble blood but
very poor. Although the [supplicant] earns the salary corresponding to his position [as lieutenant in an infantry regiment], it is
barely enough to support himself decently, and not enough to
provide any inheritance to his children other than the memory of
his great devotion to royal service; and thus to provide the aforementioned Doña Felisiana access to religious life[,] he asks your
highness . . . to favor the supplicant and the aforementioned Doña
Felisiana de Escobar y Abet [by] granting her the special grace
and license to enter as a resident of the Espíritu Santo School in
Seville when she reaches the requisite age.[41]

As this letter illustrates, Ortiz de Escobar y Abet sought to ensure
his daughter's access to a respectable adult position as a nun through the
route facilitated by the Noble Girls' School. He wrote many missives
over several years in his efforts to secure a place for his young daughter,
a campaign that began well before she even reached the age of seven at
which she would become eligible for admission. Ultimately he was successful; Feliciana was admitted to the Noble Girls' School in 1752, when
she would have been seven or eight years old.[42]

Day Students, Boarders, and Delinquents

The adult advocates, generally relatives, who sought to enroll children
in Seville's orphanages clearly spanned a broad range, from aunts and
uncles of full orphans, to indigent mothers of half-orphans, to noblemen
in prestigious military and bureaucratic positions who were the fathers
of daughters who had not lost either parent. Further adding to the diversity of orphanage populations were day students and paying boarders. By
the late eighteenth century, the Beaterio of the Most Holy Trinity was
operating a free day school to which neighborhood girls could come and
attend classes with orphanage wards. Families also sent boys to the city's
male orphanages for education and training. For example, the mother of
Antonio Nuñez paid two *reales* per day to the Toribios in 1814 for her son
to be there, but only for workdays, "since he comes to learn to be a shoemaker; and on holidays he eats at home."[43] The navigational instructors at

San Telmo also tutored private students who came to the orphanage for instruction. In 1783, San Telmo's chief internal administrator, the marquis of La Plata, complained that there were more than sixty such students. (Three years earlier another inspector had counted thirty-eight.) Institutional rules later capped the allowable number at six.[44] Rarely are the backgrounds or identities of these youths indicated, but we do know that one was the son of a judge in Seville's high court (*audiencia*).[45]

Also common were boarders who resided alongside the charity residents at the city's four principal orphanages. Boarders even resided at the Noble Girls' School, in spite of the explicit ban on such residents in the institution's founding bylaws.[46] Only the municipal orphanages do not appear to have accommodated any boarders, likely in part because families (correctly) perceived them as poor institutions that did not provide many of the services or benefits that the newer institutions did. The parents and guardians who paid to board children at orphanages did so either because they were unable to raise their children themselves or because they wanted to secure the services that orphanages provided, especially education and discipline. As an example of the former we might point to widower and carpenter Juan Manuel Carrera, who initially entrusted his two daughters to the care of neighbors then sought the advice and assistance of a clergyman who encouraged him to seek the girls' admission to Beaterio of the Most Holy Trinity, where he eventually boarded them at the modest rate of two reales per day.[47]

In other cases, it was not the push of poverty and the lack of a parent but rather the pull of educational opportunities that motivated families to pay to board children at orphanages. This was most common at the most selective institutions, which offered the best educational opportunities and prospects for postorphanage life, whether as nuns in the city's well-regarded convents or as junior officers in the Spanish fleet. In particular, San Telmo's advanced navigational curriculum attracted youths from even prominent families. For example, Captain-General of the Fleet Francisco Manxón, who in his position as San Telmo's designated "protector" endorsed several widows' requests for the admission of their sons in San Telmo, sent a young relative of his own to study at San Telmo as a boarder in 1778, alerting the administrative officers at San Telmo:

> My brother Don Joseph recently sent [to me] his thirteen-year-
> old relative and godchild Josef Turriel, from the College of

Villacaredo, with the idea that he should be looked after and that he serve me as a page[.] But having seen how bright this boy is, and [considering] that if he builds on the beginnings of an education that he already has, he might become a good mathematician[,] I have determined to send him to that Royal School [of San Telmo] so that you gentleman can put him in the appropriate class, as one of the rest, without the slightest distinction [from the others], enrolling him as a supernumerary [that is, boarder, above and beyond the 150 charity wards] with my aforementioned brother contributing the amount established for such cases.[48]

Between 1790 and 1809, another category of resident—the noble boarder (*pensionista noble*)—also resided at the orphanage, albeit in separate quarters from the charity wards.[49] As the name suggests, nobility was a requirement for this type of boarder, and the lineages of this elite group of San Telmo residents were scrupulously profiled and documented as a condition of entry.[50] Although the numbers were small compared to the charity wards, the fact that any noble families chose to enroll their sons at this institution further reflects the prominence that San Telmo had achieved by the late eighteenth century.

Perhaps the best-known boarders at Seville's orphanages, however, were the boys sent to the Toribios for "correction."[51] Gabriel Baca, who chronicled the early years of the Toribios's operations in a 1766 publication, reported that by the 1730s, families already were sending their "incorrigible" sons to the Toribios.[52] As late as 1886, a half-century after this institution had closed its doors, Sevillian Francisco Collantes de Terán speculated that "there must be few people over fifty years old who were never threatened in their childhood mischief with being sent to the Toribios."[53] Some were more than threatened. Manuel de Huelva, for example, was sent to the Toribios for a month of "correction" at the request of his widowed mother after he had gotten drunk and shown disrespect to her and a local official.[54] In the late eighteenth and early nineteenth centuries, secular and religious authorities also remanded some adults to the Toribios for punishment, though the Toribios always served primarily as a juvenile establishment. Whether a correctional ward had been committed by his own family or other authorities, parents or other relatives usually bore the costs associated with his stay at the Toribios, and they also could and frequently did pay for such "extras" as schooling, clothing, shaving, and even shackles (*grillos*).[55] Given the tiered nature of Seville's network of orphanages, it is hardly surprising that it was the Toribios, and not the more selective San Telmo or much smaller municipal orphanage for boys, that doubled as a reformatory for boys and young men; none of the girls' institutions served a comparable function. Thus, it would be wrong to conclude that all of Seville's orphanages doubled as punitive institutions or as warehouses for misbehaving or abandoned young people.

Conclusion

The residents of Seville's orphanages clearly were not an undifferentiated mass of youngsters whose parents had uniformly abandoned them to institutional care but rather a diverse group of young people who were accommodated in a fragmented network of juvenile charitable establishments in which niches existed for different groups.[56] In Seville's juvenile charitable network, we see in particular a hierarchy in which rank was closely linked to legitimacy and family status, including the distinction between nobles and commoners. Nicholas Terpstra has found similar types of status distinctions among the populations of orphanages and *conservatori* (homes for girls) of sixteenth-century Italian cities, though he also has noted that the range of wards' backgrounds could vary. Finding that the orphanages and conservatories in Florence "gathered larger numbers of children from a broader social range" than did comparable institutions in Bologna, he has speculated that the difference may be attributable to the fact that Bologna had a general poorhouse that accommodated the most indigent children, thus enabling the city's orphanage administrators to be more selective.[57] In Seville prior to 1831, however, no general poorhouse accommodated poor young people, nor do other institutions appear to have taken them in. Rather, many of the most marginal children in Seville remained outside residential welfare establishments and very likely entered the work force at much younger ages than orphanage residents.[58]

Although most of Seville's orphanages—with the exception of the Noble Girls' School—had been created for needy children, admission policies and procedures, documentation requirements, and tenacious and successful demands from family members of other children effectively kept many "marginals" out of Seville's orphanages. For example, the gypsy population—ubiquitous in contemporaries' comments on Seville's and Spain's poor—are almost entirely absent from Seville's orphanage populations; or, at least, wards were not identified as such. Children from families deemed less than "respectable" or who were outsiders or new-comers to Seville were at a significant disadvantage, as were those who lacked parents, guardians, relatives, godparents, or other adult advocates who were literate, who could secure the services of someone who was, or who had personal access to institutional administrators to press the case for a particular child's admission.[59] The active intervention of family members was often as important as the family identity of prospective orphan-age wards. Legitimacy requirements also probably worked to keep some of these children out of Seville's orphanages—including legitimate children whose families nevertheless lacked the wherewithal to prove their legiti-macy. Children from families who had been officially designated as the "solemn poor" did find their way to Seville's orphanages in large numbers, though even they were probably considerably better off than many other children, since they were by definition the "deserving poor" and moreover had access to a notary and some ability to pay (or cajole) him to certify their neediness.[60]

The kind of social selectivity that characterized Seville's orphanage admissions jibes with other research findings on early modern Spain, espe-cially concerning the importance of legitimacy and cross-generational family ties, reputation, and honor.[61] The fact that different standards of poverty and assistance existed and that these, too, depended largely on family identity and social rank also echoes the findings of scholarship on the sixteenth and seventeenth centuries, suggesting important continuities throughout the Old Regime.[62] Yet some of these same findings also chal-lenge aspects of the "common wisdom" about institutionalization and its links to reputation and social status in the preindustrial Hispanic world, suggesting possible discontinuities between the "long eighteenth century" and earlier eras, or perhaps unique standards for young people. The stigma of receiving relief, especially residential or "indoor" relief, is a familiar theme in scholarship on early modern Spain, including the eighteenth century. Scholars point to the stigma of assistance manifest in provisions of aid for the "shame-faced poor" (*pobres envergonzantes* or *vergonzantes*), who received assistance secretly in their homes so that they might be spared the ignominy of institutionalization.[63] Students of the early modern period also have long described how children deposited in a foundling home were presumed to be illegitimate, a stigma reflected in both popular prejudice and official discrimination that reforms of the very late eighteenth century finally tried—though perhaps not very effectively—to dismantle.[64] Yet in the experiences of orphanage wards we see something quite different.

In tapping the resources of orphanages, parents and other adult relatives freely admitted—and we can suspect, even exaggerated—their family's dire financial straits to secure places for their children and young kin. Moreover, they did so quite publicly. Unlike foundlings, orphanage residents' parentage was generally known, and in contrast to the secrecy surrounding the "shame-faced poor," the identity of orphanage wards and their families was not kept secret in any way. The fact that relatives from multiple socioeconomic strata, who generally were not themselves in charity institutions, publicly sought the services of orphanages for their children thus also raises a question about the "stigma" (or lack thereof) associated with institutional relief in early modern Spain and particularly with sending a child to an orphanage. We might do well to recall Stuart Woolf's claims that preindustrial philanthropic institutions helped reinforce the social status quo and protect the status of families at multiple social levels, and that it was not just those at society's lowest rungs who used and benefited from them.[65] The fact that orphanages were socially segregated, and that some came to be considered selective and indeed even exclusive institutions, undoubtedly helped preserve their usefulness to families from diverse social ranks.

Seville was not the only city where parents sought to place children in orphanages, even when this violated admission policies. Orphanages elsewhere in Europe and the Americas often housed residents with surviving parents.[66] And in a number of places, even charitable institutions not originally intended expressly for children came to accommodate large numbers of young people sent there by parents.[67] The case of Seville thus reflects not "Spanish exceptionalism" but important commonalities between this Spanish city and other urban societies. Yet historical context remains important, and the findings presented here for Seville do not support all the conclusions that scholars have reached based on investigations elsewhere. In particular, a number of scholars have argued that when parents placed children in orphanages, they did so mainly as an act of economic desperation, a temporary last resort.[68] This explanation likely describes the circumstances of some families who sent children to Seville's orphanages, but it fails to capture the diversity of backgrounds from which children came before they entered these institutions or the varied motives for which they were put there.

Seville's orphanage residents were not necessarily bereft of family, nor can they be aptly described simply as the "children of marginals." Many of them had been entrusted to orphanages as charity wards, day students, or boarders by family members, including parents. Some parents and other relatives were indeed desperate and sought the charity dispensed by orphanages so that their children could be assured basic food, shelter, and supervision. Yet for others, somewhat better off, recourse to orphanages often seems to have been part of a longer-term strategy, an attractive vehicle to provide for a child's proper upbringing and enhance his or her future prospects, whether through education, a dowry, or even appropriate discipline.

The findings reported here also prompt the question of age as a "category of analysis."[69] Life-cycle studies have suggested different roles and functions for individuals at different life stages throughout the early modern period, and this might apply as well to residential relief. The experience of institutionalization, deemed a social anathema for adults from a given family, may have been considered acceptable—and even beneficial—for a younger person. Before the advent of public schools or juvenile reformatories in Seville, orphanages fulfilled these and other functions. Families availed themselves of these services, viewing them as ways to prepare young people for respectable adulthoods outside residential relief establishments. This is an especially important finding given that the young (and the old) have often been disproportionately prevalent among the assisted poor in the Western world, though they are usually marginalized in studies of poverty, charity, and relief in preindustrial Europe.[70] The findings reported here thus challenge us both to devote more attention to the experiences of young charity recipients specifically and also to consider ways in which charity—and perhaps also other topics that we generally think of as more dependent on class or socioeconomic status than age—might have had different implications and meanings for people at different life stages.

We also must remember that not every institution provided the same services or accommodated the same populations. Seville's orphanages were sharply tiered, but together, they served children and families from multiple social strata. This reflected not only founders' and administrators' different purposes and target populations but also the actions of family members who sought the benefits of these institutions for their own children. This case study therefore illustrates the diversity of both this city's network of juvenile relief institutions and the children and families it served, cautioning against monolithic characterizations of "charity children" and the institutions that accommodated them. It also demonstrates that the images of young people entirely bereft of family ties in early modern Spanish art and literature neither adequately nor necessarily reflect the reality of Seville's orphanage wards, for whom it was not the lack of family but the continuing importance of it—through both reputation and action—that strongly influenced their access to institutional care.

Please note: All translations are mine except where otherwise indicated.

✦ NOTES ✦

1. Miguel de Cervantes Saavedra, "Rinconete y Cortadillo," in *Novelas ejemplares* (Garden City, NY: Doubleday, n.d.), 139–76; Enrique Valdivieso, *La obra de Murillo en Sevilla* (Seville: Servicio de Publicaciones del Ayuntamiento de Sevilla, 1982). See also Anne J. Cruz, *Discourses of Poverty: Social Reform and the Picaresque Novel in Early Modern Spain* (Toronto: University of Toronto Press, 1999); and Mary Elizabeth Perry, *Crime and Society in Early Modern Seville* (Hanover, NH: University Press of New England, 1980), 190–211.

2. For overviews of prominent writings on poverty and poor relief in early modern Spain, see María Jiménez Salas, *Historia de la asistencia social en España en la edad moderna* (Madrid: Instituto Balmes de Sociología, Departamento de Historia Social, Consejo Superior de Investigaciones Científicas, 1958); Elena Maza Zorilla, *Pobreza y asistencia social en España, siglos XVI al XX. Aproximación histórica.* (Valladolid: Universidad de Valladolid, 1987); and Cándido Ruiz Rodrigo and Irene Palacio Lis, *Pauperismo y educación: Siglos XVIII y XIX. Apuntes para una historia de la educación social en España* (Valencia: Martin, 1995).

   The metaphor of children as "tender plants" is taken from Antonio de Heredia Bazan, *Representación al Rey Nuestro Señor. D Philipe V . . . sobre la importancia, y facilidad de establecer cafas, y hospicios donde recoger los pobres mendicantes, niños huerfanos, y ddefamparados, y abolir la mendicidad, lograndofe adelantar las fabricas y comercio* (Zaragoza: Imprenta Real, 1744), fols. 5v–6r, my emphasis; copy in Archivo Municipal de Sevilla (hereafter, AMS), XI, vol. 30, doc. 11. For other botanical metaphors concerning children, see Archivo de la Diputación Provincial de Sevilla (hereafter, ADPS), Hospicio, bundle 3, unnumbered document, copy of poorhouse (*hospicio*) plan drafted by Seville's Economic Society of Friends of the Country, dated Seville, 5 September 1778; copy dated Madrid, 27 August 1781.

3. Katherine A. Lynch, *Individuals, Families, and Communities in Europe, 1200–1800: The Urban Foundations of Western Society* (Cambridge: Cambridge University Press, 2003). See also Katherine A. Lynch, "The Family and the History of Public Life," *Journal of Interdisciplinary History* 24, no. 4 (spring 1994): 665–84. See also Hugh Cunningham, "Histories of Childhood," *American Historical Review* 103, no. 4 (October 1998): 1204.

4. This presumption often surfaces in the literature on children and charity in the preindustrial West. Jeroen J. H. Dekker has written, for example, "Since the late Middle Ages, institutions had been founded for specific groups of

marginals, for example the ill, criminals, orphans, and the insane. Orphanages were the only institutions explicitly intended for children. Children placed in them were above all children of marginals" (Jeroen J. H. Dekker, "Transforming the Nation and the Child: Philanthropy in the Netherlands, Belgium, France and England, c. 1780–c. 1850," in *Charity, Philanthropy, and Reform from the 1690s to 1850*, ed. Hugh Cunningham and Joanna Innes [Houndmills, England: Macmillan; reprint, New York: St. Martin's Press, 1998], 131 [page citations are to the reprint edition]).

5. Alfonso Braojos Garrido, "El hospicio de Sevilla, fundación del reinado fernandino," *Archivo Hispalense*, 2d series, LIX, no. 182 (1976): 1–42. Although Seville gained a poorhouse much later than most other prominent Spanish cities, the 1830s witnessed a widespread change in the practice of charity throughout Spain, in large part as the result of the *desamortización*— nationalization of ecclesiastical property. William J. Callahan, *Church, Politics, and Society in Spain, 1750–1874* (Cambridge, MA: Harvard University Press, 1984), 145–85, especially 179; and Juan Ignacio Carmona García, *El sistema de la hospitalidad pública en la Sevilla del antiguo régimen* (Seville: Diputación Provincial de Sevilla, 1979), 452–56, 474–75.

6. Antonio Domínguez Ortiz, *Sociedad y estado en el siglo XVIII español* (Barcelona: Ariel, 1988), 495; and Cándido Ruiz Rodrigo and Irene Palacio Lis, *Pauperismo y educación: Siglos XVIII y XIX . . . Apuntes para una historia de la educación social en España* (Valencia: Martin, 1995), 105–20. Indeed, the 1830s is often identified as the boundary of Spain's "Old Regime" (*antiguo régimen*), as a cursory survey of titles and time frames of works concerning the end of the Spanish Old Regime will reveal.

7. Brian Pullan, "Orphans and Foundlings in Early Modern Europe" (originally published as *The Stenton Lecture 1988, University of Reading*, 1989; reprinted in *Poverty and Charity: Europe, Italy, Venice, 1400–1700* [Aldershot, England: Variorum (Ashgate), 1994], 5–6 [page citations are to the reprint edition]).

8. The material on Seville's foundling home is taken from León Carlos Alvarez Santaló, *Marginación social y mentalidad en Andalucía occidental: Expósitos en Sevilla (1613–1910)*, with a prologue by A[ntonio] Domínguez Ortiz (Seville: Junta de Andalucía, 1980).

9. Alvarez Santaló, *Marginación social*, [262–63] (table 1), [286] (table 15), [287–98] (table 16), and [297–98] (table 21).

10. On this policy in Madrid, for example, see J. Soubreyoux, "Pauperismo y relaciones sociales en el Madrid del siglo XVIII," *Estudios de Historia Social* 12–13, I–II (January–June 1980): 7–227, 226. But Hélène Tropé reports that in Valencia, as in Seville, only a small percentage of foundlings were

ever transferred to the Saint-Vincent Ferrier orphanage in that city. Hélène Tropé, *La formation des enfants orphelins à Valence (XVe–XVIIe siècles): Le cas du Collège impérial Saint-Vincent Ferrier*, with a preface by Augustin Redondo (Paris: Publications de la Sorbonne, Presses de la Sorbonne Nouvelle, 1998), 36–37.

11. Alvarez Santaló, *Marginación social*, 105–17.

12. For published sources on Seville's School of Christian Doctrine, see Juan Ignacio Carmona García, *El extenso mundo de la pobreza: La otra cara de la Sevilla imperial* (Seville: Ayuntamiento de Sevilla, 1993), 95–117; Francisco Collantes de Terán, *Los establecimientos de caridad de Sevilla, que se consideran como particulares: Apuntes y memorias para su historia* (Seville: Oficina de El Orden, 1886), 191–96; Juan Luis Morales, *El niño en la cultura española (ante la medicina y otras ciencias; la historia, las letras, las artes y las costumbres)*, vol. 1 (Madrid: n.p., 1960), 435–77. On Seville's municipal orphanage for girls, see Carmona García, *El extenso mundo de la pobreza*, 121–27, 133–51; Morales, *El niño en la cultura española*, 411–16; Mary Elizabeth Perry, *Gender and Disorder in Early Modern Seville* (Princeton, NJ: Princeton University Press, 1990), 49; and Collantes de Terán, *Los establecimientos de caridad*, 238–40.

13. Carmona García, *El extenso mundo de la pobreza*, 95–100; AMS, III, vol. 12, doc. 3; and James Casey, *Early Modern Spain: A Social History* (London: Routledge, 1999), 125.

14. See, for example, Donna T. Andrew, *Philanthropy and Police: London Charity in the Eighteenth Century* (Princeton, NJ: Princeton University Press, 1989), 109–15, 127–30; Brian Pullan, *Rich and Poor in Renaissance Venice* (Cambridge, MA: Harvard University Press, 1971), 263; Anne E. C. McCants, *Civic Charity in a Golden Age: Orphan Care in Early Modern Amsterdam* (Urbana: University of Illinois Press, 1997), 64–70.

15. David Goodman, *Spanish Naval Power, 1589–1665: Reconstruction and Defeat* (Cambridge: Cambridge University Press, 1997), 183–86; and Jesús Varela Marcos, "El seminario de marinos: Un intento de formación de marinos para las armadas y flotas de Indias," *Revista de historia de América* (Mexico), no. 87 (1979): 9–36. See also Antonio Herrera García, "Estudio histórico sobre el Real Colegio Seminario de San Telmo de Sevilla," *Archivo Hispalense*, 2d series, nos. 89–90 (1958); reprint, Sevilla: Imprenta Provincial, 1958, 8–13 (page citations are to the reprint edition); and Pilar Castillo Manrubia, "Los Colegios de San Telmo," *Revista de historia naval* 4, no. 13 (1986): 79–83.

16. AMS, XI, vol. 63, doc. 16.

17. The principal published work on this institution includes Francisco Aguilar Piñal, "Los Niños Toribios," in *Temas sevillanos: Primera serie*, 2d. rev. and aug.

(Seville: Universidad de Sevilla, 1992), 51–57; Vicente de la Fuente, *Los Toribios de Sevilla . . . Las adoratrices[.] Memorias leidas en la Real Academia de Ciencias Morales y Políticas* (Madrid: Tipografía Gutenberg, 1884); *Enciclopedia vniversal ilvustrada europeo-americana* (1928), s.v. "Toribio. Hist. Los Toribios de Sevilla" and "Tribunal tutelar de menores"; and Juan Luis, *El niño en la cultura española* (Madrid: n.p., 1960), 1:422; Collantes de Terán, *Los establecimientos de caridad de Sevilla*, 151–52.

18. Convento del Espíritu Santo—Seville (hereafter, CES), uncatalogued document labeled "Libro de la fundación del colegio de niñas agregadas a el Convento de Religiosas del Espíritu Santo. . . ."

19. Perry, *Gender and Disorder*, 97–98; on beatas' charitable activities in early modern Seville, see especially 95–117 (especially 102–3), 172. See also Francisco Avellá Cháfer, "Beatas y beaterios en la ciudad y arzobispado de Sevilla," *Archivo Hispalense*, 2d series, 65, no. 198 (1982): 101–2. On beatas in the broader Hispanic world, see, for example, Nancy E. van Deusen, "Defining the Sacred and the Worldly: Beatas and Recogidas in Late Seventeenth-Century Lima," *Colonial Latin American Historical Review* 6, no. 4 (1997): 441–77.

20. AMS, IV, vol. 24, doc. 3.

21. Beaterio de la Santísima Trinidad, Seville (hereafter, BST), uncatalogued document labeled "Provision Real de aprovación de las ordenanzas del Seminario de Niñas Huérfanas de la S[antísi]ma Trinidad de Sevilla," dated Madrid, 16 August 1797, article 5.

22. Archivo del Palacio Arzobispal de Sevilla (hereafter, APA), Espíritu Santo, V, unnumbered bundle [1], unnumbered document, letter from Sor Francisca del Corazón de Jesús, Seville, 22 August 1797 [to archbishop of Seville].

23. Archivo General de Indias, Seville (hereafter, AGI), Indiferente General, bundle 1647, unnumbered document, report from Universidad de Mareantes members acting as representatives (*diputados*) of San Telmo, Seville, 14 August 1699.

24. USAH, Universidad de Mareantes, book 310, fols. 38r–38v. See also Manuel Babío Walls, *El Real Colegio Seminario de San Telmo, 1681–1981: Bosquejo de su fundación: III centenario de la fundación de la Escuela Náutica de San Telmo* (Seville: Escuela Universitaria de Náutica de Sevilla, 1981), 62–71; and María del Carmen Borrego Plá, "Extracción social de los alumnos del Colegio de San Telmo de Sevilla (1721)," in *Primeras Jornadas de Andalucía y América*, 1, proceedings of a conference at La Rábida, Spain (La Rábida: Universidad Hispanoamericana Santa María de la Rábida et al., 1981), 203–4.

25. USAH, Universidad de Mareantes, books 303–8.

26. ADPS, Hospicio, bundle 1, doc. 18. Although the Toribios had been absorbed into the newly created general poorhouse in 1831, it continued to operate separately under the purview of poorhouse officials for some years thereafter.

27. Such distinctions among different kinds of orphans were not unique to early modern Spain but common to societies with high mortality rates and consequently high levels of orphanage. Even orphanages in the United States through the early twentieth century regularly distinguished between "half-orphans" and "full" orphans. See, for example, Timothy A. Hacsi, *Second Home: Orphan Asylums and Poor Families in America* (Cambridge, MA: Harvard University Press, 1997), especially 11 and 63; and Judith Dulberger, ed., *"Mother Donit fore the Best": Correspondence of a Nineteenth-Century Orphan Asylum* (Syracuse, NY: Syracuse University Press, 1996), 10.

28. The estimated numbers of five- to nineteen-year-old orphans (individuals who had lost both parents to death) are 1,141 if calculated using a life expectancy at birth of 30, and 1,423 if calculated using a life expectancy at birth of 27.5. Both estimates are based on population counts for a 1787 census and on the age distributions reported in the 1887 census (since the age distribution is not available for earlier censuses). I am grateful to Professor David Reher for providing these estimates, derived from the extensive microsimulation data set for Spain he has compiled using the CAMSIM demographic simulation-modeling program at the University of Cambridge. David Reher, e-mail to author, December 7, 1998. Other estimates are found in David Reher, *Perspectives on the Family in Spain, Past and Present* (Oxford: Clarendon Press [Oxford University Press], 1997), 297–321.

29. Due to the largely undocumented admission process at the municipal orphanage for girls (Casa de Niñas Huérfanas) and its small scale of operations, it is difficult to know with any certainty the extent to which girls with surviving mothers attended this institution. Nonetheless, in the sporadic extant lists of residents, some girls are identified explicitly as orphans (generally complete orphans) and others are not, which suggests that this institution might also have served a combination of orphans and nonorphans. (For an example, see AMS, V, vol. 247, doc. 8.) The documentation for the tiny municipal orphanage for boys (Colegio de Niños de la Doctrina) is even spottier, and for a number of years in the eighteenth and early nineteenth centuries there were no resident boys at all. AMS, VI, vol. 69, docs. 19 and 22.

30. BST, uncatalogued document labeled "Provision Real de aprovación de las ordenanzas del Seminario de Niñas Huérfanas de la S[antísi]ma Trinidad de Sevilla," dated Madrid, 16 August 1797, article 5.

31. BST, uncatalogued document labeled "Memoriales de niñas solicitando entrar unas pupilas y otras seminarias en el Beaterio de la S[antísi]ma Trinidad de Sevilla, desde el año de 1828 a 1843," letter from Gertrudis Leon, Seville, 22 January 1828 to "señor obispo ausiliar," Seville.

32. APA, V, Espíritu Santo, unnumbered bundle [1], unnumbered document, letter from Valentina Veles y Mondragón, Seville, 2 January 1798 [to archbishop of Seville].

33. Josef Gómez y Medina, *Metodo de vida, que han de observar los exercitantes, distinguidos en la nueva vivienda de la Casa Colegio de Toribios de la ciudad de Sevilla, que da al público Don Josef Gómez y Medina su Administrador* ([Seville]: Imprenta de D. Diego y D. Josef Godina, 1792), 3–4.

34. "El número de huérfanos (no todos los son pues por empeños o por inclinazión se dispensa por los mayordomos esta prezisa zircunstanzia) es al presente de 148," Archivo General de Simancas (hereafter, AGS), Marina, bundle 215, unnumbered document signed by Don Cayetano Gallego Ordoño, dated Seville, 11 January 1746.

35. A translation of this letter reads as follows:

> María Gonz[ále]z, citizen and native of Seville, widow of her husband Sebastian Gonz[ále]z, with great respect notifies your lord that she has a son, eight or nine years old, more or less, and not having any means to maintain him, I have been obliged to serve as a wet nurse, and am sacrificing to provide for him, having no help except that of God, since the nursing period is drawing to a close and I have no recourse other than to beg alms with my son. If I were alone I would go and serve [as a domestic] in a house. And [not] only this, but he is exposed to being lost to me, as a friend of mine is keeping him, so that at night he does not stay in the streets. And now that there is a chance for boys to enter San Telmo I would like you to remember this poor widow, finding myself with greater need than others as I have no help except that of God and you, not considering [my son's] merits on account of having a grandfather who was a master shoemaker at San Telmo for so many years, but only that I am a poor widow, forced to work. [A]ppealing to your great charity, whose justice I am calling upon, I devotedly ask that you receive him under the assistance of the Royal College of S[a]n Telmo; asking in the name of the heart of the Most Holy Maria, and the devoted Saint Anthony . . .

USAH, bundle 682, unnumbered document, letter of María González, Seville, 28 August 1788, [to San Telmo director, Seville]. On the "solemn poor" (*pobres de solemnidad*), see Maza Zorilla, *Pobreza y asistencia social*, 19–23.

36. AGS, Marina, bundle 216, unnumbered document labeled "Que a Josef Muñoz de edad de ocho años, hijo de Josef Muñoz, y Maria Seco, se le reciva en plaza de colegial," San Ildefonso, 5 September 1783.

37. Perry notes that women and children formed a disproportionate share of the "respectable" or "deserving" poor and as such were entitled to charity in their homes, but that they were not well represented among more public recipients of charity, such as licensed beggars and residents of charity institutions (hospitals). Based on these findings, she concludes:

> Seville did not have to confine its poor in hospitals because its charity converted so many paupers, especially women and children, into "envergonzantes," who would not beg—the shamefaced poor who would voluntarily avoid public view. Charity thus because another form of enclosure for the women of this city.
>
> Those paupers who most successfully survived conformed to expectations of respectability required by the donors. Women in particular learned to use the paternalism of the social order that considered them most needful of protection. Realizing that survival required at least the appearance of obedient submission, mothers of the poor quietly raised their children and lived out their lives, while male officials ignored their strength as survivors. (Perry, *Gender and Disorder*, 176.)

38. USAH, Universidad de Mareantes, book 313, fols. 63–64.

39. APA, V, Espíritu Santo, unnumbered bundle [1], unnumbered document, letter of Don Ygancio Chacon, n.p., n.d. [eighteenth century], [to archbishop of Seville].

40. APA, V, Espíritu Santo, unnumbered bundle [1], unnumbered document, letter of María Ana López Leyton and accompanying documentation, [Seville?], 1799 [to archbishop of Seville].

41. APA, V, Espíritu Santo, unnumbered bundle [1], letter of Pedro Ortiz de Escobar y Abet, no place or date given, but ca. October 1747 [to archbishop of Seville].

42. In addition to Pedro Ortiz de Escobar y Abet's letter ca. October 1747, already cited, see APA, V, Espíritu Santo, unnumbered bundle [1], unnumbered documents, letters to the archbishop of Seville from Pedro Ortiz de Escobar y Abet, n.p., 19 August 1749; n.p., n.d., ca. 1750; Seville, 4 April 1752; Seville, 16 May 1752. See also Convento del Espíritu Santo (hereafter, CES),

uncatalogued document labeled "Libro en que se apuntan las entradas y salidas de las niñas coleg[ial]as desde el mes de en[er]o de 1741," entry for Feliciana Escobar y Tortosa.

43. ADPS, Hospicio, bundle 18, unnumbered document, account book for 1814 labeled "Quaderno del Cargo de esta Casa de Niños Toribios, p[ar]a el año de 1814."

44. AGS, Marina, bundle 217, unnumbered document, cover dated San Ildefonso, 18 September 1783; AGS, Marina, bundle 216, unnumbered document, cover dated San Lorenzo, 24 October 1780.

45. AGS, Marina, bundle 216, unnumbered document, dated San Lorenzo, 24 October 1780.

46. CES, uncatalogued document labeled "Libro de la fundación del colegio de ninas agregadas á el Convento de religiosas del Espíritu Santo. . . ."

47. BST, uncatalogued bundle of documents labeled "Memoriales de niñas solicitando entrar unas pupilas y otras seminarias en el Beaterio de la S[antísi]ma Trinidad de Sevilla desde el año el 1828 a 1843," including letter from Juan Manuel Carrera, Seville, 9 February 1828 [to Archbishop of Seville].

48. USAH, Universidad de Mareantes, book 393, letter of Francisco de Manxon, Cádiz, 22 June 1778 to "S[eño]res y diput[a]dos de R[ea]l Colegio Semin[ari]o de S[a]n Telmo," Seville and response from Juan Manuel de Vivero et al., Seville, 30 June 1778, quotation from Manxon's letter.

49. The noble boarders were initially authorized in the 1786 revisions of San Telmo's bylaws, and reaffirmed in the 1788 version: *Ordenanzas para el Real Colegio de San Telmo de Sevilla* (Madrid: Imprenta de Blas Román, 1788), 19–20, article 27. See also USAH, Universidad de Mareantes, book 308; AMS, V, vol. 284, doc. 14.

50. USAH, Universidad de Mareantes, books 303–7. See also José Delgado y Orellana, *Catálogo de pruebas de nobleza del Real Colegio de San Telmo de Sevilla* (Madrid: Consejo Superior de Investigaciones Científicas Instituto Salazar y Castro, 1985).

51. Valentina Tikoff, "Before the Reformatory: A Correctional Orphanage in Ancien Regime Seville," in *Becoming Delinquent: European Youth, 1650–1950*, ed. Pamela Cox and Heather Shore (Aldershot, Hampshire, England: Ashgate, 2002), 59–75.

52. Gabriel Baca, *Los Thoribios de Sevilla: Breve noticia de la fundación de su hospicio, su admirable principio, sus gloriosos progresos, y el infeliz estado en que al presente se halla* (Madrid: Imprenta de Francisco Xavier García, 1766), 102–4.

53. Collantes de Terán, *Los establecimientos de caridad*, 159, no. 1.

54. ADPS, Hospicio, bundle 13b, letter from Lorenzo M[ari]a Ferreras, [Seville], 4 August 1827 to Administrator of Toribios, [Seville].

55. ADPS, Hospicio, bundle 18, account books for funds received ("Quadernos de Cargo").

56. Orphanages in diverse historical settings often have segregated young people, thus providing insight regarding social fault lines. After the Reformation, Augsburg had separate orphanages for Catholic and Protestant children. (Thomas Max Safley, *Charity and Economy in the Orphanages of Early Modern Augsburg* [Atlantic Highlands, NJ: Humanities Press, 1997], 39–44.) In early modern Amsterdam, the children of citizens were treated in a different orphanage than were the children of noncitizens, thus effectively segregating "respectable" children from the "urban underclass" (McCants, *Civic Charity*, 22–30). In the United States, not only were black, white, and Indian children treated in separate institutions but so were the white children of different religious heritages; there were Protestant, Catholic, and Jewish orphanages and even further ethnic subdivisions, such as German Catholic and Irish Catholic orphanages in St. Louis during the 1850s. The kinds of ethnic and religious diversity that defined the way that children were segregated in most of these other contexts did not exist in eighteenth-century Seville. Yet in all of them, as in Seville, it was the actual or presumed identity of the parents that largely determined where children were sent. Timothy A. Hacsi, *Second Home: Orphan Asylums and Poor Families in America* (Cambridge, MA: Harvard University Press, 1997), 18–37. For specific examples, see Nurith Zmora, *Orphanages Reconsidered: Child Care Institutions in Progressive Era Baltimore* (Philadelphia, PA: Temple University Press, 1994); Howard Goldstein, *The Home on Gorham Street and the Voices of its Children* (Tuscaloosa: University of Alabama Press, 1996); Marilyn Holt, *Indian Orphanages* (Lawrence: University of Kansas, 2001).

57. Nicholas Terpstra, "Making a Living, Making a Life," *Sixteenth Century Journal* 31, no. 4 (winter 2000): 1078–79, quotation from 1078. See also Nicholas Terpstra, "Mothers, Sisters, and Daughters: Girls and Conservatory Guardianship in Late Renaissance Florence," *Renaissance Studies* 17, no. 2 (2003): 201–29; and Nichalas Terpstra, *Abandoned Children of the Italian Renaissance: Orphan Care in Florence and Bologna* (Baltimore, MD: Johns Hopkins University Press, 2005), 70–102.

58. Valentina Tikoff, "Assisted Transitions: Children and Adolescents in the Orphanages of Seville at the End of the Old Regime, 1681–1831" (PhD diss., Indiana University, 2000), 161–65.

59. Stuart Woolf has noted the difficulties involved in fulfilling the documentation requirements for charitable assistance in societies with high levels of illiteracy. Stuart Woolf, "Charity and Family Subsistence" (originally published as a European University Institute Working Paper, no. 85/131, Florence, 1985; reprint in *The Poor in Western Europe in the Eighteenth and Nineteenth Centuries*), 200–201 (page citations are to the reprint edition).

60. Maza Zorilla, *Pobreza y asistencia social*, 19–23.

61. See, for example, Perry, *Gender and Disorder*; Callahan, *Honor, Commerce and Industry in Eighteenth-Century Spain* (Boston: Harvard Graduate School of Business Administration, 1972); Ann Twinam, *Public Lives, Private Secrets: Gender, Honor, Sexuality and Illegitimacy in Colonial Spanish America* (Stanford: Stanford University Press, 1999); Casey, *Early Modern Spain*; and the essays in Asunción Lavrin, *Sexuality and Marriage in Colonial Latin America* (Lincoln: University of Nebraska Press, 1989).

62. Linda Martz, *Poverty and Welfare in Habsburg Spain: The Example of Toledo* (Cambridge: Cambridge University Press, 1983), 202, 206–7; Maureen Flynn, *Sacred Charity: Confraternities and Social Welfare in Spain, 1400–1700* (Ithaca, NY: Cornell University Press, 1989), 79–81.

63. Martz, *Poverty and Welfare*, 206–7. Maza Zorilla, *Pobreza y asistencia social*, 23–26. For Seville in particular, see Carmona García, *El extenso mundo de la pobreza*, 45; and Perry, *Gender and Disorder*, 175.

64. *Novísima recopilación de las leyes de España*, bk. VII, tít. XXXVII, ley IV ("Los expósitos sin padres conocidos se tengan por legítimos para todos los oficios civiles, sin que pueda servir denota la qualidad de tales," 1794) and V ("Reglamento para el establecimiento de las casas de expósitos, crianza y educación de estos," 1796), 688–93. For references to this legislation and other royal initiatives on behalf of foundlings, see Joan Sherwood, *Poverty in Eighteenth-Century Spain: The Women and Children of the Inclusa* (Buffalo: University of Toronto Press, 1988), 95–124, 174–210; Alvarez Santaló, *Marginación social*, 191–203; Morales, *El niño en la cultura española*, 1:435–77; Maza Zorilla, *Pobreza y asistencia social*, 163–68; Twinam, *Public Lives, Private Secrets*, 126–83, 298–314; Susan Socolow, "Acceptable Partners: Marriage Choice in Colonial Argentina, 1778–1910," in *Sexuality and Marriage*, ed. Lavrin, 243 (n. 55); and Ondina E. González, "Down and Out in Havana: Foundlings in Eighteenth-Century Cuba," in *Minor Omissions: Children in Latin American History and Society*, ed. Tobias Hecht (Madison: University of Wisconsin Press, 2002), 102–13.

65. Stuart Woolf has argued, "There is a . . . continuity well into the nineteenth century (and, some would argue, much later) in the conviction that charity

should not be allowed to vault the gulf between ranks of a society of orders (or, subsequently, of a society based on wealth), but on the contrary should function as a reinforcement of the existing social order. The quality and quantity of charity was proportionate to the social level of the recipient, from the material living conditions within the institutions, or the repression of love affairs that ignored the social divide by reclusion of the lower-class woman in a conservatory, to the whole organization of assistance to the shamefaced poor. . . . The stability of the system was ensured by unremitting concern to uphold the moral and economic independence of the basic unit of society—the family. In this context, the institutions of charity played a dual role, not only to substitute for the absence of family (for orphans, the sick and aged, etc.), but to bolster the public reputation of individual families." Stuart Woolf, *The Poor in Western Europe in the Eighteenth and Nineteenth Centuries* (London: Methuen, 1986), 27.

66. For similar findings at an orphanage in Valencia during the seventeenth century, see Tropé, *Formation des enfants orphelins à Valence*, 112–23. For early modern Italy, see Eugenio Sonnino, "Between the Home and the Hospice: The Plight and Fate of Girl Orphans in Seventeenth- and Eighteenth-Century Rome," in *Poor Women and Children in the European Past*, ed. John Henderson and Richard Wall (London: Routledge, 1994), 94–116; and Terpstra, "Making a Living, Making a Life," 1076. For early modern Augsburg, see Safley, *Charity and Economy*, 5; and Thomas Max Safley, *Children of the Laboring Poor: Expectation and Experience Among the Orphans of Early Modern Augsburg* (Leiden: Brill, 2005), 132–33. On France, see Maurice Capul, *Abandon et marginalité* (Toulouse: Privat, 1989), 79–83, 89. For London in a slightly later period, see Lydia Murdoch, *Imagined Orphans: Poor Families, Child Welfare, and Contested Citizenship in London* (New Brunswick, NJ: Rutgers University Press, 2006), 67–119. On U.S. institutions in the nineteenth and twentieth centuries, see Hacsi, *Second Home*, 106–10; and Holt, *Indian Orphanages*, 76, 248–49.

67. Silvia Arrom, for example, has found that in late eighteenth- and nineteenth-century Mexico City, the city's poorhouse served largely as a residential school for children, and Robert Schwartz has found similar patterns at some of the poorhouses erected in early modern France. Silvia M. Arrom, *Containing the Poor: The Mexico City Poor House, 1774–1871* (Stanford: Stanford University Press, 2000), passim, especially 126–41, 247–53, 278–88. See also Robert M. Schwartz, *Policing the Poor in Eighteenth-Century France* (Chapel Hill: University of North Carolina Press, 1988), 93–131, especially 94–98.

68. Timothy Hacsi, for example, has made this argument in his examination of orphanages in the United States during the late nineteenth and early twentieth centuries (Hacsi, *Second Home*, 107–8). See also Schwartz, *Policing the Poor*, 97.

69. I am, of course, borrowing and applying this language from the influential article by Joan Scott, "Gender: A Useful Category of Historical Analysis," *American Historical Review* 91, no. 5 (December 1986): 1053–75.

70. Robert Jütte, *Poverty and Deviance in Early Modern Europe* (Cambridge: Cambridge University Press, 1994), 36, 40; and Stuart Woolf, "Introduction: The Poor and Society," in *Poor in Western Europe*, 2–3, 915.

CHAPTER THREE

Growing Up Indian

Migration, Labor, and Life in Lima
(1570–1640)

Teresa C. Vergara

∞

✢ In 1613, the notary Miguel de Contreras conducted a census of the indigenous population living in Lima.[1] He found that a considerable proportion of Indian residents were children and youths who came from almost all regions of the Peruvian viceroyalty.[2] One of these children was Inés, an eight-year-old orphan girl who lived and worked in Pablo López's home, where her parents had left her when she was "very little." And there was Juanillo, a ten-year-old boy who worked as a domestic servant in the house of Don Juan de Barrios, his Spanish colonial lord (*encomendero*). Don Juan had brought Juanillo from his *encomienda* in Chincha to work in his home in Lima. Yet another youth captured in the census was Antonio Suy Suy, a sixteen-year-old son of an Indian leader, who had lived with Spaniards since he was a very young boy. At the time of the census he was one of the youngest tailors in the city. Luisa, a fourteen-year-old slave girl, had a different life story. In 1610, when she was eleven years old, a mestizo brought her from Chile, her birthplace, and sold her to Bartolomé Nafio Girón, in whose house she now worked.[3]

These stories illustrate the diversity in the patterns of arrival, residence, and work among migrant Indian children and youths in Lima during the first decades of the seventeenth century. The massive wave of indigenous migration that occurred after conquest in the Andes has been the subject of particularly intense scholarly attention in the last two decades.[4] However, these studies mainly focus on adult cases and not the particular characteristics of youth migration and its impact on the construction of the colonial society.[5] In this chapter, I argue that rather than impeding Indian children and youths from abandoning their *pueblos*, or places of origins, as in the case of adults, Spanish authorities sought to control the indigenous population by allowing Indian children and youths to live with Spanish families in the city.[6]

Even though migrant children and youth left their natal homes for masters' homes, thereby typically breaking family links, in Spain and its colonies a master was presumed to exert fatherly care over his servants as if they were his children.[7] The fact that Indian children became members of their masters' extended families facilitated the colonial project since it ensured that they would learn the necessary economic and cultural skills to serve better the Spaniards.[8] It was expected that in their masters' houses, Indians would be exposed to the culture and religion of the colonizers as well as becoming familiar with colonial principles such as obedience, recognition of authority, and acceptance of their subordinate role.[9] As an ultimate goal, colonial authorities expected that these acculturated Indians would help maintain control and order within indigenous populations.[10]

However, education in the customs, practices, and values of Spaniards as well as Spanish technology and legislation gave Indians the tools they needed to go beyond the limits imposed on them as colonized people. Acculturated Indians, especially artisans, could construct their identities as respectable persons, moving across racial and social categories as circumstances allowed. As Lyman Johnson and Sonya Lipsett-Rivera point out, a good reputation was a kind of social capital circulated among those living at the margins of colonial society.[11]

The opening descriptions drawn from the 1613 census of Lima suggest that indigenous children and youths arrived in the capital city under a variety of conditions. Indeed, as other scholarship has shown, some had severed ties with their communities and had a difficult life in the city, and some even had been taken by force from their pueblos. Yet others arrived in the city with the permission of their parents or even were brought by them, maintained relationships with their families and communities, and counted on the support of their Spanish masters.

In spite of the different ways these children and youths arrived in the city, they all struggled to cope with the colonial system and even tried to elevate themselves socially. They used the opportunity of living with a Spanish family to improve their social and economic conditions and to avoid the dependency that limited the indigenous population in general. For instance, after becoming familiar with Spanish culture in their masters' households as youths, Indians could break into professions other than domestic service. This was particularly true of those Indian youths who established links of patronage with their masters—Spaniards who often, and ironically, aided them in becoming relatively independent economically and socially "respectable." In the case of boys, in particular, Indians might learn an artisan trade and leave the dependent position of a domestic servant.[12]

The *Padrón de los indios de Lima* provides a rich source for understanding the processes by which Indian youths became colonial adults. This 1613 census of Lima's indigenous population has been used to study demographic trends among indigenous *limeños* (residents of Lima), their migratory patterns, economic activities, and adaptation to Spanish culture.[13] Although some of these studies refer to specific topics covered in this chapter—such as the ways in which Indian children arrived in Lima, the economic activities they performed there, and the process of *ladinization*, or familiarization with the language and culture of Spaniards—unlike previous scholarship, I use the census to determine the expectations that the indigenous population, elite as well as ordinary Indians, had when they placed their children in Spanish urban households. Analyzing children's explanations of their arrival in the city, as well as examining the recollections of Indian adults who entered Lima when they were young, reveals how important it was for all Indians, not just those who arrived by choice in the city, to become familiar with the culture of the Spaniards as a strategy that allowed them to cope with the colonial system. The census also allows us to reassess the traditional assumption that those Indians who migrated from rural to urban areas severed their ties with their families and communities.[14] The *Padrón de los indios* shows this to be only partially true. In several cases recent migrants, as well as those who immigrated to the city years before the census was conducted, maintained ties with their communities.[15] Thus, to become urbanized and even "ladino" did not necessarily entail a loss of "Indianness."

Labor contracts and Indian wills are sources that complement and enrich the information of the *Padrón de los indios*. Labor contracts show the conditions under which Indian children and youths entered service and apprenticeships and shed light on the obligations assumed by both masters and children. In turn, wills provide information about the relationship between the masters and the Indian children and youths who grew up in their households. Both sources underscore the resilience of cultural links between migrants and their towns, undermining the common assumption that urban Indian migrants and those who remained in their pueblos belonged to two sharply separated worlds.

Ordinary Indian Youths

When Spanish conquerors and colonizers initially made contact with the native civilizations of the Andes, they were intrigued and fascinated by the indigenous nobility and Indian leaders, known as *caciques*, since the Spanish believed that forging alliances with the native elite would be key to their success.[16] Yet, most of the Indian boys and girls who flooded into Peru's capital city in the early seventeenth century were not elite but commoners, and they held ordinary political or economic status in their communities of origin. Ordinary Indians were beholden to work for encomenderos, or Spanish lords who had received royal title to control a given native populations, or they were subject to forced labor drafts, the *mita*, beginning at the age of eighteen.

The data from the *Padrón de los indios* shows that those who left their pueblos when they were young children did not take an active part choosing their destination, while those who moved from their towns when they were in their teens had a clear idea of both to where and why they wanted to move. The majority of Indian youths arrived in the city when they were between thirteen and seventeen years old, and these teenagers clearly intended to establish themselves legally in Lima, for most Indian adults were encouraged by both traditional community structures and Spanish law to remain in their hometowns.

These indigenous children and youths entered the city under a variety of different circumstances: some were brought by an encomendero or by their parents; others arrived on their own. Some of them were taken from their towns by force, thereby losing contact with their families, while others moved to the city to evade the labor and tribute obligations that they faced as members of the indigenous population. In general, these children came to the city to work, but their living and working conditions as well as the opportunities that were open to them for the future were not homogeneous. Rather, their situations correlated to the young migrants' gender as well as to their social, economic, and cultural status.

Indian children frequently came to Lima as domestic servants. Indigenous boys and girls often were sent from their pueblos to work in their encomendero's house in a city near the indigenous community he controlled.[17] Juan Rupay, Pedro Colloco, and María (who, like many Indian migrant children under the age of eight, lacked a last name) moved from their pueblos to the house that their encomendero, Don Fernando Niño, kept in Lima. Juan Rupay was ten years old when he arrived from Don Fernando's encomienda of Surco, Pedro Colloco was twelve years old when he arrived from another encomienda in Huaylillas, and María was eight years old when she arrived from Don Fernando's encomienda of Chuqui.[18] It was not only young children who moved to Lima to serve in their encomendero's house; young men also came to the city to work for their encomenderos.[19]

Indian boys and girls also worked in the homes of their encomenderos' relatives. Such was the case of the two girls, Catalina and Inés, who reportedly lived and worked in the house of the daughter of Doña Inés de Villalobos, their encomendera. It appears Doña Inés sent the girls to work for her daughter when they were quite young since, at the time of the census interview, Catalina was fourteen years old and Inés was eleven. The girls came from Cuenca and Coria, respectively, both towns quite distant from Lima.[20] Children such as Catalina and Inés who arrived in the city in their early years and came from distant towns were the most prone to sever ties with their families and communities.

Nonelite Spaniards who lived in the city also desired the status associated with commanding the labor of Indian children, whom they would employ in their houses and orchards. Colonial authorities allowed Indian boys and girls to live with nonencomenderos in part because there was a high demand for cheap labor in the city and in part, as indicated previously, as a means to exercise control over the indigenous population. In fact, in the labor contracts for Indian youths, it frequently appears that the Lima's colonial authorities themselves put Indian children to work with masters.[21] For instance, one of the Lima's *alcaldes* (municipal officials) put a ten-year-old boy in the service of Alonso Pérez de Villamediana. The contract specified that the youth had to work for Pérez de Villamediana for two years; in exchange he would receive lodging, food, and a small salary and would be instructed in the Catholic doctrine.[22]

According to information in the *Padrón de los indios* and the labor contracts, children began to work in Spanish households when they were around nine or ten years old. Therefore, Antonio Carama's age—he was a ten-year-old boy who had arrived in the city the previous year to work in the house of Francisco de Araujo—did not make him exceptional.[23] Orphaned children often moved to Spaniards' homes at even younger ages. For example, Juan Churque, a ten-year-old orphan boy, told Contreras that he began to live with his master when he was no older than four years.[24]

Although these children began living and working in their Spanish masters' households when they were very young, they frequently were paid for their services only after age ten, when they could legally sign a contract with their masters, as did Juana de Ordoñez. In 1597, she agreed in writing to serve Doña García Ordoñez. However, information in her contract shows that the relationship between Juana and her mistress did not commence at the time they signed the contract but instead had been established earlier. Since Indian children often adopted their masters' surnames, the fact that Juana had the same last name as her mistress indicates that Juana was raised in her mistress's house. What is more, Juana was a *ladina*, which means that she spoke and understood Spanish very well, and we might guess that she had learned the language in her mistress's house. Finally, Juana did not know what pueblo she came from or the names of her parents, a situation that was common among orphaned children and those who were removed from their towns when they were very young.[25]

How did these children physically get to the city? Inés, an Indian woman in her thirties, reported that many masters who employed youths prior to coming to Lima generally brought these same youths to Lima.[26] Inés herself had been brought to Lima as a child by her Spanish mistress.[27] The same was true for twelve-year-old Francisco Arguello, who came to Lima from the northern city of Guayaquil, his birthplace, with his master, Francisco Zamora.[28] In addition, Indian children, especially orphans, arrived in the city with travelers, merchants, and priests who were often asked by Lima's residents to bring them an "*indiecillo*" (little Indian).[29]

Many Indian youths retained strong recollections and even active ties with their community of origin. For example, a youth named Juan could not remember who his encomendero was because, he said, he left the town when he was a small boy. But he told Contreras that he not only knew where his mother was but also that his cacique was a man named Don Agustín.[30] Juan's memory does not appear to have been unusually strong. The information in the *Padrón de los indios* shows that 35 percent (n=196) of the children and youths interviewed knew, like Juan, where their parents were and/or the names of their caciques.

It is possible that some of these children maintained ties with their relatives and communities through those people who moved between their towns and Lima to fulfill the compulsory labor obligations that all Indians had to perform for the Spanish state. What is more, the people who transported products for their encomenderos and sold their own products in Lima's market undoubtedly also carried hometown news to the city's Indians, helping sustain strong community links despite migration.[31] Isabel de Umay, a twenty-year-old married woman from San Miguel de Urcomay in Chinchacocha, grew up in Lima in the house of a Spanish woman, where she was still working in 1613. Although she spent all her life in the city, she had married an Indian from her community of origin. At the time of the interview, Juan, her husband, was not in the city but back in San Miguel, their pueblo, where he traveled frequently.[32]

The fact that some Indians who grew up in Lima still paid tribute to their caciques in their pueblos of origin also reveals the importance they assigned to keeping ties with their communities. The payment of Indian tribute in particular assured them their right to maintain use of their community's resources. The cases of Francisco de Chávez and Francisco Huarachaico illustrate this very well. Francisco, a twenty-year-old artisan from Cajatambo, arrived in Lima when he was twelve years old. At the time of his interview with Contreras, he said that he had been paying tribute to his cacique for two years, which indicated that he had begun fulfilling his tribute obligations promptly at the mandatory age of eighteen. Juan Guamán had lived in Lima for four years before he turned eighteen in 1611. Even so, he still owed his home community obligations as an Indian, and his father, who remained in his town, paid tribute for him.[33]

Indian wills also showcase how Indian migrant children and their parents maintained close relationships over distances. This was especially true of those Indians who moved to the city when they were children but inherited lands and other belongings that their parents possessed back in their pueblos. Catalina de Vargas came from the valley of Umay, located in the central coast, where her parents and the rest of her family lived. Although she grew up working as a domestic servant in Lima, thanks to the connections she maintained with her family, she knew when her parents died and learned that she had inherited part of their lands.[34]

Nevertheless, it was easier for those Indian children and youths, and in general for all migrants, to maintain a relationship with relatives and communities whose pueblos were located a short distance from the city.[35] This is why Isabel, a twelve-year-old girl who had lived all her life in one Dr. Guardiana's house, knew the names of both her encomendero and her cacique. The proximity of Ica, her hometown, to the capital city probably made it easier for her to receive news about her relatives and about political authorities.[36]

For those children who came from distant territories, news from their relatives and towns was rarer. The distance between Lima and Jusepe de la Cruz's community of origin, Zaña, which was located in the northern part of the viceroyalty, undoubtedly contributed to his lack of knowledge about his pueblo. Thus, it is not surprising that he could not tell Contreras whether his parents were still alive, and when he was questioned about the native authorities in his community, he said that he heard that his cacique was someone named Don Martín, but he did not know for sure, nor did he know the name of his encomendero.[37]

Indian youths' ties with their communities were severed not only by distance and the vagueness of children's memories but also by abandonment and parents' deaths.[38] However, in some cases, even orphaned children such as Cristóbal Gutiérrez, a twelve-year-old boy who worked in a Spanish woman's orchard since he was very young, did know who their caciques were.[39] Cristóbal's intriguing case raises a set of questions. Did his cacique place him in his mistress's house? Was it his cacique who gave permission for someone to bring him to the city? Did his cacique continue watching over him after his parents had died?

Indeed, labor contracts in notary records indicate that caciques from the towns near Lima sometimes brought orphan children from their communities in order to place them with Spanish masters to learn a trade.[40] By doing so, these indigenous leaders fulfilled their obligation to care for orphan children and, at the same time, made sure that people from home communities would live in the capital and therefore grow up to provide the community representation and help their leaders and other townspeople. Thus, it is possible that, rather than only a process of breaking away from Indian communities, indigenous child migration sometimes could be a strategy that Indians employed to protect their ethnic groups and defend the rights of their pueblos in the face of colonialism.

Indian children often arrived in the city with their own parents, a practice that is well documented in the *Padrón de los indios* as well as in Indian labor contracts dating as far back as the sixteenth century. It was not until the second half of the seventeenth century, however, that Indian parents could count on the protection of the law when placing their children with Spanish masters. It was at that point that King Charles II prohibited his subjects from impeding Indian parents who wished to send children under the age of eighteen to learn a trade or to engage in any other activity that they deemed appropriate.[41] The king undoubtedly enacted this law because for some time Spanish authorities in charge of governing Indians in the rural areas (the *corregidor* and the priest), as well as landowners who lived in these areas, had been requiring Indians to send their children to serve the Spanish population without any economic compensation. Thus, prior to the law's enactment, Indian parents could view sending their children to Lima as a way of preventing their offspring from forced unpaid labor elsewhere as well as protecting them from the abuses of local authorities and other groups who lived near their towns.

It is clear that the notion of child labor was not new to Andean peoples. Most likely, in the rural areas of the Andes, Indian children performed different types of tasks according to their age within their own communities. In addition to helping in their homes with domestic chores, most also worked alongside their parents in Spanish enterprises such as mines and textile workshops. For example, in the mining regions of the Andes, older children worked outside the mines, picking up small pieces of silver that their mothers later sold to Spaniards, while in the textile workshops, boys and girls spun wool.[42]

But when economic times were hard in the countryside, the ancillary labor children performed did not provide sufficient hope for the future, so Indian parents looked to urban centers for a solution. Indian parents knew that by leaving their children with a family in a city they were assured that the children would at least receive food, lodging, and clothing. We might imagine that this was what Juan and María thought when they left Inés, their daughter, in the house of Pablo López. According to Inés's recollection, her parents left her there when she was a very young girl. She could not remember their last names, since at the time of the census she was

OTABA CALLE
PVCLLACOCVAMRA

3.1

SETIMA CALLE
PAVAV·PALLAC

3.2

SESTA CALLE
CORO·TASQVE

3.3

only eight years old. Pablo López said that Inés's mother was from the town of Sayán, located in the Lima highlands.[43]

For those Indians who already lived in a city other than Lima, however, their objective in migrating seems to have been specifically to move to the capital, which was the largest city in the region and promised indigenous migrants the greatest economic and social opportunities (and, perhaps, presented them with the most difficulties). It is very likely that Lima's prestige as a city of opportunities not only circulated among Spaniards and mestizos but also among Indians. Indians who already lived in urban areas knew the Spanish language and were familiar with the culture of Spaniards. They would feel themselves prepared to succeed in Lima. Such a consideration may well have led Catalina Quispe Chuque, an Indian widow, to bring her son from the highland city of Huancavelica to the capital to serve Don Francisco de Saavedra. At the time of the census, her eleven-year-old boy had a Spanish hairstyle and dressed like a Spaniard, clear signs of his acculturation and good omens for his quick adaptation to both the capital city and his new life there.[44]

If we assume that Indian parents brought their children to Lima in order to give them a better life, then we can also assume that they tried to put them in the homes of people they trusted and who would treat them well. Some Indian parents also signed a labor contract with their son's or daughter's master in which the master promised before a local colonial authority to give good treatment, which meant food, lodging, clothing, and medical care. However, for some ordinary Indians it was not easy to

3.1–3.3. Felipe Guamán Poma de Ayala's Stages of Childhood. The illustrations on the facing page by early colonial Indian chronicler Felipe Guamán Poma de Ayala depict three *"calles"* (literally, "roads" or "stations") in the Andean life cycle. Note that the stations are counted in descending order, with the seventh and sixth roads (*séptima* and *sesta calles*) representing progressively greater age, when adolescents began to help with agricultural work and to travel on their own. The eighth road (*otaba calle*) depicts an age of five years when play competed with emerging responsibilities for children. The drawing is subtitled *"pucllacoc uarma,"* which in Quechua means "playful female," but the caption reads "serves her mother." Source: Felipe Guamán Poma de Ayala, *Nueva córonica y buen gobierno*, ed. Franklin Pease G. Y. (Caracas: Biblioteca Ayacucho, 1980), 160, 159, 157.

establish connections with Spaniards in the cities. A woman named María, for example, brought her nine-year-old son Juan to Lima to serve Mayora, a free black woman. Mayora lived in the predominantly "black" parish of Santa Ana, staying in a rented room in a house in which Indians from various regions of the viceroyalty also lived. It is likely that all of them helped Juan adapt to life in the city, but it is also probable that his understanding of Spanish culture was different and perhaps was acquired more slowly than if had he been employed in a Spanish household.[45]

More ambitious parents brought their sons to the city to learn a trade. Indian parents knew that as apprentices their sons would live in their masters' households, where they would be trained in job-related skills as well as initiated into the social and religious life of the craft. After two to six years, depending on the trade, apprentices would become journeymen and thereafter function as independent wage earners. According to guild regulations, after an additional two- to four-year period, Spanish journeymen were eligible to be examined as masters; when they were approved they could own shops and sell directly to the public. These Spanish guild regulations, however, did not apply to Indians. Indian journeymen were exempted from the master examination and could open their own shops immediately after their apprenticeship period if they had enough money to rent a workshop and to purchase their own tools and materials.[46]

Indian parents who were aware of the possibility of fairly rapid advancement within a particular trade apprenticed their sons, knowing that by becoming artisans their offspring would be considered respectable members of society.[47] In 1613, Juan Antonio Quipián came from Jauja to Lima with his twelve-year-old son so that Juan Antonio could work as a sacristan in the Monastery of La Concepción, a female convent that, as an entity, held the encomienda of his town. Although Juan Antonio's job indicates that he was substantially integrated into Spanish culture, he must have intended the same for his son when he placed the boy as a shoemaker's apprentice to Diego de Brizuela, in whose house the child lived. After Juan Antonio finished his service to the nuns, he would return to Jauja and to the rest of his family, while his son would stay in the city three or four more years to finish his apprenticeship.[48] At that point, the youth, as an artisan, would be able to establish himself legally in any place.

Other Indians who became artisans took advantage of such possibilities, and they often moved from one place to another until they found a situation that maximized their opportunities to improve their economic and social situation, as Martín Guamán did. Martín, an eighteen-year-old button maker, was born in the highland community of Huamanga, grew up in Huancavelica, and came to Lima when he was fourteen years old. After learning the button-making trade he moved back to Huamanga, where he stayed for a while and then decided to return to Lima.[49]

Indian parents who already lived in or near the city of Lima, such as Miguel Morales, were the most familiar with the advantages their sons would garner by becoming artisans in the capital. Morales was an Indian fisherman who lived with his family in Callao, the port of Lima. Among Indians, fishing was a traditional occupation usually passed from fathers to sons. But Spanish legislation allowed anyone to fish in areas that local Indians once had controlled. This meant that being a fisherman increasingly lost its appeal as an occupation for Indians, who faced competition from Spaniards and mestizos who often had better boats and employed other fishermen.[50] Morales likely took all of this into consideration when he decided that his son, Juan Pérez, would not be a fisherman but rather an apprentice of Garcí Hernández, a Spanish tailor. Because Lima was so close by, young Juan still lived in Callao with his family, but he went daily to Lima in order to work for his master and learn the craft.[51]

Elite Indian Youths

Elite Indians who lived in Lima can be divided into two groups: caciques and their families who for various reasons decided to live in the city; and members of the Indian elite who lost their noble privileges after the Conquest and with the establishment of the colonial regime. Especially after the fifth viceroy of Peru, Francisco de Toledo (1569–81), reorganized the viceroyalty and began Indian resettlement projects, the situation of several members of the Indian elite, known as *principales*, changed for the worse. Viceroy Toledo reduced the number of Indians who could claim rights as part of the indigenous nobility, recognizing only the cacique and the *segunda persona* (lesser noble) and their sons as part of the Indian elite. All other elite Indians, according to Toledo's legislation, had to work for a living and pay tribute to both their local leaders and to the Spanish colonial government.[52]

Indian elites who were not wealthy enough to live without working, including some principales and even caciques, sought to establish their children in Lima as guild masters. This position would give them social recognition as well as a chance to participate both in local government as Indian authorities and in the church as supervisors (*mayordomos*) of Catholic confraternities.[53] In other words, many elite indigenous families sought to regain what conquest had taken from them by ensuring that their children found new routes to power and prestige within the colonial system.

The steps that other elite Indian parents followed to establish their children in Lima were similar to those taken by commoner parents. The children of principales arrived in the city with their parents or with a trusted person who usually placed them with Spanish masters. Pedro Guevara, the fifteen-year-old son of a cacique in the province of Huaylas, arrived in Lima in 1610 in order to learn the trade of tailor with a Spanish master. But Pedro did not come with his father; he came with an Indian tailor from his pueblo, and the tailor told Contreras that he, too, had grown up serving Spaniards. At the time of the census both were working in a local tailor's workshop.[54]

Although male Indian youths often gained familiarity with the Spanish way to behave at the table, to dress, to pray, and to talk as they learned a trade in a master's workshop in the capital city, many parents decided to acculturate their sons first, before coming to Lima. Don Andrés Panta, cacique of the town of Caton in the province of Zaña, placed his son, Don Francisco, with a Spanish family when he was seven years old. According to Don Francisco's interview, after eight years with the Spanish family, he moved to Lima. In 1613, five years after his arrival, Don Francisco was twenty-two years old and worked as an embroiderer in a Spaniard's workshop, a prestigious occupation.[55]

The information about elite Indian girls that can be gleaned from the census of 1613 shows that a full 98.2 percent (n=13) lived with their families and did not work, and only one girl who was alone in the city—a fourteen year old—lived and worked in a Spanish home.[56] Other parents preferred to put their daughters with elite Indian families in Lima related to them by blood, place of origin, or simply by social-class standing. For instance, Don Francisco de Talavera, an elite Indian from a pueblo located in the Lima Valley, took his seven-year-old daughter Catalina to live in Lima with the son of a cacique from a different pueblo. There is no indication in the census that Catalina worked as a servant in the home of the cacique.[57]

Elite Indian parents also sometimes placed their daughters in monasteries or lay female spiritual houses. Although the *Padrón de los indios* does not provide information about elite Indian women living in nunneries in

Lima, recent studies have shown that caciques brought their daughters to provincial cities such as Cuzco and Huamanga precisely in order to place them in spiritual houses.[58] Some simply wanted their daughters to become Hispanicized. Others, though clearly a minority, were more ambitious and hoped that their daughters would be accepted as nuns. While most Indian girls could not become black-veiled nuns because of the caste restrictions established during the sixteenth century in religious houses, sometimes the daughter of a rich and influential Indian cacique, who could pay the significant dowry necessary to profess as a nun, was accepted into a female religious order. The caciques knew that their daughters could never obtain a black veil, a status reserved for elite Spanish women who ran the nunnery and managed its revenues and property. Nevertheless, the position of these caciques' daughters as nuns of a white veil bestowed prestige on their families and provided the social networks that elite Indians needed to move successfully in Spanish society.[59]

Those elite Indians who maintained their political and economic power after the Conquest were also interested in bringing their sons to Lima so that they could learn to read and write in Spanish, as well as receive further training in Catholic doctrine. They also undoubtedly expected that during the period that their sons lived in the city, the youths would acquire the social networks they needed to interact with Lima's colonial authorities.

Ensuring that caciques' sons learned the Spanish language and Catholic doctrine was also part of the agenda of the colonial administration. In 1569 Viceroy Toledo ordered that schools for caciques be opened in the cities of Lima and Cuzco, but this measure was implemented only in the second decade of the seventeenth century. For that reason, when Don Pedro Guacra Yalli, an elite Indian of Canta, decided that his ten-year-old son should learn to read in Spanish, he placed him in the school for children run by Juan de Mendoza, a Spanish teacher, in Lima.[60]

Caciques and principales, however, more often placed their sons in monasteries or in the houses of lawyers, notaries, and priests than with trained teachers. Noble Indian parents sometimes paid these individuals to instruct their sons, while in other cases the boys had to work in exchange for their education. The case of Don Francisco de Vergara, cacique of Ocros, illustrates the efforts of elite Indians to become literate Christians. Don Francisco explained that he began his Spanish education when he was young, while he was living with the canon Dr. Padilla as "his boy." With

Dr. Padilla, Don Francisco learned to read and write in Spanish and to count, as well as receiving lessons in Catholic doctrine. After the canon's death, Don Francisco was entrusted to Don Juan Félix de Padilla (who might have been related to the canon), with whom he lived for more than twelve years until the Indian got married and assumed the position of native leadership of his town.[61] Other elite indigenous males reported that they too received an education at the hands of church officials or in male monasteries.[62]

Some caciques and principales wanted their children to master Spanish legislation as well as Catholic doctrine, undoubtedly so that they could help their communities in the numerous civil suits that made up the core of Spanish colonial politics. That was what Don Martín Talpachin, cacique of the town of Huamantanga, aimed to do when he brought his two sons, ages twelve and ten, to Lima. Don Martín had chosen the notary Navamuel to teach the boys legislation as well as Spanish reading and writing, and at the time of the census, they were living in the notary's house.[63] Don Martín knew that learning to read and write in Spanish, as well as understanding Spanish legislation, would give his sons the tools they needed to be recognized as legitimate Indian authorities by the Spanish population as well as by their own people.[64] The son who did not inherit a position of leadership could perform some specialized task such as translator or prosecutor in Indian cases, and in the city he could work as an interpreter in the town council (*cabildo*) and the Royal Audiencia (Royal High Court) as well as assist the people from his town with their lawsuits.[65]

Enslaved Indian Children

In the first decades of the seventeenth century, enslaved boys and girls represented 9 percent of the Indian children and youths in Lima, and most belonged to ethnic groups that were at war with the Spaniards, such as Chilean Araucanians.[66] The Spanish crown had prohibited the trade in and enslavement of Indians in the sixteenth century, but due to Chilean Indians' continued resistance to Spanish rule, the crown permitted those captured in territories still at war to be sold as slaves.[67] Children and young women from these ethnic groups were sold and distributed throughout the viceroyalty of Peru.

The rules that regulated the Indian slave trade prohibited the sale of boys under ten and a half and girls under nine and a half years old.[68] Nonetheless, commercial trafficking in Indian children was so profitable that the rules were ignored. For example, in 1611 the archbishop of Lima sold Pedro, a six-year-old boy from Chile, to the painter Martín Alonso Mesa.[69] The adults who sold these children were usually those who traveled to war territories frequently, such as soldiers and sailors. For instance, Doña Magdalena de Andrada told Contreras that she bought Ursulilla when the girl was five years old from a Spanish sailor who came from Chile and sold the girl to her for one hundred pesos.[70]

These enslaved Indian children were brought to the city primarily to work as domestic servants, and like other children who worked in Spanish houses from a young age, they grew up as part of their Spanish masters' families. By 1613, eleven-year-old Lucía de Carvajal and sixteen-year-old Francisca Carrillo had lived and worked in the house of Doña Leonor de Carvajal for several years. Both girls were slaves from Chile and had been sent by Doña Leonor's son, Don Fernando Carrillo, to his mother when they were very young.[71] As was usual in the case of Indian children who grew up in Spanish homes, both girls had added to their names the surnames of their masters.

Even though children became part of the imagined "clan" of masters' families, it is difficult to believe that their lives would not be marked by the same kind of brutality and exploitation as were the lives of African slaves. Although black slaves could incorporate themselves into Spanish families, as Lucía and Francisca appear to have done, the violent way in which they arrived in the city and the rupture of their ties with family and ethnic groups had to have made assimilation psychologically, and perhaps socially, difficult for these children. In addition, their condition as slaves placed them in the lowest social and legal position in colonial society. That may have been why María Magdalena, a fourteen-year-old girl, rejected her mistress's identification of her as an Indian slave from Santa Cruz de la Sierra, a war territory. María Magdalena insisted that she was from Majes in the highland province of Arequipa—an area far from the war territories—where, she said, her parents lived.[72] Clearly, securing a reputation as a free Indian, particularly by insisting on that status before a census taker such as Contreras, was critical to her.

Life and Work in the City

As is now obvious, there was tremendous variety in the conditions that brought young Indian migrants to the capital of colonial Peru. Once they arrived and established themselves in the city, the possibilities they faced were as multiple as the factors that brought them to Lima.

These possibilities reflected the young migrants' social status within Indian communities as well as their gender. Elite boys generally entered as craft apprentices immediately after arriving in the city. They also experienced better working conditions and could be sure that at the end of their apprenticeship they would become journeymen or even guild masters. Commoner Indian boys, in contrast, had very limited opportunities to obtain an urban apprenticeship directly. They had to work first as domestic servants in the city or in other places before beginning to learn a trade.

All Indian boys who entered apprenticeships performed a variety of tasks both in workshops and in their masters' houses. Some of them signed written contracts that specified the rights and duties of both parties, but a significant percentage of apprentices made only verbal agreements concerning work conditions. This situation surely allowed some masters to take advantage of their apprentices. Indian youths who arrived in the city by themselves were most vulnerable to masters' manipulation of the terms of the contract, which contrasted sharply with that of Spanish, mestizo, elite-Indian, and even slave apprentices.

The majority of documented cases reveal that young Indian servants were placed with master artisans by their parents, relatives, or masters, who signed contracts that protected the apprentices' rights.[73] These contracts specified that the master would treat his apprentice well, taking care of him in case of illness, and would teach him the "art of the trade." The contracts also stated how long the training would last. This was a very important clause in the standard apprenticeship contract, for it guaranteed that the master would certify that the apprentice knew the trade and would prepare him for the exam to become an official journeyman.

If many indigenous youths were denied the guarantees that other castes enjoyed when entering apprenticeships, Indian apprentices who were under the age of ten were also deprived of a salary during the first two years of their training. According to the law, Indian apprentices from eight to twelve years of age were to be paid twelve pesos a year, and those older than twelve fourteen pesos a year in addition to the goods and services specified in the contract.[74] But masters often justified their failure to pay young Indians by declaring that "because of his young [corta] age he was not a useful person during his first years," and it was enough if "he receives the necessary food, clothing, medicine, and instruction in Catholic religion and good manners [*buenas costumbres*]."[75]

Many Indian parents seemed to accept masters' failure to pay their children an apprentice salary. In 1601, Francisca Beltran placed her son Andrés as a carpenter's apprentice. The signed contract specified that Andrés would be an apprentice for four years, during which time, in addition to teaching Andrés the trade, the master artisan would give him room and board, medicine, and instruction in Catholic doctrine. As the contract stated, Andrés was to receive no money during his apprenticeship or at the end of the contract, a condition to which Francisca agreed.[76]

Parents accepted the lack of pay because the opportunity to become a journeyman put these youths in a better position in Spanish colonial society. Once they became journeymen they could dress in Spanish-styled clothing and were recognized as acculturated Indians by other members of colonial society.[77] This was one of the reasons why it was so important for commoner Indians to learn a craft, but artisan status gave them other rights as well. To begin with, Indian craftsmen were exempt from working in the mines and textile workshops. In addition, artisans had the right to establish themselves wherever they wanted. They could live in the city without worrying that the Spanish colonial officials might force them to return to their towns. Becoming an artisan also improved one's economic position. A journeyman received from his master around forty pesos a year in addition to food, clothing, and medical care.[78]

The social and economic advantages that young, male, Indian commoners achieved by becoming artisans are particularly notable if we compare their situation with that of elite Indian boys who also came to Lima to learn a trade. After becoming journeymen and artisans, both groups situated themselves in very similar social and economic positions. Although entering a trade made it possible for commoner Indians to improve their social and economic position, for elite Indians the choice to come to the city narrowed their chances of maintaining themselves as members of a separate, prestigious social group. Thus, for the latter, entering a trade in the city represented a decline in their social position, even though elite Indian artisans tried to control those institutions, such as religious confraternities and guilds, that could give them power and prestige.

Indigenous children and youths also signed contracts as domestic servants. Although these contracts had the advantage of providing information about Indian girls as well as boys, they were far less numerous than those of apprentices. The duties of the servant children were not specified in the contracts with any precision, but it is clear that they were hired to help in different tasks both at home and in the orchards common in Lima at that time. During sowing and harvesting seasons some of the children also had to help on the lands that their masters owned in the urban hinterlands. If the master had a *pulpería* (grocery store), they also worked there, waiting on customers and keeping the place clean. For instance, the contract of Miguel, a twelve-year-old boy from the southern coastal town of Pachacamac, stipulated that he would serve Enrique de Figueroa for one year in all that was needed as well as in "those tasks that Indians do." Ana, a ten-year-old girl from La Magdalena, signed a contract equally ambiguous. She was to serve her master's wife and daughters "in all they order her to do."[79] As in the case of apprentices, servant children aged ten years and younger infrequently received pay during the first years of their service. For instance, ten-year-old Juana de Ordoñez would receive twelve pesos a year only after two years had elapsed from the date she signed a contract with her mistress. In other cases, young servants received less money than was stipulated by the law. Ana, mentioned above, was paid only three pesos per year.[80]

Servant children could enjoy better working conditions, however, if the contract was signed in the presence of one of their parents or before a Spanish official. That was why Miguel, whose contract was drawn up before a Spanish official in charge of protecting Indian rights, received twelve pesos at the end of the year in addition to the standard room and board, medical care, and two pieces of Indian clothing.[81] The domestic servant Francisca more than likely received a similar payment since her father, an Indian silversmith, was present at the time she signed a year-long contract.[82]

According to the law, the length of children's contracts could not exceed one year. In reality, however, contract periods frequently lasted more than two years. The duration varied according to the age of the child, with the youngest children usually signing contracts for the longest period. Juana de Ordoñez's contract, for instance, stipulated that she serve her mistress for six years, until reaching sixteen years of age.[83]

Because learning a trade was closed to women in Lima, it was usually girls who remained in their masters' houses until they married.[84] Those who began working when they were young girls were considered members of the household, and in addition to learning the duties of a domestic servant, they also received other kinds of instruction from their mistresses. For instance, Ana, the Indian girl from La Magdalena, learned to sew as well as to tend to domestic chores such as cleaning and cooking.[85] Both activities prepared Ana not only to tend to her own family but also to perform economic activities other than domestic service. Were she to decide to work as a seamstress, she could have earned money with an occupation that early modern Spaniards considered respectable for women.

By becoming part of the extended family, girls and youths also received the protection of their Spanish masters. According to the patriarchal system, the head of household had the responsibility to care for female dependents when they became adults, particularly by making their marriage arrangements. In some cases, masters also provided female dependents, including those who were not daughters, a dowry.

It was not only Spanish men, however, who felt the weight of patriarchal responsibilities to marry off females raised in their homes. Since she was a young girl, María de Corona, an Indian woman from Chilca, had lived and worked in the house of Doña Leonor de Corona. When María decided to marry Mateo, an Indian painter from her hometown, Doña Leonor gave her a dowry valued at 166 pesos and four reales "to aid to support the burden of the marriage." The dowry included sixty pesos in cash, clothing, and household items. Some of the objects, such as tablecloths and plates, had been part of Doña Leonor's own dowry. Besides giving her a dowry, Doña Leonor went with María to appear before the notary in order to register the items she would take into the marriage.[86] Doña Leonor's actions tell us about her care for María as well as about the possibility that loving relationships could be established between masters and their servants. They also tell us that these relationships could facilitate the transfer of Spanish gender and economic norms associated with marriage to Indian youths.

Sometimes "protection" involved more than putting Indian girls into good marriages; it also involved encouraging them to stay in bad ones. Juana Chumbi came to Lima when she was a young girl to serve Don Martín Pizarro, her encomendero. Juana only lived in Don Martín's home until she married, but she maintained ties with her encomendero and his family for years afterward. For that reason, when her husband hit her, Juana sought protection in Don Martín's home. She stayed there while recovering from her wounds, during which time Don Martín brought the couple together. After twenty days in Don Martín's house Juana returned to her husband and marital home.[87] Although Don Martín Pizarro clearly cared about Juana, the way in which paternalistic relationships between Spanish masters and Indian servants were established reinforced the dependency of Indians, especially women, on both Spanish masters and Indian husbands.

Conclusion: From Growing Up Indian to Growing Up Colonial

At the turn of the seventeenth century, colonial officials and Lima's elite incorporated Indian children as members of Spanish households in order to ensure colonial control and indigenous dependence. Yet by living with their Spanish masters, these children became ladinos and colonial Christians, not necessarily docile and dependent. The fact that Indian children culturally integrated into the capital city of Peru was not only the result of an imposition from above but also of the pursuit of a goal from "the bottom up." Indian parents put their children in Spanish households in order to see future generations master the language, trades, and culture of their colonizers. And sometimes Indian children themselves made the decision to enter a Spanish home.

In general, young, male, Indian commoners had different and arguably even better opportunities to demonstrate their integration into colonial culture and to assert their social status as ladinos than did their female counterparts. Girls spent their youth living and working in Spanish households and were subject to their masters' authority and protection. As proof of belonging to their masters' household, girls tended to assume their masters' surnames. Even though boys also assumed their masters' surnames, many showed more outward signs of acculturation in their dress and hairstyle. And when young, male, domestic servants turned fourteen or fifteen, they tended to move from their masters' households in order to learn a trade, which gave them the possibility of eventually becoming economically independent.

In practice, the experiences of commoner boys in Lima differed little from the experiences of the sons of the Andean indigenous elite also in the city. In the process of learning a trade, however, commoner youths improved their social and economic condition while elites lost their right to be considered a separate, superior group. Thus, the process of migration to Lima, and especially the possibility of learning a trade, particularly benefited commoner Indians.

By moving to live with Spaniards in Lima, all Indian children and youths ultimately improved their ability to negotiate the colonial system and broadened, at least in some measure, their social and economic opportunities. Even the elites who lost status might become literate and familiarize themselves with Spanish legislation, reinforcing their own political power in native communities. Commoners, by becoming artisans, gained the right to live freely in the city, leaving the dependent position in which they were placed by the colonial administration. Without a doubt for all of them, however, the most important consequence of establishing a relationship with Spaniards was the fact that they might count on the support of their patrons regardless of their own circumstances.

Although many Indian children and youths who migrated to Lima grew up separated from their families, several maintained stronger relationships with their relatives and towns than historians have recognized. At least those Indian boys and girls from towns located near Lima remained attached to native authorities, families, and friends, and they retained familiarity with the traditions and practices of their people. What did they do with the cultural background they received from the two worlds to which they belonged? It seems that in the process of becoming adults and ladinos, they reelaborated both indigenous and Spanish traditions and practices. In the workshops of Lima, many immigrant Indian youths not only made artisan products, but also refashioned themselves into colonial Indians—Indians still, but culturally colonial.

✢ NOTES ✢

I am grateful to Susan Porter Benson for her encouragement and for her comments on earlier drafts of this paper. Different versions of this paper were presented to the workshop "Marking Difference" (Connecticut College, New London, April 2003 and 2004). I thank participants, in particular Rachel O'Toole and Leo Garofalo, at those meetings for their insights, comments, and suggestions. Special thanks also to the editors of this volume for their comments and queries. Karen Spalding deserves particular thanks for her insights and her helpful editorial suggestions. And last, but not least, I thank Francisco Quiroz for reading more drafts of this paper than he probably would like to remember and especially for his emotional support without which finishing this paper would not be possible.

1. Viceroy Montesclaros appointed the notary Miguel de Contreras to register the indigenous population living in Lima. The main objective of this measure was to ensure that the Indians who were living illegally in the city would return to their towns to pay tribute and work in mines, in textile workshops, and on agricultural lands.

2. According to the census, 576 Indian children and youths lived in Lima in 1613. I consider seventeen as the age limit in the case of boys because Indian men were legally considered adults at the age of eighteen and began to pay tribute and work in the labor drafts. I also consider fifteen years to be the age limit for girls due to the fact that the majority (62 percent) of the sixteen-years-old girls counted in the census were married. Indian children and youths comprised almost 30 percent of the indigenous population living in the city.

3. Noble David Cook, ed., *Padrón de los indios de Lima en 1613* (Lima: Universidad Nacional Mayor de San Marcos, 1968), 38–39, 42, 111–12, 133, 285, 317.

4. See, in particular, Nicolás Sánchez-Albornoz, *Indios y tributos en el Alto Peru* (Lima: Instituto de Estudios Peruanos, 1978); Thierry Saignes, *Caciques, Tribute and Migration in the Southern Andes: Indian Society and the 17th-Century Colonial Order (Audiencia de Charcas)* (London: University of London, Institute of Latin American Studies, 1985); Noble David Cook, "Patrones de migración indígena en el virreinato del Perú: Mitayos, mingas y forasteros," *Histórica* 13, no. 2 (1989): 125–52; Ann Wightman, *Indigenous Migration and Social Change: The Forasteros of Cuzco, 1570–1720* (Durham, NC: Duke University Press, 1990); Lynn B. Lowry, "Forging an Indian Nation: Urban Indians Under

Spanish Colonial Control (Lima, Peru 1535–1765)" (PhD diss., University of California, Berkeley, 1991); Karen Vieira Powers, *Andean Journeys: Migration, Ethnogenesis, and the State in Colonial Quito* (Albuquerque: University of New Mexico Press, 1995); Thierry Saignes, "Indian Migration and Social Change in Seventeenth-Century Charcas," in *Ethnicity, Markets, and Migration in the Andes: At the Crossroads of History and Anthropology*, ed. Brooke Larson, Olivia Harris, and Enrique Tandeter (Durham, NC: Duke University Press, 1995), 167–95; Ann Zulawski, *They Eat from their Labor: Work and Social Change in Colonial Bolivia* (Pittsburgh, PA: University of Pittsburgh Press, 1995); and Paul Charney, "Negotiating Roots: Indian Migrants in the Lima Valley During the Colonial Period," *Colonial Latin American Historical Review* 5 (1996): 1–20.

5. Charney "Negotiating Roots" is an exception. Yet, he identifies migration of Indian children as mainly illegal and coercive.

6. Formally, the mobility of Indian adults was restricted, especially after the building of Hispanized Indian towns during viceroy Francisco de Toledo's rule (1569–81). In his *ordenanzas* (decrees) Toledo ordered that Indians who left their towns for reasons other than to serve the labor drafts or to work temporally for Spaniards be fined and whipped (Francisco de Toledo, *Disposiciones gubernativas para el virreinato del Perú, 1569–1574* [Seville: Escuela de Estudios Hispano-Americanos, 1986], 1:263–64, 1:467, 2:245, 2:416–17). However, colonial officials undermined resettlement programs by issuing a series of decrees allowing urban migrants to become permanent residents, immune to repatriation, and exempted from the obligations of their home communities. For instance, in 1551 Juan Quiñones, the prosecutor of the Royal Audiencia, pointed out that he was appointed by the Royal Audiencia to put capable as well as vagabonds Indians with masters in the city in order to learn a trade (Archivo General de la Nación, Protocolos Notariales [hereafter, AGN, PN], 117, fol. 25). This practice of changing legal status was one of the strongest attractions for adult migrants to urban centers.

7. For the characteristics of the family in Spain and colonial Latin America, see James Casey and Francisco Chacon, eds., *Familia y sociedad en el mediterráneo occidental. Siglos XV–XIX* (Murcia: Universidad de Murcia, 1987); Pilar Gonzalbo Aizpuru, *Familia y orden colonial* (Mexico City: El Colegio de México, 1998); and Pilar Gonzalbo Aizpuru and Cecilia Rabell, eds., *La familia en el mundo iberoamericano* (Mexico City: Universidad Autónoma de México, 1994). For the "Spanish model" of family and household as part of the general Western European pattern, see Peter Laslett, *Family Life and Illicit Love in Earlier Generations: Essays in Historical Sociology* (Cambridge: Cambridge University Press, 1977).

8. Viceroys' letters to the king and travelers' accounts underscored the crucial political role these Indian children served as adults. It was also the argument used by the members of the cabildo and the royal audiencia of Lima to oppose the compulsory return of those Indians who lived in the city and served Spaniards. See Archivo de Municipalidad de Lima, Libro de Cédulas y Provisiones de Lima 4, fol. 152v. For a more detailed analysis about this topic see Teresa Vergara Ormeño, "La Lima indígena: Migración, trabajo y vida cotidiana, siglos XVI y XVII" (master's thesis, Pontificia Universidad Católica del Perú, in process).

9. Labor contracts consistently state that one of the most important obligations of a master was to teach the Catholic religion to the Indian under his or her service. In general, this source has no information on how the master had to carry out this task. However, some contracts include details. For instance, the contract between María Lazatina and Gaspar de Gamboa and his wife for one year stipulates that Don Gaspar and his wife were to teach María Christian doctrine and send her to mass (AGN, PN, 102, fol. 88).

10. The official practice of taking children from ethnic groups that the state sought to control and placing them with masters was not new. It was used in Spain to exercise control over the peasants and the urban poor. It was also used after the reconquest of the kingdom of Granada to control and assimilate the Moorish population. The case of the Moorish children was the model followed with the Chilean children captured in war territories. See Richard Konetzke, *Colección de documentos para la historia de la formación social de Hispanoamérica, 1493–1810* (Madrid: Consejo Superior de Investigaciones Científicas, 1958), II, vol. 1:135–38.

11. See Lyman L. Johnson and Sonya Lipsett-Rivera's introduction to *The Faces of Honor: Sex, Shame, and Violence in Colonial Latin America*, ed. Lyman L. Johnson and Sonya Lipsett-Rivera (Albuquerque: University of New Mexico Press, 1998), 1–17; Stuart B. Schwartz, "Colonial Identities and the Sociedad de Castas," *Colonial Latin American Review* 4, no. 1 (1995): 185–201; Douglas Cope, *The Limits of Racial Domination: Plebeian Society in Colonial Mexico City, 1660–1720* (Madison: University of Wisconsin Press, 1994).

12. Certainly, artisans—especially shoemakers, or *sastres*—were not at the top of urban colonial hierarchies, however the fact that they were specialized workers who had their own workshops and worked independent from a master placed them within the group of those who were considered respectable people.

13. See Noble David Cook's introductory essay to *Padrón de los indios de Lima*; Alvaro Barnechea, "Marginación, informatización y cambio cultural en la ciudad de Lima en el siglo XVII," Memoria de Bachiller en Ciencias Sociales,

Pontificia Universidad Católica del Perú, Lima, 1985; Miguel Jaramillo, "Formación de un mercado laboral urbano e indígena en Lima a principios del siglo XVII," Memoria de Bachiller en Ciencias Sociales, Pontificia Universidad Católica del Perú, Lima, 1985; Paul Charney, "El indio urbano: Un análisis económico y social de la población india de Lima en 1613," *Histórica* 12, no. 1 (1988): 5–33; Lowry, "Forging an Indian Nation"; Charney, "Negotiating Roots"; and Teresa Vergara Ormeño, "Migración y trabajo femenino: El caso de las indias en Lima," *Histórica* 21, no. 1 (1997): 135–57.

14. See, for example, several of the works cited in Note 5, above.

15. On the rural and urban interactions in the bishopric of Cuzco, see Wightman, *Indigenous Migration*, especially chapters 4 and 5.

16. See Karen Spalding, *De indio a campesino. Cambios en la estructura social del Perú colonial* (Lima: Instituto de Estudios Peruanos, 1974); Steve Stern, *Peru's Indian Peoples and the Challenge of Spanish Conquest Huamanga to 1640* (Madison: University of Wisconsin Press, 1982); Karen Spalding, *Huarochirí: An Andean Society Under Inca and Spanish Rule* (Stanford: Stanford University Press, 1984); and María Rostworowski, *Costa peruana prehispánica* (Lima: Instituto de Estudios Peruanos, 1989).

17. In Spain, too, it was common for noble families to recruit their servant children from the towns they controlled; see Carmen Sarasúa, *Criados, nodrizas y amos: El servicio doméstico en la formación de trabajo madrileño, 1758–1868* (Madrid: Siglo Veintiuno Editores, 1994), 74–75.

18. Cook, *Padrón de los indios*, 121, 123–24.

19. Ibid., 229–30, 231.

20. Ibid., 239–40. Also see the case of Juan, 231–32.

21. I reviewed eighty-three Indian labor contracts involving children from 1570 to 1630 and found that in fifty-one of the contracts Spanish authorities in charge of the Indians in the city—the *alcalde ordinario* (mayor), *protector de naturales* (prosecutor of Indians), *corregidor* (judge-administrator of an Indian district)—put Indian boys and girls to work with Spanish masters. This information explains why more than 80 percent of Indian children and youths registered in the *Padrón de los indios* worked in Spanish households.

22. AGN, PN, 102, fol. 695.

23. Cook, *Padrón de los indios*, 132. For other examples, see the cases of Pedro, Juana Payco, and Andrés Conde, 150, 320–21, 376. It seems that at ten years of age children were considered mature enough to assume some responsibilities. See, for instance, Viceroy Toledo's comments in *Disposiciones gubernativas*, 1:291, 1:295–96.

24. This example and the similar case of Indian orphans Isabel and García can be found in Cook, *Padrón de los indios*, 82, 244, 291–92. Other cases of orphaned Indian children are those of Luisa Ana, Francisca de Icalla, Juan Alonso, Cristóbal Gutierrez, and Juana Montalvo (ibid., 67–68, 85, 153–54, 260, 277).

25. AGN, PN, 4, fol. 1043.

26. Alonso was born in Espíritu Santo in the province of the Huamalies and was fourteen years old at the time of the census (Cook, *Padrón de los indios*, 268).

27. Ibid., 38.

28. Ibid., 93. That was also the case of Martín Guaman, Pedro Lacuanda, and Juana Payco, 171, 320–21.

29. Ibid., 150, 300, 291–92. Similar cases were those of Jusepe de la Cruz and Cristóbal Bautista, 300, 315. Due to the lack of information about the condition in which Pedro, Jusepe, and Cristóbal arrived in Lima, it is not possible to know if they were forced to come to the city. In other cases, the information that children gave about their parents indicates that their parents gave authorization to bring them to Lima.

30. Other cases are those of Alonso Yana, Juan Rupay, Pedro Colloco, and María (ibid., 268, 121, 123–24).

31. See Vergara Ormeño, "La Lima Indígena," chapter 3.

32. Cook, *Padrón de los indios*, 71–72. A similar case was that of Mateo and María de Corona from the town of Chilc. See AGN, PN, 34, fols. 217–17v.

33. Cook, *Padrón de los indios*, 458, 500, 501. Ann Zulawski finds a similar pattern in the mining city of Oruro (Alto Perú) ("Wages, Ore Sharing, and Peasant Agriculture: Labor in Oruro's Silver Mines, 1607–1720," *Hispanic American Historical Review* 67, no. 3 [1987]: 410). See also Saignes, "Indian Migration and Social Change," 177–79.

34. AGN, PN, 3, fols. 266r–67.

35. However, there are also children who arrived in Lima from places that were not very near the city but who still had information about their parents, such as Hernando de Guzmán, a nine-year-old boy who came from Huáraz (the present-day capital city of Ancash) and Alonso Velásquez, a thirteen-year-old who came from Huamanga (the present-day capital city of Ayacucho). Their parents brought them to the city and maintained contact with them (Cook, *Padrón de los indios*, 272, 309).

36. Ibid., 90.

37. Ibid., 300. According to Paul Charney, the majority of orphan Indians were abducted from their towns to work as servants for Spanish residents in Lima. See Charney, "Negotiating Roots," especially 5.

38. See, for instance, the cases of Luisa Ana and Francisca de Icalla (Cook, *Padrón de los indios*, 67–68, 85).

39. Ibid., 260.

40. Francisco Quiroz Chueca, "Artesanos y manufactureros en Lima colonial" (master's thesis, Universidad Nacional Mayor de San Marcos, Lima, 1998). See especially the thesis's appendixes. I would like to thank Francisco Quiroz for letting me use his tables on *limeño* artisans' labor contracts.

41. See *Recopilación de leyes de los reynos de Indias* (Madrid: Consejo de la Hispanidad, 1943), 2:192, bk. IV, tít. I, ley XI.

42. See Ann Zulawski, "Social Differentiation, Gender and Ethnicity: Urban Indian Women in Colonial Bolivia, 1640–1725," *Latin America Research Review* 25, no. 2 (1990): 93–113.

43. Cook, *Padrón de los indios*, 38–39.

44. Ibid., 279. Also see the case of Francisco Pasqual from Trujillo, 297.

45. Ibid., 37. According to the *Padrón de los indios* only 10.8 percent (n=36) worked with a master who was not a Spaniard. See, specifically, Cook, *Padrón de los indios*, 250–51.

46. See Lyman Johnson, "Artisans," in *Cities and Society in Colonial Latin America*, ed. Louisa S. Hoberman and Susan M. Socolow (Albuquerque: University of New Mexico Press, 1986), 227–50; and Francisco Quiroz Chueca, *Gremios, razas y libertad de industria. Lima colonial* (Lima: Universidad Nacional Mayor de San Marcos, 1995).

47. Indian artisans often placed their sons to learn their same craft. For an example see AGN, PN, 61, fols. 371, 372v.

48. Cook, *Padrón de los indios*, 295, 453–54.

49. Ibid., 427.

50. For information about Peruvian Indian fishermen before and after the Spanish conquest, see María Rostworoski, *Costa peruana prehispánica* (Lima: Instituto de Estudios Peruanos, 1989), 264–72.

51. Cook, *Padrón de los indios*, 292–93.

52. Toledo, *Disposiciones gubernativas*, 1:256. Indeed, Toledo's legislation was only one of the causes of the Indian elite's loss of their social and economic status. Other internal causes such as the enrichment of common Indians played an important role in this process.

53. Information from *Libros de Cabildo de Lima* and the documents of the section of *Cofradías* in the Archivo Arzobispal de Lima (hereafter, AAL) show that during the sixteenth century and the first decades of the seventeenth century the caciques and principales who lived in Lima controlled the offices and *mayordomías* in the city. Most of these elite Indians were artisans.

54. Cook, *Padrón de los indios*, 136–37. Other cases are those of Cristóbal Pusa, Alonso Sánchez, and Agustín Flores, 59, 240, 281.

55. Ibid., 22.

56. Of these girls, 69.2 percent (n=9) were under the age of three.

57. Cook, *Padrón de los indios*, 254, 255.

58. The first lay pious house, known as beaterio, for indigenous women was funded in Lima in 1691. See Nancy van Deusen, *Between the Sacred and the Worldly: The Institutional and Cultural Practice of Recogimiento in Colonial Lima* (Stanford: Stanford University Press, 2001), 172.

59. See Stern, *Peru's Indian Peoples*; Kathryn Burns, *Colonial Habits: Convents and the Spiritual Economy of Cuzco* (Durham, NC: Duke University Press, 1999).

60. Cook, *Padrón de los indios*, 340.

61. AAL, Idolatrías y Hechicerías (hereafter, IH), leg. IV, exp. 18, 1662: fol. 12v.

62. See ibid., 327–28, 489.

63. Cook, *Padrón de los indios*, 164.

64. There is important literature on caciques moving between the Spanish and Andean worlds. See Spalding, *De indio a campesino*; Stern, *Peru's Indian Peoples*; Spalding, *Huarochirí*; and Franklin Pease G. Y., *Curacas, reciprocidad y riqueza* (Lima: Pontificia Universidad Católica, 1992).

65. For instance, in 1617 Don Juan Chuquia, an elite Indian man well known for his knowledge of Spanish language and Catholic religion, was elected prosecutor by the members of the Indian municipality of Paucartambo (AAL, IH, leg. 1, exp. 4, 1617: fol. 2).

66. According to the notary Contreras, forty-nine Indian boys and girls were slaves in 1613.

67. In 1608, Philip III authorized the war against the Chilean Indians and their sale as slaves due to their attacks on the Spaniards and rejection of the Spanish authority. In 1610, the war was suspended at the request of the Jesuits. In 1625, Philip IV authorized the war again for the same reasons as his predecessor. See Juan de Solórzano y Pereira, *Política indiana*, Libro II (Madrid: Companía Iberoamericana de Publicaciones, 1647), 139.

68. According to the law, these children had to remain slaves only until the age of twenty. See Konetzke, *Colección de documentos*, 2:1, 2:135–38.

69. Cook, *Padrón de los indios*, 277.

70. Ibid., 259. Other similar cases are those of María de Chile, Ana, Bárbara, and María, 106, 107, 222, 276–77.

71. Ibid., 235. Also see the case of Luisa del Salto, 319.

72. In this instance, Contreras accepted the girl's story and noted that she was from Majes (ibid., 344).

73. For instance, see the contract for a shoemaker's apprentice in AGN, PN, 1166, fols. 12v–13v.

74. J. M. Ots Capdequi, *El estado español en las Indias* (Mexico City: Fondo de Cultura Económica, 1965), 99–100. For information about the different forms of payment, see Francisco Quiroz, "Formas de pago en el artesanado, Lima siglo XVI," *Cuadernos de Historia Numismática* 5 (1993): 41–59.

75. See, for example, AGN, PN, 61, fols. 34, 210v, 237v.

76. AGN, PN, 106, fol. 398v. See also AGN, PN, 61, fols. 371, 372v.

77. Some economic activities acted to mask racial/cultural identities that permitted the upper mobility. See John K. Chance and William B. Taylor, "Estate and Class in a Colonial City: Oaxaca in 1792," *Comparative Studies in Society and History* 12, no. 4 (1977): 454–87, and the response to this study by Robert McCaa, Stuart B. Schwartz, and Arturo Grubessich, "Race and Class in Colonial Latin America: A Critique," *Comparative Studies in Society and History* 21, no. 3 (1979): 421–33; Patricia Seed, "Social Dimensions of Race: Mexico City, 1753," *Hispanic American Historical Review* 62, no. 4 (1982): 569–606; Christopher H. Lutz, *Santiago de Guatemala, 1541–1773: City, Caste, and the Colonial Experience* (Norman: University of Oklahoma Press, 1994); Elizabeth Anne Kuznesof, "Ethnic and Gender Influences on 'Spanish' Creole Society in Colonial Spanish America," *Colonial Latin American Review* 4, no. 1 (1995): 153–76; Stuart B. Schwartz, "Colonial Identities and the Sociedad de Castas"; Muriel Nazzari, "Vanishing Indians: The Social Construction of Race in Colonial Sao Paulo," *Americas* 57, no. 4 (2001): 497–524.

78. Forty pesos a year was considered a good income. For instance, the rent for a room, where officials often lived, was around one and a half pesos per month. However, the rent of a house with a workshop, where masters and officials could open their own business, was more expensive—around eight pesos per month. For that reason, officials who sought to work independently frequently worked in their own rooms. See AGN, PN, 25, fols. 387, 487, 647v.

79. See Miguel's contract in AGN, PN, 43, fol. 127v and Ana's in Archivo Histórico del Museo Nacional de Antropología, Arqueología e Historia (hereafter, AHM) A190, 1586, fols. 1v–2.

80. See Juana de Ordoñez's contract in AGN, PN, 4, fol. 1043, and Ana's in AHM, A190, 1586, fols. 1v–2.

81. AGN, PN, 43, fol. 127v.

82. Ibid., 151, fol. 460.

83. Ibid., 4, fol. 1043. More commonly, however, children signed contracts for two or three years and renewed for two or three more years. See, AHM, A190, 1586, fols. 1v–2.

84. Indian women with connections and money became seamstresses, *chicheras* (vendors of corn liquor), or food sellers in the plaza, but most of the time they began these activities after they married. See Vergara Ormeño, "Migración y trabajo femenino."

85. AHM, A190, 1586, fol. 2.

86. AGN, PN, 34, Folios Sueltos, fols. 216–17v.

87. AGN, Real Audiencia, Causas Civiles, L83, C310, 1631, s/f.

CHAPTER FOUR

Ursula

The Life and Times of an
Aristocratic Girl in Santiago, Chile
(1666–1678)

JORGE ROJAS FLORES

TRANSLATED BY BIANCA PREMO

∞

⸭ WHEN URSULA SUÁREZ WAS BORN IN SANTIAGO, CHILE, IN 1666, infant mortality was extraordinarily common, there existed no market in children's toys, child-care manuals did not circulate, schooling was limited, and the upper classes frequently relied on wet nurses to breast-feed their infants. This historical panorama is relatively well known. But what do we really know of the intimate lives of little girls such as Ursula: about the relationship she might have had with her parents and with other adults, about her feelings and thoughts, about how she spent her time? These questions are much harder to answer than those about the general environment. Indeed, for this reason most historians tend to focus on transformations in perceptions or representations of childhood—or better said, changes in related concepts that might affect children such as illegitimacy or childhood death—rather than on children themselves.

This chapter is an exploratory effort to examine both of these aspects of the history of children: how colonial Chileans represented and understood childhood, and how children lived their youth. It also takes on another challenge: the chapter attempts to illuminate some of the methodological possibilities that analytical attention to a single historical source can offer. It examines the life of Ursula, an upper-class girl in seventeenth-century Santiago, through the autobiography she wrote as an adult Clarist nun. Her text is of the genre known as *vidas*, or spiritual autobiographies, which the Catholic Church required of individuals engaged in confessionary processes surrounding (often suspect) mystical experiences.[1]

A priest-confessor directed the autobiographical story contained in the vida and, with his intervention, literate readers would judge the purity of the author's behavior. As other authors, including those who have studied Ursula, have pointed out, vidas are formally imprinted with self-justifications for taking on a religious vocation, affirmations of love and fear of God and faithfulness to the church, and a worldview in which Providence is a main protagonist.[2] But vidas are far from crude manipulations of a literary formula. They are also profoundly introspective texts that served as written confessions. It is obvious that in her *Relación* Ursula exerted genuine effort to convey the particulars of her life and that she did more than follow a confessionary boilerplate. Thus, while it is a public document, her text is also, at its heart, an intimate gesture. Through it, we can see a range of everyday childhood experiences with relative clarity—experiences that allow us to draw closer to childhood as not only an ideological category but also as an historically lived experience, albeit the experience of an upper-class girl.

Ursula was indeed a upper-class girl who lived in a house full of servants and whose parents would one day offer the dowry necessary for her to become a nun. Her *Relación* cannot tell us about the life of an "average" child in colonial Santiago. How then do we use her story in a way that no other historians have—as a description of colonial childhood? An autobiography can be understood as an entity within itself, a terrain etched with details that give it unique depths and contours. For that reason, we must examine the vida intensively, attentive to its own internal logic and its purpose as an intimate confession.

Reading such a rare testimony in this way risks falling into anecdote or forced generalizations, so I will conclude by considering the scholarship on spiritual autobiography in Spanish America and on the history of childhood. Along the way, analysis will be supplemented with secondary sources about the era—including a classic work by Benjamín Vicuña Mackenna, a nineteenth-century Chilean historian, who incidentally is also one of the rare scholars who mentions childhood in the country's colonial past.[3] The point is not, however, to use comparison and contextualization to argue that certain aspects of Ursula's life were representative. In fact, what might be most illuminating is to focus on what made Ursula unique.

This chapter will concentrate on Ursula's life from birth until 1678, when, at age twelve, she left her parents' home and entered the convent. By following Ursula through her childhood years, this chapter aims to demonstrate that careful use of a single source can yield a valuable history of a single child in colonial Latin America as well as suggest something about the history of childhood more generally. Let us begin in the cradle.

Birth

Ursula María was born on October 20, 1666, in the heart of Santiago in a house that sat on the corner of the downtown streets of Moneda and Morandé. The house belonged to Ursula's paternal grandparents, Martín Suárez Madrigal and María del Campo Lantadilla.[4] Santiago was a small and simple city that could not compare with the major colonial capital cities. According to a report submitted to the king in 1657 the population was only five thousand, and it grew to about ten to twelve thousand by the time Ursula lived.[5] The sense that one was living on the margins of empire was palpable in this place that survived off of commercial activity with Upper Peru and the area bordering the south and where agricultural expansion was limited and artisanal production barely met the market demands of urban inhabitants. Even the aristocrats of Santiago lived relatively simply and frugally, aware that they could not afford the lavish lifestyles of those who inhabited, for instance, the viceregal court of Lima. The city's rich would not come to know true ostentation until the middle of the nineteenth century.

Ursula's parents were Don Francisco Suárez and Doña María de Escobar. Theirs was a marriage of business and status. Don Francisco came from a family of successful merchants and bureaucrats. Doña María, for her part, was one of those colonials who was short on wealth but long on genealogical roots, and hers stretched back to the Spanish conquerors. It was for this reason that she married well but brought no dowry to the match.[6]

Ursula's paternal grandmother, María, not only provided the house of her birth but also served as her godmother, while her maternal grandfather, Antonio de Escobar, served as her godfather. It was the godparents who, in the expression of the day, "*sacaron la pila*"—meaning they paid for the baptism. And they did so joyfully since Ursula was the first child to whom her mother had given birth, although she was not her mother's first child. Her mother had prematurely delivered a baby after eight months of pregnancy and the baby died without being baptized.[7]

We can guess that the name Ursula was selected to invoke the protection of the saint whose feast day was celebrated around the infant's birthday.[8] Other close family members, such as Ursula's mother and grandmother, shared her common second name, María. Choosing a name often was intended to honor a godparent or important relative, and early in the eighteenth century it became custom to bestow two or three names on a child. A child's name was therefore selected at the same time that godparents were chosen, an act that reflected the status of the parents.[9] Colonial inhabitants seeking to move up social hierarchies would select *compadres* who could help elevate their families to a superior rank, but surely María and Francisco needed no such hand up. For this reason, they chose godparents based on intimacy rather than status.

Death Looms Close By

When Ursula was born, one of her aunts, Mariana de Escobar, hung a rose of Jericho in the birthing room, a detail that Ursula undoubtedly heard from family members.[10] This plant, hardy and able to survive drought, was known for supernatural properties related to love, health, and childbirth. These properties were imparted to Ursula through various magic rituals with Christian, biblical foundations. The protection of such supernatural forces to guard baby Ursula's health, it turned out, was sorely needed.

During Ursula's infancy, her life was in constant jeopardy, as were those of many babies during this period. In fact, memories of dramatic battles against childhood diseases left their mark on the relationship between Ursula and her mother. Every time María scolded her daughter, she reminded the girl about the difficulty she had faced in keeping her alive: "Your life has cost me so many difficulties; there is not one saint left who has not heard my pleas to make you healthy."[11]

Surely, María's efforts to save her little girl's life also constituted a common theme in family lore, and Ursula was descriptive about this

4.1. Baltasar Jaime Martínez de Campañón, *Españolas de luto* (Spanish women in mourning), Peru, late eighteenth century. Source: Baltasar Jaime Martínez de Campañón, *Trujillo del Perú* (Madrid: Ediciones Cultura Hispánica, 1978), 6.

in her vida. She reported that her mother went "from convent to convent" to pay for "novenas at masses and to offer alms for my life at altars because, she said, I had *hética* (a fever and rash associated with consumption) three times and ran such high fevers that I would not eat or drink." After going to a several churches, baby Ursula's condition did not improve. Her mother, "crying a sea of tears" and "sad and afflicted" by the possibility that her only daughter would perish, visited the shrine of Saint Nicolás and put the baby on the altar, begging the saint for a cure. With this, Ursula recalled, "I started to come back [to life]." Paternal grandmother María also participated in this spiritual quest to save Ursula; she too gave alms for the only child of her only child from her second marriage.[12]

In later years, illness remained a concern. The long periods of sickness grandmother María experienced, due to the consumption that finally killed her, fueled mother María's anxieties about her daughter's health. Ursula had slept with her grandmother, raising fears that the old woman was the source of contagion. Her mother had tried several times to prevent them from sleeping together, and Ursula recalls her crying, "Ay, child of my womb, who too shall die."[13]

Volumes have been written about the emotions—or absence thereof—that the proximity of death inspired in premodern times. But, in Ursula's situation, the threat of death generated sentiments quite different than stoic Christian resignation in the face of the possibility of losing a loved one. We have seen a mother's desperation when her child was sick, and the state of medical science in seventeenth-century Santiago was such that treatment by a physician did not appear to be an option for María. In fact, Ursula never mentioned the possibility that her mother would seek the attention of *meicas* (healers) but instead sought out divine intercession through the cult of saints.

The proximity of another illness and death offers another telling detail about attitudes toward death, this one through the eyes of a child. Ursula's grandmother was the adult to whom she felt the most emotional closeness when young, and the nun would later remember how her family tried to ensure that she would not suffer too greatly when the old woman died. For example, it was forbidden to mention her deceased grandmother María's name in her grandfather's house so as to avoid invoking the old woman's memory. But no matter what the family tried, Ursula discovered that nothing could console her and relieve her grief.[14]

Rearing

The procedures surrounding caring for an infant in the days after child-birth followed precepts of Chilean tradition, and nineteenth-century historian Vicuña dismissed these practices as nothing more than evidence of the ignorance and superstitions of the colonial period. Various displays of maternal sacrifice lasted forty days. The mother avoided the region's traditional drink, *mate*, until the second day of nursing and at the beginning of the forty-day period could add neither sugar nor herbal powders to the drink, though she could add an infusion made of twigs to the beverage. Flowers and other aromatic waters were banished from the house, and mothers avoided cold water completely.

As Vicuña has written, colonial child rearing was an act of servitude as well as sacrifice. Children grew up "tucked in the arms of the country's Indian wet nurses, and from their course lips learned Quechua and the Araucanian language before the 'national language' [meaning Spanish]."[15] María, Ursula's mother, followed the practice and used *amas*, or wet nurses, to nurse her infant daughter. Historians have long studied the meanings given to the practice of breast-feeding (including the belief that nursing harmed or weakened the mother), female preoccupations with the aesthetic consequences of nursing, its contraceptive effects, and the idea that breast-feeding demeaned noble women.[16] In Ursula's case, there is no insinuation that sending an infant to nurse with an ama was due to disinterest or neglect but rather only to the belief that nursing would restrict her parents' sexual activity. Her mother also had an inflammation in her breasts after pregnancy, which undoubtedly led her to continue using wet nurses. Ursula's short illnesses were blamed on the fact that she had nursed from "pregnant milk," and her wet nurses were changed several times with Ursula showing no significant health improvement.[17]

Ursula would later report that between the presence of wet nurses and her close relationship with their grandmother, "I was not under my mother's power until my grandmother died even though they lived in the same house. But I hardly ever was carried around by my mother; I stayed only with my grandmother."[18] Mother María found reason to resent the situation. Ursula would recall that fights between María and the woman's mother-in-law, who shared the same house but were competitors in the rearing of the little girl, lasted until Ursula's grandmother died.

Ursula's mother took issue with the grandmother's indulgences in rearing Ursula and worried, "What will become of this girl, whom the señora does not discipline [*doctrina*]?" In mother María's opinion, children "should be taught from the time they are little, and the trouble is that I cannot spank her because the señora will get angry."[19] The emotional closeness between Ursula and her grandmother also caused jealousy among the other grandchildren of the house. In the nun's words, her grandmother raised her "with so much love that never, never was there a quarrel [over what I wanted]; everything had to be as I wished and nothing was not to my liking so that I would not become sad and become more ill."[20]

The distance between the mother and mother-in-law, and the closeness between child and grandmother, placed Ursula in a strategically central position in terms of household power dynamics. Ursula understood the influence that she exercised over the older women. At times, her own mother would also try to use the situation to gain some leverage in family politics. Since she ultimately had no control over the home owned by her parents-in-law, when she needed something, she encouraged her child to intervene on her behalf. At other times, however, the child acted on her own against her mother's interests, provoking her ire.[21]

In sum, the tension between the two Marías—Ursula's mother, María de Escobar, and her grandmother, María del Campo—conditioned how the girl was treated and reared. What is significant is that, in the grandmother's opinion, Ursula's mother acted less as mother and more like a stepmother.[22] Clearly, there was an ideal role for a mother to play in her child's life, and Ursula's mother was judged lacking. While this was the emotional world in which Ursula was raised, the little girl's social universe consisted of more than emotion; it also contained a physical world.

Punishment, Pats on the Head, and Penitence

In Ursula's case, her mother was the enforcer of physical punishment. In no instance did Ursula ever mention her father as a disciplinarian, and her grandmother figured far more often as a protector shielding her from her mother's castigation, than as an authority meting out punishment. In Ursula's memories, physical punishment did not register as abusive. She almost always conveyed a belief that her own childish mischief was justification for her mother's anger. And, in many instances, often because of her grandmother's mediation or the intervention of another adult, Ursula was able to avoid altogether being whipped or otherwise physically punished.[23]

Physical punishment comprised chiefly spanking or whipping; or at least this is what Ursula later remembered and wrote about it. And she usually recalled threats rather than actual punishment. The nun made scant reference to being struck with blows, although she did remember ducking a few slaps that her mother tried to give her when the woman was furious and spouting threats. It was this kind of physical treatment that, according to Ursula, her grandmother and father denounced as especially cruel.[24]

How did Ursula view the punishments her mother gave her? There are indications that she saw it as natural in terms of generational order, for she wrote, "When I got older, it wasn't necessary to hit me." This did not mean she always submitted to punishment. Ursula later wondered, "Why did I love my mother—such a tyrant—who wanted to bend my will?" and reported that on some occasions she tried to escape her mother's blows.[25] But, in general, she rarely questioned the woman's authority over her.

In fact, Ursula seems to have believed that only her mother had the right to spank her. On one occasion she describes how her mischief (*averías*) inspired punishment by "someone who was not my mother." One of the household servants got angry when she saw little Ursula playing rather than tending to her chores and gave her "two strokes with a riding crop on the back." Ursula reported that she felt "strong emotions that she dared to whip me" and began to plot revenge. Ursula broke into tears as though she had been brutally punished. Her staged theatrics worked so well in drawing the scorn of the servant's own adult relatives that Ursula eventually had to come to the servant's defense.[26]

Elsewhere in the text, we find another event when a servant, this one in the home of Ursula's aunt, attempted to physically discipline the girl. Ursula again reacted with surprise at the "daring" displayed by an Indian nanny/teacher (*maestra*). Crucially, it was not only the notion that a non-white servant or nanny might raise her hand to an elite child that shocked Ursula; it was the corporeality of the punishment itself. Ursula complained to her aunt, but rather than mentioning the servile status of her Indian servant, she mentioned the fact that she was too young (*chiquita*) to be punished in such a way. The Indian teacher never punished Ursula again because she never taught Ursula again. Ursula's aunt intervened after Ursula complained, but it is not certain that the woman removed the girl from the Indian servant's control. In fact, it is possible that the servant herself decided to withhold the service of teaching Ursula since her disciplining methods were not respected.[27]

Ursula's childhood was also marked by displays of tenderness. Despite all of the friction between mother and daughter, the *Relación* provides abundant examples of a mother who was caring and close to her child. Ursula recalled small moments of tenderness, such as admiring her mother's hair as she sat in the woman's lap and listened to her loving words. She also recalled a day when her mother called her in from the patio to praise and flatter her, and, in Ursula's words, she "put her hands on my head, so happy." When Ursula's grandmother died, the girl was reared directly by her mother, ending the years of contest over Ursula. This seems to have made María greatly happy, and Ursula reported that her mother treated her with a "thousand signs of affection, never wanting to let me out of her arms."[28]

Ursula's father occupies far less space in her vida, and it is difficult to tell how much emotional space he occupied in her life. Historian Armando de Ramón describes Ursula's world as dominated by women.[29] The domestic arena was a feminine space, and it is possible that Ursula's autobiography simply reflects this fact rather than to convey something particular about the women in her life. Still, when Ursula does mention her father, it is obvious that he was far from absent or emotionally distant.

Ursula was, by her own admission, her father's favorite. "My father loved me in the extreme," she wrote, "and even after they had my sister, I was always the most loved, especially, as I have said, by my father." One incident in particular illustrates the point. During a meal, Ursula's mother got angry and began to threaten her in front of all the family. As things escalated, Ursula's father turned on his wife and told her that when she scolded Ursula, it pained him personally since "I was the child of his heart [*niña de sus ojos*] and all his love." In fact, Ursula's next recollection is remarkable, for she remembered that her father's affection for her made her mother jealous and provoked her mother to accuse her father of an excess of physical pampering. He responded that the girl was his "little girl" and carried her off to his room "where I gave him my signs of affection" (*Donde le hacsia yo mis halagos*).[30]

Ursula's testimony is indeed striking in its conveyance of the many physical gestures of emotion between adults and children: she mentions caresses, "signs of affection" or "flatteries" (*halagos*), and pats. We have already seen that mother and father took on different physical roles, with her mother meting out punishment. Yet, while she designated different physical expressions to different adults in her life, all adults seemed comfortable in physical contact with the girl. Even her grandfather, who was a relatively stoic figure, displayed physical tenderness on the day when she entered the convent by taking the adolescent girl into his arms. His gesture evinced a sign of admiration from all the family members who had gathered to see Ursula off.[31]

We might expect that in this era disciplining a child held some relation to the Catholic notion of purification through physical penitence. In Ursula's text, however, punishment of this type is not mentioned. Adults' anger flared when Ursula got into predicable childhood trouble, and most castigation figured as momentary displays of adult authority rather than premediated impositions of penance for sinful activity. Instead of a discussion of how sin inspired punishment, what we find in the *Relación* is Ursula's own slow, personal discovery of the meaning of sin and penitence.

Throughout the text, Ursula referred to the evil that undergirded her actions, even when she was a child: "In my infancy and childhood years, I was perverse"; "I was the epitome of evil since the light of reason still did not shine in me when bad inclinations grabbed me[;] if Divine Providence had not subjected me to grave illnesses my life would have been a disaster." These passages clearly place the vida in the confessional genre. But other details also reveal an intimate side of the autobiography that conforms less neatly to contemporary notions of sin and redemption.[32]

Penitence-style punishment was only mentioned in the context of self-sacrifice, and it was portrayed as part of the ritual warm-up to Holy Week. Gestures or rituals of self-mutilation and physical sacrifice appear to have been incorporated early into children's lives, taking the form of a kind of game that led to Christian socialization. During Lent, Ursula recalled, "we walked on our knees around the patio; these were the penances of a little girl, for I still had no discipline." She also recalled that she and her cousin self-flagellated with cornstalk sheaves and crops in front of a block of wood with a nail in it that had been set up in the patio—an impromptu mock-up of the Stations of the Cross.[33] Although the *Relación* could have fallen into an idealization of Ursula's religious past in these passages, the text breaks away from predictable paths and displays a kind of sincerity in reconstructing a child's incomprehension of the meanings of ritual acts of religiosity. Ursula did not crown her recollections of these penitences with a halo, but instead remembered her acts of devotion as "childish games" (*niñerías*).

Sleeping In, Nightmares, and Magic Wands

Ursula's *vida* both chronicles her childhood behaviors and imposes post-facto self-judgments on these behaviors. She characterized her child-self as sickly, naughty, "lively to the extreme," as well as "streetwise," and "presumptuous and bossy." She also portrayed herself as a relatively spoiled child, particularly in that she was permitted to sleep in all morning. She was, she said, a "big sleeper" (*gran dormilona*), and she recalled how her mother would chastise her: "At noon you don't want to move from the bed and it is a huge chore to try to get you up."[34]

While she slept, Ursula wrote, she frequently dreamed of witches. She woke up with a fright on various occasions, keeping her mother and servant up into the night. In a recollection not atypical among religious women of the era, Ursula once believed that she saw the devil in a mirror—he appeared as a black man who shot fire through his eyes. In the beginning, María blamed the vision on her daughter's late nights and tendency to sleep in late. But the little girl was so consistently upset by nightmares that her mother grew alarmed.[35]

In late colonial and early republican Latin America, pedagogues tended to blame servants for instilling these kinds of nightmares in elite children. Fears and fantasies were attributed in particular to the influence of African and native Andean religious beliefs, and since children spent a good portion of the day with nannies of Indian and African descent, such ideas took on layers of meaning. Vicuña, with his inimitable sarcastic style, stated that "the countries neighboring the cradle of our forefathers were the Araucanian frontier and the Congo," and that "from these places appeared such fantastic traditions and frightful stories of spirits, specters, penitents, and [wandering] souls."[36]

Regardless of the origin of Ursula's night frights, they did concern her mother, who lamented aloud, "What will I do with this girl? Where shall I put her, Lord of my life, this child, consumed by frights, souls and the devil, who has me so worried?" Indeed, it appears Ursula's mother was of the opinion that the child should be removed from the house and sent to live with aunts in order to calm her.[37]

Although Ursula's personal story highlights fears rather than fantasies, we also gain a glimpse of some of her more pleasant childhood imaginations and activities in her spiritual autobiography. The *Relación* is relatively silent on the subject of games. Perhaps this is because, during Ursula's early years, she was close to her ill, bed-ridden grandmother, and this meant that she was quite sheltered. She hardly left the home even to play, as her cousins and sister did. What is interesting here is that Ursula's failure to participate in communal play gave others the perception that she behaved like a "little old lady."

Nevertheless, in some passages, Ursula referred to games played with her sister, although these were normally discussed in a vague, generic way. She related, for example, the trouble she and her sister got into one day when her mother went calling on neighbors and family, leaving the girls in the house alone with a servant. Ursula described no specific toys except to say that her sister, at some point, was playing "with water in a jug." Ursula also remembered "having heard of a magic wand [*varilla de virtud*], with which one could perform miracles." She regularly left her house alone in search of the mysterious wand.[38]

But, most critically, we learn that Ursula recalled playing at being a nun. She enclosed herself in a room as though in the cloister and let no one into her make-believe cell. When she later entered a real convent, she would regret that she had lost the opportunity for other kinds of play since, even at the age of twelve, her days as a novice became filled with tasks and teaching. She lamented that as a child "to punish myself for being small and to avoid the misbehavior that conformed to my age, I had to be big like the others."[39] Ironically it appears that just as Ursula played at being a nun while she was a child, after she became a novice she eventually played at being a child again. A year into her novitiate, she recalled, "I left and began playing," "getting into mischief" with other novices.[40]

This contradictorily mischievous, spoiled child who acted like an old lady reported that she had to change her behavior radically when she was sent to live with a great aunt, who taught her to read. It is unclear what brought about the change—whether it came from Ursula herself or from the influence of a specific adult, or whether it is part of the conversion narrative common in writings of this genre. But Ursula reported that she stopped leaving the house to go into the street, avoided all instances that could result in physical punishment, and learned "not to raise my skirts for anyone who was not my mother." The context for this last comment is unclear; it could refer either to a growing recognition of norms of sexual modesty and danger, or to punishment.[41]

This brings us to the question of sexuality and rites of passage for the young Ursula, who did not provide us much direct evidence of her experiences in this realm save a few incidences, all which serve to portray her as an individual with a strong disinclination or disdain for marriage. At the age of five or six years, Ursula devised a game of playing the role of an adult woman: she would cover herself with a *mantilla*, put on all of the "adornments," sit in front of the widow facing the street, and wait for men to pass by. After only a few instances of playing this game, a man approached the window, began a conversation with her, and offered her some coins. At that point, the little girl gave up her disguise and tried to grab the money out the stunned man's hand. One of her aunts heard about Ursula's trick and, although she tried to muster anger, she ended up breaking into laughter at the girl's wit. Ursula's mother was hardly amused.[42]

Within the narrative logic of the autobiography this incident may convey disdain for marriage or rejection of men. Ursula also provided another "early sign" of her future vocation when she discussed her childhood belief that women became the living dead upon matrimony. She reported that when she saw brides, she "was convinced that all who married were dead."[43] At some point Ursula stopped socializing with and entering the presence of female relatives after they had married "even if they [too] were children."[44]

Her professed rejection of adult men and belief that marriage was tantamount to death were countered by her mother's insistence that the young Ursula be married. Ursula included many passages designed to demonstrate that she was so committed at even a young age to her monastic vocation that she battled her mother over the issue. For example, one holiday, after mass the women had gathered to chat. When the subject turned to marriage, Ursula reported that she "saw fit to get up . . . and walk out." She was probably somewhere around the age of ten when this occurred.[45]

Certain features of Ursula's narrative of her childhood—particularly her self-criticism and her dogged insistence that she never wanted to marry—follow established conventions for spiritual autobiography. Yet these elements are not consistent throughout the text. For example, Ursula not only cast herself in the role of a spoiled child who would one day adopt virtue, she also remembered being prudish and withdrawn. Furthermore, she reported performing acts of charity and kindness. She said that if a household object was broken she would accept the blame so that the servants would not be punished. And she reported that her sister did the same.[46] She also recalled finding bread to give to servant and slave children in the household when they were hungry.[47]

Ursula as Elite

Although offered only in fragments, Ursula's text reveals that she recognized her social status at a young age and grew up concerned with displaying and maintaining it. This preoccupation translated into unabashed expressions about the importance of material life, especially clothing. It also structured her relationships with servants and endowed her with an acute sensitivity to matters of inheritance.

The *Relación* offers hazy but telling examples of Ursula's love for gala events, such as dances (although she disliked feeling as though she was up for sale on the marriage market), and her fascination with jewels and clean, elaborate clothing.[48] Ursula also liked to dress up (*andar galana*), decked out in white dresses and mantillas embellished with pearls. Perhaps this was simply no more than an expression of a child's tendency to play adult roles. But Ursula did not just dress as an adult; she dressed as an elite Spanish adult. Thus, dress-up in colonial Santiago was fraught with caste-based meanings that positioned children alongside their parents in the city's social hierarchy.

Ursula's relationship with servants was further evidence of her entrenchment in the upper echelons of the colonial hierarchy. The perceived need to be served and to have individuals ready to cater to needs was an element of Ursula's life since she was young. There is reason to believe that slave families could be relatively intact inside of elite households such as Ursula's, and the presence of slave children was not at all uncommon.[49] Those slave children might be paired with owners' children. Ursula remembered that her grandmother assigned a fourteen-year-old *mulata* servant to serve only her and that she had a personal servant by the age of five.[50]

If being served held social significance for the upper classes of seventeenth-century Santiago in terms of status to the outside world, it also had an internal meaning within the home of Ursula's grandmother. In 1672, when Ursula was about six, the family unit was made up of four adults and two children, but the household also counted fourteen servants of various ages, and the distribution of their labor was a signal of the family members' social position within the household. The grandmother made sure that upon her death one slave woman was distributed to each of her granddaughters, and Ursula remembered this vividly since she was a witness when the old woman dictated her will and testament.[51] The grandmother originally wanted to leave a slave only to Ursula, her favorite. But

Ursula's mother worked indirectly to make sure that her other daughter too was left a servant. In the end, Ursula received the services of a "little black girl" named Juanilla, and at least from that point on young slaves were ubiquitous in her life.[52]

It appears that even when she was quite young, Ursula had a clear idea of what she had coming to her by way of inheritance. She wrote that before she was twelve years old, she and her mother debated Ursula's preference for entering a nunnery, and her mother tried to dissuade the girl with material incentives. María promised to give her daughter "more than ten slaves and silver." Ursula quickly retorted that she already had a legal claim to more than that since she was a legitimate child of her father and therefore eligible for a set portion of inheritance.[53] In another incident Ursula considered the possibility that her mother might disinherit her for entering the convent. But she comforted herself with her certainty that she needed nothing from her mother and that her father would never disinherit her.[54] The issue of property and inheritance was critical, since even entering a convent did not erase a woman's class status in colonial Latin America. Ursula would need to provide a hefty dowry to a convent in order to become a black-veiled nun—a position in convents reserved for the colonial elite.[55]

In fact, one of the arguments her mother made in attempts to dissuade young Ursula from entering the convent was that she would have to abandon the "good life" (*vida regalada*), especially since the order would not allow Ursula to bring a servant into the cloister. As María began to give in to Ursula's life choice, she said that she would feel best if her daughter could enter a convent where some of her female relatives resided and if she could bring in a servant that she already knew to take care of her.[56]

María's concern that Ursula would have difficulty adjusting to the austere life of a nun was well founded. When the twelve-year-old girl first entered the convent, she was "disgusted" that all of the comforts of her home were missing and that she did not eat off of "silver plates" but instead from earthenware. Her mother earlier had offered to send her into the convent with all the material adornments, but Ursula had not thought it necessary. Now, looking around and watching as nuns were served from "trays made of mud," she wondered what she had done by entering "such an ugly convent" where nuns "have no pillows." She sent word that she needed a silver dish, a basin, and a silver jug.[57] Although she adjusted, Ursula was deeply aware that she was less "served and cared for" in the nunnery than in her home. The knowledge that she could so easily go from the good life to the comparatively austere life of nun was, ultimately, bitter for her.[58]

Spaces

In Santiago's upper-class homes, spaces were reserved for children only from the second half of the nineteenth-century when bourgeois norms began to promote separate children's bedrooms and the establishment of playrooms within the house. During the turn of the twentieth century, playgrounds outside of the home began to spring up around the city.[59] But before this, spatial segregation by age within the domestic realm was unknown.

The colonial household generally was architecturally structured around two or three areas. Depending on the economic situation of the family and the physical dimensions of each *solar*, or residence measuring between one-fourth and one-eighth of a city block, each house might have two or three patios. In the case of wealthier homes, the first patio opened to the street from a hallway that led to a spot for mounting horses and into the roadways. The second patio housed the heart of the home, which consisted of private rooms for the family, including the living room, receiving room, and antechambers. The kitchen, pantry, and servants' rooms were situated around the third patio that was located within the interior of the residence.[60]

Ursula never mentioned in her vida whether her childhood home was built around two or three patios. We only know that, located to the east of major city thoroughfares, it took up half a solar. Nor do we know if she was confined to the interior of the house. In fact, it appears from her various references to watching the bustle of the city streets through the window that Ursula spent considerable time in the outer rooms.[61] What we do know is that the home of her grandmother, where she was raised, was large enough to accommodate fourteen slaves and three generations of family: her grandparents, her parents, who undoubtedly gave shelter to various dependents within their residence, and herself and her sister.

Ursula also seems to have spent considerable time in the central living room with other women.[62] During the era, it was typical for women to gather in this room and to sit on the cushions of an *estrado* while they chatted. The estrado was a long reclining platform that normally measured about fifteen centimeters high and several meters across, and it was covered with rugs or sheepskin pelts. The lady of the house often sat in the center of the estrado on a stool. Ursula recalled in passing that she frequently rested in the room "as was the custom of girls."[63] There, pretending to be asleep, she listened to the adult conversations of the women and particularly to their tales of love affairs. She later recalled that it was on the estrado, listening to the women talking about their behavior with the opposite sex, that she developed her abhorrence of marriage.[64]

Ursula did not seem to have had her own bedroom. She slept with her grandmother every night, even while the woman was gravely ill. After her grandmother's death, on various occasions she spent the night in her mother's bed. Shortly before entering the convent at the age of twelve, Ursula recalled listening to her mother "whispering" at night, indicating that she still slept with her and that it would not have been unusual for a child to have regular physical contact with adults during the night.[65]

Ursula's memory of the spaces where her childhood took place stands in contrast to more traditional descriptions of colonial childhood like those that Vicuña offers. His words give the impression that elite youths spent their childhood years "piled up" in the rooms of servants, neglected by their parents and other adults of their class.[66] This nineteenth-century historian also underscored the power of the *pater familias* as guardian of the household. In his narrative, a central part of each day was the nightly *recogida*, or lockup, when the key to the door facing the street was hung up and monitored by the father.[67] Ursula mentioned no such ritual.

The reported practice of the recogida brings us to the salient question about whether the world of children, particularly elite female children, ever extended beyond the home. Clearly, upper-class residences structurally faced inward, for internal patios and the thick exterior walls enclosed private homes. Nevertheless, in the colonial period, the house, the church, the plaza, and the street merged into an integrated ambit of social relations and ritual. Although it is possible that children were kept inside when they were small, once they reached a stage of relative autonomy, they began to frequent all those other social sites.

Ursula parents' residence was not the only home she inhabited during her childhood. She was sent to live with a great aunt when it came time for her to learn to read. She also occasionally was shuttled to other relatives, including her grandfather—where she reported her mother sent the girl to "rest" after her diabolical visions. All these relatives' homes were located in the center of the city, only a few blocks from Ursula's principal residence. Ursula also recalled social visits to the homes of other city inhabitants, but these were mainly inspired by events such as the marriages of her young relatives.[68]

The possibility of leaving the house for other reasons also existed. At times, the girl accompanied her servant on chores. And, in one undoubtedly impressive incident at the age of around seven, Ursula went to visit the convent of the nuns of Santa Clara.[69] The convent was located in the center of the city, making it possible to conjecture that the girl also witnessed aspects of public life, including civil and military activities, in the streets.

The street was more than a transit point to the young girl from Santiago. It was also a place of adventure. It is unclear if this would have been a common experience for all upper-class children, but Ursula went out into the street enough to call herself streetwise, or *callejera*. She ventured through Santiago looking for her magic wand, and in order not to get lost, she learned to follow the irrigation streams. "Every afternoon this was my job, and I would return home when the chapel bells rang [*a horas canónicas*]," usually around nine o'clock or nine-thirty each evening. "Sometimes," she reported, "they would spank me so I would not go out and get run over by a horse."[70]

During one of these outings, she encountered an establishment that seems to have served as a brothel. As she described it, this was a house "with empty rooms without doors, where so many shameful acts were committed that it was dreadful . . . and not only two people were engaged in this evil but eight or ten; and no other eyes than the eyes of an innocent who had no idea what sin they were committing witnessed this. I thought they were marriages, so I went every day to see it." One day Ursula told her mother what she was watching, and her mother responded, "Little girls do not talk about such marriages nor do they get involved in them." Ursula learned from her mother's comment only that she should not mention what she saw, but she continued to go visit the house.[71] It was not until the girl went to live with her great aunt that she stopped going out into the streets, indicating that enclosure in the home developed alongside education and maturity for girls.[72]

Education and the Struggle over Marriage

It is conventional wisdom that women's education during the colonial period was rare and superficial, and that girls in particular were shut out of the world of letters.[73] Yet Ursula's text is filled with references to education. Even though she was part of a small minority of female children in the city to learn to read and write, it is important to remember that education extended beyond the written word into the broader world of female skills, marital expectations, and Christian indoctrination.

A chief goal of Ursula's educators was to familiarize her with reading and writing, though she made no mention of being taught arithmetic. Ursula learned from relatives and from teachers. Her great aunt, Josefa Lillo, taught her to read at the age of six but not without some difficulty. Doña Josefa employed a method of teaching using primers, and once Ursula had learned to write sufficiently she began to practice with the Mercederian friars' *libros de propósito*. While staying with her aunt, Ursula also learned embroidery. Later the job of teaching her this particular female skill was turned over to an indigenous woman who served as *maestra de labor*, then to another servant woman when she moved to the home of other aunts.[74]

The fact that María had delegated the responsibility for teaching her child to other women did not mean that she was unconcerned with Ursula's education. But she viewed her primary responsibility to marry her daughter off, and thus Ursula summed up her mother's pedagogy in the following way: "All that a woman must do she made me learn." The primary lessons mother María's taught her daughter were about morals, starting with "fear of God and doctrine."[75] This education in Christian ethics also included instilling the value of charity. Ursula recalled crying when her mother attempted to give away clothes belonging to her and her sister; these were, she said, special *polleras*, or skirts, although they lacked the silver embellishments of the best of such garments. Her mother reprimanded the child and began a lesson in the proper conduct toward the poor. "Look," Ursula recalled her saying, "if a pauper asks you for the shirt off your back, even if you have nothing else to give, you must give it and if you do not, God will not help you."[76]

Lessons that would prepare Ursula for married life also included teaching her about financial affairs related to household governance. María permitted Ursula to take charge of the weekly allowance for supplying the pantry and handed over its keys to the girl. Indeed, she and

Ursula's aunt praised Ursula, albeit in a patronizing way, for her ability to manage money. At the time, Ursula was quite young and her ability to count was limited, so she freely gave the female servants all the money they requested without much accounting, and she also recalled gladly giving her mother money for alms from the pantry fund.[77]

Thus, many elements of female education and social life were ultimately oriented toward the goal of marriage and administering a household. This was because marriage in the colonial period was not only a personal decision. It served a complex function for a family, filled with cultural, social, and economic dimensions, not to mention its emotional aspects.[78] The relationship between Ursula's education and the possibility of her future marriage became increasingly charged with conflict as mother and daughter began to clash over the course that the girl's life would take.

"My mother's desire to see me married grew just as I grew," Ursula wrote, although María was willing to wait until her daughter reached the age of twelve, which in the Catholic Church was the canonically sanctioned age for marriage.[79] Few girls actually married at this young age in the colonial period, although parents often began to plan daughters' futures after puberty. Adults, especially the women chatting on the estrado, spoke of Ursula's future marriage in her presence. But even when she was young, Ursula later recalled, she had other plans and began to voice them publicly. Her aversion to marriage and her clear desire to enter a convent incited her mother to threaten her on various occasions.[80]

In other regions of Spanish America, some women forced daughters more intent on entering convents than marital life to marry against their will.[81] But in Ursula's case, her mother's efforts only redoubled the girl's refusal to marry, producing dramatic family squabbles. Ursula met her mother's threats of using violence to change her mind with dramatic threats of her own. If she were to have to marry and sleep with a man, she said, "I will hang myself"; "I will cut my throat, or slice open my chest with a dagger."[82] It seems that the special interest Ursula's mother had in her daughter's future was not shared by the adult men in the child's life. During one of many fights mother and daughter had over the decision between marriage and the female monastery, Ursula's grandfather tried to intervene and convince María to "leave her be if she does not want to marry."[83] In the end, María gave in, and it was she who took her daughter to enter the Convent of Santa Clara in the Plaza de Armas in the center of Santiago. It was 1678 and Ursula was twelve years old.[84]

Final Words: A Colonial Child
and Colonial Childhoods

It is worth noting that, in an era that has never been particularly well known for the agency or importance of children, at least one woman remembered a childhood in which she was able to exert considerable weight in everyday household politics, even at five and six years old. The manner in which the child Ursula formed a focal point of adults' attention and care, inspiring contests between adults, concerns about her future, and contortions to conform to her desires, does not seem to be so different from what we might see in a similar household today.

This is not to say that "modern" notions of childhood were beginning to develop during this era, for we still need more precise studies of whether and how new concepts of youth and new pedagogies—European or otherwise—were developed and disseminated among the inhabitants of colonial Latin America. Nevertheless, Ursula speaks to another possibility though her vida. Perhaps the place children have occupied within family life has not changed so radically over recent centuries.

Thus Ursula presents challenges to historians of childhood who emphasize dramatic changes with "modernity," as did Ariès. As early as the dawn of the nineteenth century, Vicente Pérez Rosales, in his *Recuerdos del pasado*, displayed a typical historical fascination with transformations in childhood. The chronicler, growing old and standing on the brink of an epochal shift from colonialism to republicanism in Chile, recalled dramatic changes in the way elite children lived during the course of his life. He believed he was viewing the end of an era of childhood marked by an absence of rigid formalism and the lack of prescriptive, restrictive social roles for children. He was nostalgic for the simpler, freer, more authentic childhood of the past.[85]

Pérez Rosales's nostalgia for days gone by easily presages one of the primary arguments about the "invention of childhood" in the modern period and rising regimentation of children's lives. Contemporary scholars of childhood also point to a lack of spatial segregation between adults and children in premodern times, which Ursula's *Relación* confirms. It is illustrative that Ursula had no toys designed only for children but nonetheless engaged in imaginative games with the world around her. What is more, she lived in an upper-class world where household spaces seemed relatively open to her, and she was never relegated to playrooms and children's bedrooms. It is clear that, to some degree, Ursula lived in a way in which segregation from adults was unknown, and children were not assigned clear social functions or spatial limitations.

Yet unlike nineteenth-century Chilean historian Vicuña, who described elite children's abandoned in servants' quarters, and unlike twentieth-century British historian Lawrence Stone, who portrayed premodern child-rearing practices as abusive, we do not have to interpret this freedom as adult indifference or neglect. At the same time that the elite adults in Ursula's life permitted her a certain degree of freedom in daily activities, they also expressed concern for the girl's rearing, education, and well-being in an era marked by high infant mortality. Adults' protective attitude toward Ursula and her possible death due to illness is notable. For example, rather than to react defensively by emotionally distancing herself from her sickly baby, María went from saint to saint to save her daughter. What is more, to face the death of even the old and infirm was considered a traumatic experience for children; Ursula was sent to live with her paternal grandfather when her maternal grandmother finally succumbed to illness, and the adults in Ursula's home tried to shield her from grief. Parental interest in children's health, social restrictions placed on excessive physical punishment, and the instinct to protect children from certain types of harm in fact may be phenomena that are shaped by cultural and historical circumstance but not in and of themselves artifacts of any particular point in time. Thus, although important changes in perceptions and rates of childhood mortality, rearing, and education undoubtedly occurred along with modernity, these changes might be best viewed as shifts in emphasis rather than as revolutions in practice.[86]

Ursula's *Relación* offers other correctives to current scholarship. In particular, it tells historians of gender—particularly scholars of colonial Latin America—something rather unexpected. We know that, particularly among the upper classes of colonial Spanish America, high value was placed on female enclosure (*recogimiento*), which had both spiritual and sexual connotations.[87] Yet Ursula's refusal to go out and play with her fellow children and her preference for staying inside earned her not praise for her virtue but instead the nickname of "little old lady." The way Ursula told it, colonial Chileans believed that recogimiento was a mode of behavior that was to develop only with maturity and that any young girl who practiced it was behaving in a way inappropriate to her age.

References to Ursula as a "little old lady" may be a narrative device that she employs to underscore the early development of her virtuous traits. Indeed, Cristina Ruiz revealed the importance of the saintly arche-type when she studied hagiographies of Mexican nuns.[88] Clearly, many narrative elements in hagiographies and vidas—for example, Ursula's aver-sion to marriage and even her self-criticism for being a spoiled child—may tell us more about normative models of gender, conversion, and religiosity than about her unique experience and behaviors as a child. But should we therefore conclude the authors of vidas have somehow "tainted" their own recollections of childhood with an artificial hue of saintliness?

Too many signs point in the opposite direction. Many details in Ursula's vida do not fit neatly within the paradigmatic notions of saintli-ness Ruiz lays out. For example, Ursula recalled both good and bad behav-ior. She was both charitable and spoiled. She was a sheltered "little old lady" but also reported being streetwise and staying out into the dark of the evening searching for a magic wand in Santiago's streets.

Dismissing Ursula's vida as pure formula also risks overlooking rich detail about childhood in the text of her autobiography. Consider, as one final example, how she reports that adults addressed her with diminu-tive nicknames that mimicked the speech mistakes of a toddler, such as "Urchula" or "Ursuleca." The nuns of Santa Clara teased a seven-year-old Ursula when she visited the convent because the convent's abbess and president was also named Ursula, and they called the little girl *pechidenta*, a childish rendering of *presidenta*.[89] These small details speak to us as evi-dence that a childhood existed in the colonial period—or at least one colo-nial childhood existed for Ursula—and that memories of it can stray from the well-worn paths that writers of spiritual autobiography took when they searched for a saintly personal history.

The insistence that we can see something of the experience of a wealthy seventeenth-century Chilean girl through Ursula's *Relación* does not, of course, mean that we can understand colonial childhood in the aggregate. Understanding childhood among Santiago's popular classes rather than elites, for example, requires other archival tools, some of which have been devised by Gabriel Salazar.[90] Yet my sense is that those who rely on popular sources that can be quantified, such as criminal cases, should be just as cautious about the limits of their sources as those who use a single source generated by the elite, such as spiritual autobiography. For example, legal cases from the colonial period are abundant and reveal a great deal about the lives of ordinary children. But they tend to be limited in their representative nature because they cast light only on children who somehow transgressed social norms. This would explain the attention thus far in the historiography to social transgressions such as illegitimacy, abandonment, and infanticide. Ultimately, it is attention to multiple sources together—without dismissing any as too formulaic—that is the best methodological option for those who wish to understand the history of children as opposed to childhood as a unified category.

Analyzing multiple sources together may reveal yet one more surprise for historians of childhood. Perhaps any assumption that there is a great distinction between popular and elite childhoods is overdrawn, or at least does not do justice to the fact that the diverse people of colonial Latin America did not always live in isolation from one another, particularly in cities. If there was physical segregation between different social groups in colonial cities such as Santiago, it had not reached anything of the divided nature that it would in later centuries. Ursula made it clear that in the realm of material life and in the ambit of her home, the contact between people of different social ranks was intimate, particularly through ties of servitude.[91] Thus the definitions and experiences of childhood held by the elite would have intersected at multiple points with those of the masses.

It is true that the characteristics of childhood revealed in Ursula's memory best represent an elite childhood. Yet ultimately, and ironically, analyzing childhood memories that an elite nun in Santiago left in her autobiography more than three hundred years ago has opened, rather than closed, the possibility that there were certain values, practices, and meanings attached to colonial childhood that would have been understood and reproduced by many colonial Latin Americans.

✦ NOTES ✦

1. The growing use of vidas as historical sources has produced some important comparative studies that have broadened our understanding of their defining characteristics. See especially Kristine Ibsen, *Women's Spiritual Autobiography in Colonial Spanish America* (Gainesville: University Press of Florida, 1999).

2. The vida of Ursula Suárez has been a focus of many recent studies, most notably Ibsen, *Women's Spiritual Autobiography*; Manuel Durán S., "Sor Ursula Suárez: Estrategias y espacios de poder (siglos XVII y XVIII)," *Mapocho* 54, no. 2 (2003): 159–77; and Carolina Ferrer, "Sor Juana Inés de la Cruz y sor Úrsula Suárez: ¿Modelos de autobiografías de monjas?" *Nomadías*, Serie Monográfica 1 (1999): 85–104.

3. Benjamín Vicuña Mackenna, "La era colonial," in *Historia crítica y social de la ciudad de Santiago: 1541–1868*, vol. 2 (Santiago: Editorial Nascimento, 1926), chapter 20.

4. Úrsula Suárez, *Relación autobiográfica*, Prólogo y edición crítica de Mario Ferreccio Podestá, estudio preliminar de Armando de Ramón (Concepción, Chile: Biblioteca Nacional, Universidad de Concepción, Academia Chilena de la Historia, 1984), 91; de Ramón, "Estudio," in *Relación*, 48–49.

5. Diego Barros Arana, *Historia general de Chile*, vol. 5 (Santiago: Editorial Universitaria, Centro de Investigaciones Diego Barros Arana, 2000), 216–17; Armando de Ramón, *Santiago de Chile (1541–1991): Historia de una sociedad urbana* (Madrid: Ediciones Mapfre, 1992), 95–99; *Historia urbana: Una metodología aplicada* (Buenos Aires: Clacso, Comisión de Desarrollo Urbano y Regional, Ediciones SIAP, 1978), 88.

6. De Ramón, "Estudio," 54–60.

7. Ursula, *Relación*, 49.

8. In fact, the day of Saint Ursula is celebrated on October 21 rather than October 20, when Ursula was born. For saints' days and naming, see de Ramón, "Estudio," 48–49; Mario Góngora, "Sondeos en la antroponomia colonial de Santiago de Chile," in *Estudios de historia de las ideas y de historia social* (Valparaiso: Ediciones Universitarias de Valparaíso, 1980), 277–304.

9. Vicuña, *Historia*, 427–30. Also see Armando de Ramón, "La sociedad española de Santiago de Chile entre 1581 y 1596 (estudio de grupo)," *Historia* 4 (1965): 191–228.

10. Ursula, *Relación*, 91. In Christian culture, the rose of Jericho is also called the "resurrection flower" because of a legend about how it continually flowered during Christ's life, dried up during his crucifixion, and reflowered after the resurrection.

11. Ursula, *Relación*, 92.

12. Ibid., 92–93.

13. Ibid., 101.

14. Ibid.

15. Vicuña, *Historia*, 431. Vicuña points to the commonly used Quechua terms *guagua* (baby), *nana* (grandmother), and *taita* (father), in *Historia*, 433.

16. Elisabeth Badinter, *¿Existe el amor maternal? Historia del amor maternal. Siglos XVII al XX* (Barcelona: Paidós-Pomaire, 1981), 74–78.

17. Ursula, *Relación*, 89–90. "*Leche preñada*," or "pregnant milk," seems to refer to milk supposedly ruined by sperm (Badinter).

18. Ursula, *Relación*, 93.

19. Ibid., 94.

20. Ibid., 93–98, 100.

21. Ibid., 97–98.

22. Ibid., 101.

23. For example, see ibid., 100, 119, 124–25, 116.

24. Ibid., 94, 98, 100, 111, 112, 115, 116, 100, 118, 119, 121, 124.

25. Ibid., 122, 124.

26. Ibid., 129–32. Note that Ursula's mother also rejected the idea that the girl would be punished by someone other than her when she entered the convent (Ursula, *Relación*, 144–45).

27. Ursula, *Relación*, 113.

28. Ibid., 103, 120.

29. De Ramón, "Estudio," 60.

30. Ursula, *Relación*, 124–25.

31. Ibid., 139.

32. Ibid., 90.

33. Ibid., 116.

34. Ibid., 92, 110–11, 129.

35. Ibid., 106–7, 109.

36. Vicuña, *Historia*, 434.

37. Ursula, *Relación*, 110.

38. Ibid., 107–8.

39. Ibid., 100, 151.

40. Ibid., 109–10, 126–27, 146–47.

41. Ibid., 110–11.

42. Ibid., 113–16.

43. Ibid., 126.

44. Ibid., 126.

45. Ibid., 122.

46. Ibid., 137.

47. Ibid., 137–38.

48. Ibid., 117, 121. For children's dress in Chile, see Isabel Cruz, *El traje: Transformaciones de una segunda piel* (Santiago: Ediciones Universidad Católica de Chile, 1996), especially 70, 214; Vicuña, *Historia*, 514–16.

49. According to Vicuña, *Historia*, 491–93, slave children performed a wide range of domestic tasks. Also see Alejandra Araya, "Sirvientes contra amos: Las heridas en lo íntimo propio," in *Historia de la vida privada en Chile*, ed. Rafael Sagredo and Cristián Gazmuri, vol. 1, *El Chile tradicional: De la conquista a 1840* (Santiago: Taurus, 2005), 161–97; and Rosa Soto Lira, "Negras esclavas: Las otras mujeres de la Colonia," *Proposiciones* 21 (1992): 21–31.

50. Ursula, *Relación*, 99.

51. The ages of the slave fluctuated between three and forty-five (de Ramón, "Estudio," 49–50).

52. Ursula, *Relación*, 102–3.

53. Ibid., 121. According to Spanish law, twelve was the age for matrimonial consent for girls. See Bianca Premo, *Children of the Father King: Youth, Authority, and Legal Minority in Colonial Lima* (Chapel Hill: University of North Carolina Press, 2005), 22. Still, demographic information principally from the eighteenth century does not show a high number of marriages among minors younger than eighteen. For the Chilean case, see Eduardo Cavieres and René Salinas, *Amor, sexo y matrimonio en Chile tradicional* (Valparaiso: Instituto de Historia, Vicerrectoria Académica, Universidad Católica de Valparaíso, 1991).

54. Ursula, *Relación*, 124.

55. See Kathryn Burns, *Colonial Habits: Convents and the Spiritual Economy of Cuzco, Peru* (Durham, NC: Duke University Press, 1999); and Asunción Lavrin, "Values and Meanings of Monastic Life for Nuns in Colonial Mexico," *Catholic Historical Review* 58 (1972): 367–87.

56. Ursula, *Relación*, 133.

57. Ibid., 140–41.

58. Ibid., 143.

59. On the creation of playgrounds in the 1910s and 1920s, see my "Juegos y alegrías infantiles, 1900–1940," in *Historia de la vida privada*, ed. Rafael Sagredo y Cristián Gazmuri, vol. 2, *El Chile moderno: De 1840 a 1925* (Santiago: Taurus, 2005).

60. Eduardo Secchi, *La casa chilena hasta el siglo XIX* (Santiago: Cuadernos del Consejo de Monumentos Nacionales, 1952), 8–9; Vicuña, *Historia*, 470–85.

61. De Ramón, "Santiago de Chile, 1650–1700," *Historia* 12 (1974–75): 277–78.

62. Secchi, *La casa chilena*, 8–9.

63. Ursula, *Relación*, 113. Ursula reported that she often ate separated from adults with her sister on a "small table" in the estrado. On one occasion, she was surprised to be invited to the bigger table, but it is unclear whether adult men also sat at the table or if it was only for women gathered in the estrado (Ursula, *Relación*, 119).

64. Ursula, *Relación*, 113, 122; and Vicuña, *Historia*, 479–80.

65. Ursula, *Relación*, 98, 101–2, 122–23, 138.

66. Vicuña, *Historia*, 433.

67. Ibid., 454.

68. Ursula, *Relación*, 110, 125, 129, 131, 134, 138; De Ramón, "Santiago de Chile, 1650–1700," 150–51, 212; and De Ramón, "Estudio," 45.

69. Ursula, *Relación*, 105.

70. Ibid., 108.

71. Ibid.

72. Ibid., 111.

73. Vicuña, *Historia*, 455.

74. Ursula, *Relación*, 111–13, 129–31.

75. Ibid., 116.

76. Ibid., 117.

77. Ibid., 117–18.

78. Asunción Lavrin, ed., *Sexuality and Marriage in Colonial Latin America* (Lincoln: University of Nebraska Press, 1989); Daisy Rípodas Ardanaz, *El matrimonio en Indias: Realidad social y regulación jurídica* (Buenos Aires: Fundación para la Educación, la Ciencia y la Cultura, 1977); and Pilar Gonzalbo Aizpuru and Cecilia Rabell, eds., *La familia en el mundo iberoamericano* (Mexico City: Instituto de Investigaciones Sociales, Universidad Nacional Autónoma de México, 1994).

79. Ursula, *Relación*, 118.

80. Ibid., 118–19.

81. Premo, *Children of the Father King*, 62–63.

82. Ursula, *Relación*, 118–20, 122–24.

83. Ibid., 119.

84. Ibid., 138–39.

85. Vicente Pérez Rosales, *Recuerdos del pasado (1814–1860)* (Santiago: Imprenta Barcelona, 1910), 11–12. "Good manners" became a dominant preoccupation among the upper classes in the nineteenth century, when apprenticeship in moral and doctrinal issues alone was no longer judged sufficient. For example, one of the first guides to manners, published in 1819, proclaimed, "It is not enough to know one's moral obligations toward men but [we must] also know the rules of urbanity so that our acts are pleasing and others do not flee from us as rustics and brutes [*mal criados*]," cited in Sebastián Cataldo, *Moral, urbanidad y sociedad en Chile durante la segunda mitad del siglo XIX* (unedited), Santiago, 2001.

86. Indeed, Linda Pollock argues that watersheds in the history of childhood are less revolutions in practice (the way children are treated, educated, and loved) than transformations in the way that treatment is understood and articulated (Linda Pollock, *Forgotten Children: Parent-Child Relations from 1500 to 1900* [Cambridge: Cambridge University Press, 1983]).

87. Nancy E. Van Deusen, *Between the Sacred and the Worldly: The Institutional and Cultural Practice of Recogimiento in Colonial Lima* (Stanford: Stanford University Press, 2001).

88. Cristina Ruiz Martínez, "La memoria sobre la niñez y el estereotipo del niño santo. Siglos XVI, XVII y XVIII," in *La memoria y el olvido: Segundo simposio de historia de la mentalidades* (Mexico City: n.p., 1985); and her "La moderación como prototipo de santidad: Una imagen de la niñez," in *De la santidad a la perversión: O de porqué no se cumplía la ley de Dios en la sociedad novohispana*, ed. Sergio Ortega (Mexico City: Enlace Grijalbo, 1986), 49–66.

89. Ursula, *Relación*, 99, 112, 137, 105.

90. Gabriel Salazar, "Ser niño guacho en la historia de Chile (siglo XIX)" *Proposiciones* 19 (1990): 55–83.

91. On social ties between children and adults of different social groups, see Premo, *Children of the Father King*.

CHAPTER FIVE

Consuming Interests

The Response to Abandoned Children in Colonial Havana

ONDINA E. GONZÁLEZ

∞

✢ SO DESPERATE WERE SOME COLONIAL CUBAN MOTHERS TO RID themselves of unwanted children that they "would go to the country-side and would leave their children there, sometimes throwing them alive into wells, other [times] into the sea (of which there were many and frequent examples) and other [times] putting them in the doorway of some house, leaving them exposed so that dogs would tear them apart and eat them."[1] Thus wrote the late seventeenth-century Cuban bishop Diego Evelino Hurtado de Compostela to Charles II, king of Spain, in the prelate's attempt to gain royal permission to open a house for foundlings in Havana.

Some twenty-four years later, at one o'clock in the morning on Friday, July 15, 1712—just one year after Havana's foundling home, Casa Joseph, finally opened—someone walked up to the door of the *casa cuna*, or foundling home, placed a two-day-old baby boy in the turnstile (*torno*) located in the wall next to the entrance of the house, rang the nearby bell, turned, and walked away. Inside the building the undoubtedly tired resident wet nurse came to the door, pushed the torno around, collected the abandoned child, and went back to her room with the baby in her arms. And so began the life of Juan de Buena Beritura. The next day Juan was baptized and anointed with oil by the resident priest. Later that same day the priest noted pertinent information about the infant in the house registry, including the fact that Juan had been left "with a new red shirt."[2] More than likely that same day, or perhaps within just a day or two, Juan went to live with a wet nurse employed by the casa cuna to care for him.

As with so many of the children left in the torno of Casa Joseph, the records do not tell us what happened to Juan. We do not know even if he reached five years of age, the point at which the foundling home ceased to be responsible for the children and left them on their own, hopefully to experience "the kindness of strangers." We know only that Juan's parents, like so many parents in similar situtions, had few choices. Among them were to leave the baby at Casa Joseph or to commit infanticide. Juan's parents choose to give him a chance at life.

The foundling home played a crucial role in the care of abandoned children in Havana, and as such its early record is a solid indicator of the history of at least certain children, such as Juan, at the beginning of the century. This chapter attends to these children's history—as much as information in the aggregate allows—as well as revealing links between the evolution of Casa Joseph and developments in the concepts and practices of charity in Havana. What we will also find is that church-state struggles over funding for the house mirrored societal attitudes toward children that were characteristic of the era.

In the chapter that follows this one, Ann Twinam also looks at the story of children abandoned at the *casa cuna* in Havana but largely during the latter half of the century. If the foundling home was a flashpoint for clashes over notions of charity and public good during the first half of the century, in the closing decades of the 1700s, issues of abandonment become entangled not only with attitudes toward charity but with policies of race and social status as well.

The history of Casa Joseph and the foundlings abandoned there present us with at least two ways of viewing Havana's society: through the experiences of the children themselves and through evidence of conflicting yet concurrently developing responses toward the children. Although it is the former that we shall examine first, some general comments about both are necessary by way of an introduction.

First, the very fact of abandonment results in near invisibility of the individual in historical records, and thus actual stories about any one foundling are scarce if available to us at all. However, these children—in the aggregate—do come to us through entries and notations in the few government and church logs that recorded their presence. These sources allow us to know something of the experience abandoned children in Havana all shared. What follows include some of the bits and pieces we can glean about a few of the children as well as the general picture that emerges of the early days in the lives of Havana's foundlings.

Second, there is much more documentation about the adults and institutions charged with responding to the plight of these children. From these sources we can trace changing attitudes toward foundlings and even the place of abandoned children within Cuba's colonial society. Briefly, on the one hand, we find that over the course of the 1700s the crown increasingly employed secular rhetoric in its decrees regarding foundlings in Havana, ultimately with Charles III (r. 1759–88) declaring the need to train these children to be good subjects and thus benefit the empire. Charity in this era became a tool for enforcing the power of the royal state rather than a response to the poor. Centuries-old royal rhetoric of paternal concern for its subjects shifted in the latter half of the eighteenth century to one that held that it was more important for subjects to be good residents than to be well cared for. On the other hand, we also see that the wealthy citizens of Havana were moved from inaction in the face of abandoned children at the beginning of the century to significant, yet inadequate, levels of support for Casa Joseph at the end. This change was occasioned by a late-century emphasis of the elite on the salvific effects of acts of charity. Although such notions certainly long predated the end of the century, for reasons that will be examined later, they were unimportant to the wealthy denizens of the city until late in the 1700s.

The case of the foundling home in Havana suggests that the Spanish crown, particularly in the person of Charles III, responded to the needy in an effort to exert social control over both the elite and the poor, in effect altering the definition of charity from an individual's act of religious devotion to a state function toward a group. The crown's actions, however, should not be surprising as such control was key in the king's push to amass power across the empire. Interestingly, the elite in Havana seemed oblivious to these attempts at curtailing their actions, as is evident in their

change in attitude from near hostility to the problem of foundlings ultimately to an intimate involvement in raising capital for Casa Joseph.

In addition to the elite, the crown, and the children, there were two
other actors in the drama surrounding Havana's abandoned children: the
church and the local government. Unlike the crown and the elite, ecclesiastical authorities and municipal officials remained static in their positions toward foundlings. Throughout the history of Casa Joseph, these
two groups fought bitterly, trying to foist responsibility for providing
funds for the care and sustenance of unwanted children onto the other.
The animosity between the two went far beyond issues of funding for
Casa Joseph, but in this case, the children became yet one more battle-
ground for long-standing rivalries. These children who were abandoned
at Casa Joseph, as unlucky as we may believe them to be, were probably
the fortunate ones, for they were left at a place that gave them hope for
a life. Their reality, though, was anything but bright as the story of the
home reveals.

There was one point, however, that the four powerful entities seemed
to have in common, even over the course of the entire century: the children themselves were, at best, a secondary issue. Ecclesiastical and royal
actions often belied rhetoric that drew on the church's charge to care for
the needy and the king's role as "father" to foundlings. Local secular officials—who were from elite circles—did not want the financial burden of
supporting abandoned children. And the elite in general were so absorbed
with their own self-interest that the foundlings did not even register with
them until the children could be of some purpose to them. Indeed, for the
foundlings of Havana, abandonment took many forms, most of which had
dire consequences. Were it not for the tenacious work of Bishop Valdez—
Compostela's successor—in the early eighteenth century, the home would
have remained an idea instead of becoming a reality.

The Beginnings

Sixty-year-old Gerónimo de Valdez arrived in Cuba in April 1706 as the
island's new bishop. Among the many royal decrees he carried was one
ordering the creation of a home for abandoned children in Havana.[3]
Perhaps, at first, this particular decree might not have seemed of any more
importance than the others. Shortly after his arrival, however, he reported
back to King Philip V (r. 1700–17) that

in the short time I have served I have recognized and experienced the great lack [of a foundling home]. . . . In [this city,] with the frequent Armadas and diverse passengers being in transit, some hardships and errors are experienced by some good women whose husbands are away, as by some virtuous and circumspect maidens who, in order to conceal their defects [pregnancies], go out to the country sides, and they leave their children there.[4]

So moved was Valdez by what he witnessed that he immediately requested the needed royal license to open the foundling home "under the royal patronage of Your Majesty and [to] establish this house with the privileges and exemptions that in similar occasions you have conceded to the rest, in these kingdoms as in Spain."[5] In his petition, however, the prelate recognized that the reality of Havana, and the New World in general, was such that the children of slaves, *mulatas*, and free blacks needed to be excluded from the foundling home if the racial and social lines of Cuban society were to be maintained even within the confines of the casa cuna. These limitations were necessary, he argued, to ensure that undeserving children, so designated because of their lowly births, would not accede to the social standing of legitimate birth and noble privileges granted by royal decree to all foundlings. Furthermore, in the case of slave children, the bishop sought to protect the assets of the elite by making certain that slave mothers had no safe place to abandon their offspring. He feared that "in order not to see their children as they are, they [the mothers] would take them to the house."[6]

The bishop was granted his license, with these restrictions in place, and in 1710 paid eight thousand pesos to the estate of Don Lucas Riso for a house one block south of the Plaza Nueva, Havana's principal plaza. Valdez then began renovations, making "all the accommodations necessary for a house of abandoned children."[7] He chose the site in part because it was removed from the center of activity but still close to the city's most important real estate.[8] As a testimony to the need for the home, even before renovations on the house were finished, Bishop Valdez began receiving abandoned children. Barely four months into the project, the bishop wrote, "they have already left some five or six foundlings [that] I have being cared for in various parts [of the city]."[9]

Such impromptu beginnings, however, did not preclude the need for an official opening. The city gathered for the dedication of the casa cuna on March 19, 1711, the feast day of Saint Joseph. Priest Don Balthazar Gonzales de Betancourt celebrated mass in the home's newly built chapel; in attendance that day were Bishop Valdez and Dr. Don Pablo Cabero, as well as a lieutenant, general auditor, and the governor of the city. Among the "many people" in the crowd were perhaps some women who would eventually work for the casa cuna as wet nurses.[10] If the congregation and the celebrants had any idea of what lay ahead—the struggle for revenue, the overwhelming expenses, and worst of all, the plight of the children themselves—the occasion would have indeed been a somber one, for it was one thing to open a home and quite another to ensure that it had the requisite resources for continuous operation.

The Children

How needed was the house? From 1711 to 1752, 938 children were left at the foundling home. While an average of 22 children were abandoned annually over that period, 1717 saw the peak at 40 children left in one year and 1740 had the fewest number—only 4—placed in the house's turnstile.[11] Of the 744 for whom there is pertinent information (for example, dates of abandonment and death and baptismal records), the picture is truly bleak: from among that group, the death rate between 1711 and 1752 was 72.8 percent (n=542).[12] Of the 176 we know survived, 152 reached at least five years of age.[13] The other 24 left the care of the house alive before they were five years old. From these, some "were returned to their parents because they came for them; some, who being mulattoes were returned to their mothers; and some [people] took them [the foundlings] to be raised for free because of the usefulness of [their] service if they [the children] reached the competent age" to become servants.[14]

Just as with Juan, whose story opens this chapter, when children were left at Casa Joseph information about their deposition was noted in the *libro de partidas*, or birth book. This registry included the day, date, time, and location of abandonment. From this source we know that children were left at Casa Joseph throughout the year, with minimal seasonal fluctuation. Nearly 70 percent of them were left between seven and eleven o'clock in the evening, perhaps in an effort to conceal the identity of the abandoner, perhaps a desperate parent. One piece of information that appears only rarely in the registry is the age of the child at deposition. Of those whose age is noted (n=22), twenty (90.9 percent) were newly born;

the remaining two were only one or two months old.[15] The boy or girl (for a foundling was as likely to be female as male) might be left with new shirts and blankets made of silk or with a coverlet of old rags, with just a rosary or with nothing at all. Although the condition in which a child was left at Casa Joseph might reflect parental economic status, there was little else to mark the child's place in the world.

Occasionally a note was left giving the child's name and indicating whether the child had been baptized, but usually there was nothing about the child's parentage or familial affiliation noted in the registry. This omission does not mean, of course, that the decision to leave a child at the casa cuna was a painless one for anyone involved. On the contrary, the few notes that were found with abandoned children are often poignant, revealing the depth of sorrow over having made a difficult decision. The infant Ana María was left on March 5, 1720, with such a note: "Her parents ask that to this little child you give help for the love of God."[16] Other parents must have felt similarly. Certainly those parents who came back for their children (n=10) or who paid for their offspring's care (n=8) felt an ongoing commitment to their children, as might well have the eight who indicated that their children had been baptized by a priest before being left at Casa Joseph.

Once children were abandoned, it was the practice of the foundling home to have the resident priest baptize and anoint them with oil unless a note left stated that a baptism by the hand of another priest had already taken place. Again as with Juan, shortly after the religious rite the children would be transferred to the care of wet nurses, or amas, who would take them into their individual homes. To answer the bell and to care for and suckle the children during their brief time in the casa cuna proper there was a wet nurse, or *madre ama*, who lived at the house. While the children were in the homes of their respective amas, however, the babies remained under the guardianship of Casa Joseph, which was responsible for paying the wet nurses and overseeing the care of the children.[17]

At least 270 of the children abandoned at Casa Joseph during the early years were sent to amas who took care of only one child; but, of course, there were amas who had more than one charge. Such was the case with the wet nurse Thereza Lujan. On May 12, 1745, when Juana Josepha was abandoned at the foundling home, Lujan already had fourteen years of service to the house. And it was into Thereza's care that the baby girl was placed.[18] Two weeks later Juana was dead. A few years earlier the same fate had befallen Joseph de la Concepzion. Like Juana he was placed in Thereza's care shortly after being left at the foundling house. He lived one year, seven and one-half months.[19]

The earliest records of Thereza Lujan working for the foundling house date from 1731. We lose track of her when she disappears from the records in November 1752. However, we do know the fate of Juana, Joseph, and nineteen more of the twenty-four children for whom Thereza was responsible over her twenty-two years of employment with Casa Joseph. They died, nine of them living a month or less. Of the remaining three we know only that they survived five years in her care. After that, they too disappear from the records. Was Thereza murderous, neglectful, or unlucky? We simply do not know.

Although Thereza represents the most extreme case of an ama with multiple charges from Casa Joseph, the experience of ama Anna María de Estrada and her sole charge, Joseph Gerónimo, was more typical. Joseph was abandoned at eleven o'clock on a July evening in 1712. With him was a note stating only that he was named Joseph, having been entrusted to the care of the saint of the same name. The next morning the man chosen by the resident priest to act as Joseph's godfather was holding the baby as the infant was baptized and anointed. On July 20, 1712, just one day later, Joseph was given over to Anna María, a married woman living within the city, to act as his ama. The baby stayed with Anna and her husband for the next three years and five months, dying three days before Christmas 1715.[20]

All foundlings were under the guardianship of Casa Joseph only until they reached the age of five, at which time they were discharged from the care of the house.[21] Although we do not know their fates at this point, we can speculate that some may have been taken in by new families to be raised as servants; others may have found places as apprentices to learn a trade. Some probably remained with the wet nurses who had raised them. But undoubtedly many others died quickly once out of the care of the home or lived out a short Dickensian life on the streets, for more than likely many children were simply left to fend for themselves.

The Struggle for Funding

From the day it was founded, Casa Joseph rarely rose to the level of stability, and, as Bishop Valdez had anticipated, the institution encountered constant financial difficulties. Initially, the bishop asked the king for a one-time gift of twelve thousand pesos from the ecclesiastical *vacante*, or episcopate income generated during an episcopate vacancy, in New Spain. Knowing he would need ongoing financial support, the bishop further requested that income for the maintenance of the children and the house be awarded from the excise and sales taxes of the city.[22] Indeed, according to the terms of the papal bull *Eximae devotionis* (1501), the crown had the "responsibility to make up from the royal treasury any deficits" in the financial operations of religious institutions under royal patronage, such as Casa Joseph.[23]

After granting the first petition without hesitation, the king instructed the bishop to convene a meeting of the secular *cabildo*, or town council, the governor, and the bishop to discuss from which income source funds for the house should be drawn. The king further ordered this same group to draw up a constitution that would govern daily operations of the house.[24] The meeting was singularly unsuccessful with no agreements being reached as to the source of funding or the governance of the house.

The prelate reported:

> I convened the mentioned governor and captain general and the commissioners of the cabildo of this city in order to confer and deal with the referred [topic]. I made the mentioned royal decree known to them so that they would decide on the necessary means so that from the property and income of the city they could help with whatever is possible in the maintenance of abandoned children.[25]

Apparently the commissioners remained unmoved by the bishop's appeal or by the fact that his requests enjoyed royal backing. The city's financial obligations were such, argued the secular authorities, that there was no surplus to support the casa cuna. The commissioners also contended that the constitution of the house and the terms under which it would operate were within the purview of the bishop; they refused to become involved in determining the internal structures or guiding principles of Casa Joseph.[26]

The bishop, undaunted, suggested that the revenue raised by an excise tax on soap imported from New Spain and on livestock brought for sale to Havana from the interior of the island would be a good source of funds.

He further suggested that some of the monies collected to maintain the royal waterway, or *zanja*, which was the city's main water supply, could be used to fund Casa Joseph. In trying to deal with a problem that had plagued Havana for almost 150 years, the cabildo argued that all those funds were necessary to ensure the cleanliness of the waterway, which was constantly being contaminated by the collapse of its dirt walls and by cattle and human waste introduced upstream. There were no resources left for support of Casa Joseph according to the secular authorities. The opposition of the council notwithstanding, in 1718 the king ordered that an annual payment of one thousand pesos be taken from the collected excise tax for the waterway until the cabildo determined another, more suitable source of funding for Casa Joseph.[27]

The king's one proviso was that the paying of this subsidy should not impinge on the operations of the cabildo. Moreover, the king and his advisors retained authority to determine if demands on the cabildo's resources were onerous, thereby limiting the council's decision-making power. Though the secular leaders accepted the king's authority in theory, in this case, as in others, they acted in their own interest, only reluctantly and sporadically sending the mandated funds to Casa Joseph.

The cleanliness of the waterway was more than a question of public health. It was crucial to the maintenance of Havana as a key port in the route between the Indies and Spain. It is important to note that if ships could not be properly victualed in Havana, the city would suffer a severe economic blow. In the face of losing the city's preeminence as a port, foundlings mattered little to local officials. By contrast Philip V repeatedly reiterated his personal concern for the foundlings. The monarchs of Spain, who were considered parents of the poor, orphans, and foundlings, had for centuries taken this role seriously, and Philip V was no exception.[28]

Transatlantic communication makes it clear that very little was ever settled between the civil authorities and the church in matters concerning the foundling home. Indeed, from the beginning, the house became embroiled in Bishop Valdez's difficult relations with the civil authorities. His interactions with the governor were particularly bad. Repeatedly, Valdez excommunicated Governor Martínez de la Vega only to lift the ban when the governor bowed to the bishop's demands. Finally, the governor complained to the king that "taking advantage of the remedy of excommunication, there has been no year, from the time of my predecessor, that he [the bishop] does not use such a sacred sword in cases that do not merit even the threat of a fine."[29] The bitterness between the two men was such that much of Valdez's concern for the children, like his frequent decrees of excommunication, may have been designed simply to antagonize the governor.

An attempt to discredit the local government, combined with the very real needs of Casa Joseph, prompted Bishop Valdez to write Spain in 1719, in 1720, and again in 1721, complaining that no subsidy from the waterway tax collections had been delivered. Despite repeated directives from the king, only a total of five hundred pesos of the nearly four thousand pesos due had been sent to the casa cuna during almost four years.[30] Perhaps as a result of these protests, beginning in 1722 the royal treasury made good-faith efforts to pay Casa Joseph in a timely manner, at least for a while.[31] In a 1724 response to royal inquiry into the status of payments to the casa cuna, the *contador* (treasurer) of the island reported that only seventeen hundred pesos remained in arrears. He also explained that although the king wanted the burden of the house's subsidy spread among all the city's income sources, only the waterway tax generated sufficient revenue to support Casa Joseph.[32] Though the payments finally were made, the controversy continued, this time instigated by the government. In 1728 cabildo officials petitioned the king to suspend payments to Casa Joseph. They requested "that after contributing so many years to the mentioned house . . . [and] being the work of enclosing the waterway so useful to Your Majesty's service and the public good of this city, that you [the king] are served to order that the mentioned contribution be suspended."[33]

To gather support for this request, Governor Martínez de la Vega sent two notaries to investigate the condition and current status of Casa Joseph. They reported to the governor that the home's "main door as well as the turnstile were closed" and had been for more than two years.[34] Following this report, the governor's dispatch to the king smugly informed him that the foundling home was closed.

Upon receiving this alarming news, the king ordered local treasury officials to give their own account of the state of the casa cuna. This report contradicted that of the governor and outlined the financial woes of Casa Joseph. It also reported the number of children admitted to the institution during the years in question.[35] It is clear from the treasury's information that the foundling home was indeed operating but could not continue without added royal patronage in the form of further financial support. This time the king exercised his right to supersede all decisions by a local cabildo, weighing one public good against another: the needs of Casa

Joseph against the city's need for a clean water supply. At the same time that he sought information about the foundling home, the king also asked for the estimated cost of enclosing the waterway and any other local needs that had to be met with the excise tax.[36] The information was provided in excruciating detail. Ultimately the king decided in favor of the house, declaring that support for it created no undue hardship on the royal treasury in Havana and ordering that the city could and should meet its other needs while subsidizing Casa Joseph.

The discussions among the king, the cabildo, and the church were always conducted within a framework of ostensible concern for public welfare. The church argued that the plight of abandoned children superseded the needs of the local population and represented the greatest good. To bolster this point of view, a counselor reviewing Bishop Valdez's case for the king relied on centuries-old laws that demanded succor for abandoned children. The counselor, drawing on sixteenth- and early seventeenth-century law codes that addressed the responsibilities of a community—either its wealthy or its government—to care for abandoned children, noted that "the cause and the necessity of the maintenance of the house for children [in Havana] . . . should not have less attention and preference than whatever other public works."[37] Furthermore, he added, even if privileging Casa Joseph in the distribution of public funds proved harmful to other municipal projects, the decision was justified because the house was "so public, necessary, and pious" that it trumped the cabildo's concerns.

Cuban civil authorities, however, disagreed and argued that enclosing the royal waterway represented the greatest need and therefore the greatest good. They contended that years had passed without their being able to address the serious problem of water contamination. The water supply was so filthy that it was foul smelling and "gravely pernicious for the sailors."[38] A potable water supply was needed, they stated, not only for the residents but also for "the *flotas*, the galleons, the Armada de Barlovento and the many other unescorted ships which pass on to the kingdoms of Castile," stopping in Havana to take on fresh water.[39] By connecting this local need to the welfare of the entire empire, the cabildo members clearly hoped to sway the king. They did not succeed; the king remained committed to the casa cuna.

Underlying the cabildo's position was the considerable influence of Havana's merchant elite, many of whom were cabildo members. These government officials, often the wealthiest citizens of the town, were feeling pressure from their fellow merchants to use the tax revenue for infrastructure improvements that would aid commercial growth.[40] Although the proposed improvements to the waterway never occurred, the funds were commonly used for other public works. Financial support was given to Casa Joseph only grudgingly. Unfortunately, the elite's lack of the interest in the welfare of abandoned children in Havana went further than just bristling at tax revenue being used to fund the house. The elite also did not directly support the casa cuna with their own funds.

Even though there are no documents that directly address why wealthy *habaneros* did not patronize the house in its early years, the description of Havana and its denizens by Pedro Augustín Morrel de Santa Cruz, a mid-eighteenth-century bishop to the island, suggests that affluent citizens were interested solely in personal comfort. Whereas in other cities throughout the Indies wealthy residents routinely supported the local cathedral, resulting in ornate, beautifully appointed churches, in Havana Morrel found the city's cathedral "a spot that uglifies [the city] a great deal."[41] However the elite residents of the island's capital had no problem spending lavishly on ostentatious shows of finery both in clothing and in furnishings for their homes, often leaving well-connected families in near states of poverty.[42] Even Bishop Valdez, in 1713, had written the king asking for royal financial support in ministering to the poor of Havana because of the "penury of resources of the elite residents [*vecinos*] of this city."[43] Additionally, last wills and testaments of members of the Havana elite were replete with financial gifts to endow masses to ensure their salvation or to endow ecclesiastical offices, usually for one of their children. These bequests also rested heavily on the estates of upper-class residents.[44] It certainly seems that Havana's elite were prepared to wait until after death to take care of matters of the soul. Since wealth in Cuba depended largely on agricultural production and therefore could be difficult to acquire, elite individuals may have preferred to spend their hard-earned money on themselves and only reluctantly give to charitable endeavors.

By the 1710s Casa Joseph was experiencing the consequences of a dearth of personal and corporate philanthropy. In fact, most of the money committed to Casa Joseph—other than the funds from the waterway tax—came from Bishop Valdez himself. In the course of three years (1715–18) Valdez sold fifteen *solares*, or plots of land, belonging to the church at one hundred pesos each and placed the income under a *censo*, or annuity, whose interest of 5 percent was payable to the foundling home.[45] An examination of eleven other censos whose interest income was used for support of the house once again reveals a decided lack of interest on the part of Havana's elite. Nine of those censos were given directly to Bishop Valdez, presumably for whatever ecclesiastical purpose he chose. He assigned them to Casa Joseph.[46] Only the remaining two censos, generating five hundred pesos, were specifically designated by the donor for the house.[47] It should come as no surprise, then, that Valdez pursued the matter of funding from the cabildo with such vigor, since the wealthy citizens of Havana were clearly not a source of support.

The bishop also left as a bequest two thousand pesos in censos from his *spolium*, or the estate of a prelate. These additional funds, however, did not result in Casa Joseph's financial stability, far from it.[48] Moreover, another of the bishop's bequests to Casa Joseph presented problems for the house. The casa cuna became enmeshed in litigation with the Colegio de la Compañía de Jesus and the cathedral over a piece of property that Valdez left the home. The school and the church both wanted the land because it was prime real estate, but the house would not relinquish it to either. Again, the king ruled in favor of Casa Joseph. He determined that the home was the primary heir to the property and stipulated a settlement in order to lessen the financial drain on the house caused by the civil suit.[49]

Dealing with financial strain was a common experience for Tomás de Heredia, administrator of Casa Joseph from 1729 to 1759. Annual expenses of the house always exceeded annual income generated from the censos and from rental income of four rooms within the walls of the casa cuna itself.[50] After just five and a half years (January 1728 to June 1733), the house owed Heredia 1,082 pesos and 2 reales, almost an entire year's income for the house from all sources.[51] Nor did receiving the city's subsidy become a matter of routine. According to the treasury's own records, by 1739 the city had fallen behind in its payments.[52] In 1742 Philip V ordered the royal officials in Havana to pay overdue support because the house for abandoned children "is found reduced to the greatest misery" due to lack of funds.[53] Again, in 1744 Heredia wrote the king that "although 1,000 pesos was granted to [the house] each year for its maintenance and subsistence, a great deal was owed in arrears."[54] Furthermore, Casa Joseph's administrator requested that the king issue new decrees for Bishop Juan Lasso de la Vega (1731–52), the governor, and the *contadores de cuentas*, ordering that the bishop "dedicate himself to [the house's] permanence because it . . . [was] inherent for his pastoral duties" and that the two secular officials make the overdue payments.[55] The arrears were especially vexing, claimed the administrator, because the waterway tax was annually generating 3,450 pesos beyond what it had generated when the initial grant of 1,000 pesos was made.[56] Despite the 1744 royal decree ordering the governor and other royal officials to pay the casa cuna these arrears, the funds needed for support were not forthcoming.[57]

By 1752 Casa Joseph was near fiscal collapse. So dire was the situation that Heredia closed the home, placing a note stating that until further notice no new children would be taken in.[58] Even more pressing than the financial needs of the house, however, were the needs of abandoned children. A reported increase in the rates of infanticide quickly forced Heredia to reopen Casa Joseph, but the house remained deeply in debt with almost 7,000 pesos owed to nursemaids and to Heredia. Finally, in 1756 Ferdinand VI (r. 1746–59) ordered that the 18,803 pesos and 7 reales needed to pay the house's debts be taken from an accumulated *vacante* in Havana.[59] As a result, all the foundling home's debts were paid and its wet nurses received their back wages.

Despite decades-long royal attention to the casa cuna in Havana, at no point in its history was Casa Joseph on firm financial footing, even in the last years of the century when the home raised 95,343 pesos and 4 reales as endowment.[60] According to Cuban historians César Mena and Armando Cabelo, the need for a foundling home was so great at the end of the century and Casa Joseph so ineffective in meeting that need, primarily due to its financial problems, that "finally public charity was awakened."[61] Havana had indeed witnessed an upsurge of child abandonment; for example, in 1772 alone ninety-four children were left at Casa Joseph with annual abandonment rates between 1766 and 1775 reaching seventy-one children. Money for the children under the care of the foundling home was raised through pledges and gifts, unfortunately to little effect since so very much was needed. In the early 1800s, Casa Joseph and the Royal Beneficence House, founded in 1792 to shelter young girls, were merged and formed the Casa de Beneficencia.[62] In 1852, the Casa de Beneficencia merged with the Casa de Maternidad, remaining a single entity well into the twentieth century.[63]

As difficult as the experiences of Casa Joseph were, they were not unique, as studies of foundling homes throughout the Spanish American colonies indicate. René Salinas Meza, in writing about Santiago's Casa de Huérfanos, noted that "rising expenses and endless budget deficits never allowed the institution to acquire necessary resources to program expansion or improvements in the orphanage."[64] The financial situation of the Buenos Aires home was no better. In a 1788 royal response to the administrator's appeal for additional funds, Charles III directed the viceroy to secure needed resources as quickly as possible in order to sustain the foundling home so that it "does not come to total ruin."[65] "The economic state of the foundling home could not have been more pitiful," the king acknowledged.[66] Finally in 1838 the *porteño* house closed its door due to its dire financial situation.[67]

Mexico City's house for abandoned children, the Casa de Niños Expósitos, fared better economically than did those in Buenos Aires, Santiago, or Havana. Initially resources were scarce, but within six years of its first depositions (1766), the Casa de Niños Expósitos was under the care of the Congregación de La Caridad and Señor San José. The members of this group took their responsibilities seriously, ensuring that there were sufficient funds for the work of the house. But toward the end of the eighteenth century, "the attitude of the congregants changed," and the economic situation of the house deteriorated.[68]

The Response

In the habaneros' response—or more accurately lack of response—to the city's foundlings in the first half of the eighteenth century, what we see is that personal salvation was not tied to traditional acts of charity; rather, it was a function of one's personal piety, not one's action. In early eighteenth-century Cuba good works increasingly became the responsibility of the church, and for the wealthy individual economic self-interest in the temporal world superseded the needs of the abandoned children. Additionally, among the elite in Havana there seems to have been a heightened sense of corporate social structure, which may also have led to a near blindness to foundlings. As Ann Twinam discusses in her chapter in this volume on Havana's foundlings and the *gracias al sacar*, in the late colonial period there was an increased elite rigidity in terms of social class. The foundlings' ambiguous standing within that social structure undoubtedly contributed to the elite's initial disregard of their plight. In spite of royal decrees granting all the privileges of lofty and legitimate birth to foundlings, the realm's subject, at least in Havana, refused to honor these royal edicts. The unknown parentage of abandoned children left them in social limbo, and the lack of concern by the government and the elite in Havana left them in dire circumstances.

Casa Joseph remained the source of concern for Spanish monarch after the mid-eighteenth century, but the reasons for the concern were different than those expressed earlier by Philip V. In 1763, in the midst of what are known as the Bourbon Reforms, Charles III called for the creation of a beaterio, or home of lay religious women, to be named María Santísima de las Mercedes and to shelter the young girls no longer under the care of Casa Joseph. He also called for the boys from the foundling home to be placed under the care of the Bethlemite religious order.[69] Girls were to stay with the eight holy women in the beaterio until they married or took vows to become nuns. Boys were to be educated and learn a trade or sent into maritime service. Charles's clear intent was to create good subjects: as he wrote, "The children are released and in their most tender infancy they remain destitute of all human care and in an absolute and total abandonment. . . . If they reach adulthood, far from being of some good, they are outlaws and very harmful for the republic."[70] His predecessors' reasons for decreeing ongoing support and care of abandoned children were expressed with, and seemingly based on, religious sensibilities. Yet Charles, breaking with the past, reasoned that it was better to care adequately for vulnerable children in order to ensure that they acquired skills necessary for self-sufficiency than it was for society, in later years, to contend with lawless, indigent adults.

The changes in both royal rhetoric and public response to the horrors experienced by foundlings in Havana parallels Silvia Arrom's findings about the Mexico City Poor House that opened in 1774. Arrom argues that the largely secular founding of the home reflects a shift from traditional styles of charity, usually orchestrated by the church and meted out as part of one's religious convictions, to a modern style in which social welfare becomes the primary tool used by the state in response to the needy. However, Arrom also finds that, ironically, the "experiment [the Poor House] had made few inroads into the traditional 'moral economy' of begging, in which the needy had the undisputed right to receive alms and the affluent considered it their duty to dispense them."[71] Arrom's work reveals a dichotomy between the public welfare efforts of the state and the religious goals of wealthy individuals.

In Havana's case, we find the same dichotomy in responses by the crown and by individuals to foundlings. In the mid-eighteenth century Charles III used his concerns for the general state of the empire to justify the creation of a support system for foundlings released from the care of Casa Joseph. However, thirty years later, the need for the home was as great as ever. At that point, local bishops in Havana were successful in raising funds from wealthy individuals by reminding them of their Christian obligation to the needy and the importance of acts of charity, charges which they now took seriously, in stark contrast to their earlier indifference to such matters.

What caused this change in attitude of the elite? Beginning in mid-century, Cuba, and specifically Havana, became increasingly important to the crown primarily as a key defensive site for the Spanish American colonies. As a result, the crown poured money into the capital to increase local fortification and bowed to pressure from local elite who sought special privileges. Island merchants and planters wanted trade limitations eliminated, a restructuring of the taxes, and an increased number of slaves brought to the island for sale—so necessary, they claimed, for the ever-expanding sugar production.[72] The crown was generally only too willing to grant the requests. With sugar becoming ever important, trade and commerce flourished in the latter half of the eighteenth century, and with them came increased capital accumulation among the elite. The island's increasing importance within the empire and the corresponding elevation of Havana as one of the realm's principal and wealthiest cities surely spurred the elite to charitable acts, now that money was more available. As a result it was only when the elite habaneros became secure in their own wealth and social position that they saw value to themselves as patrons of abandoned children.

Conclusion

The story of Casa Joseph reveals much about the place of abandoned children in colonial Havana society. The debates over funding, the constant struggle for money, and the lack of interest on the part of the wealthy residents of the community until the late eighteenth century indicate that, at the very best, these unwanted children were a passing consideration. For the church, the children were an obligation over which other priorities could easily take precedence. For the local government, the children represented an unwarranted and unnecessary diversion of funds. The friction between the administrators of the casa cuna and the cabildo should be seen within the context of a long, bitter battle between the church and the government for power, a battle that included repeated excommunications, the withholding of funds, and a steady stream of transatlantic correspondence filled with accusations of misconduct, often fabricated. Therefore, for these two powers, the children were not of primary concern. In fact, these unwanted children simply became another field of struggle for control of the city. For the crown, the concern for abandoned children evolved from care for the children's welfare based on a deep religious sense of obligation to a concern over the potential drain on and damaged to the empire that unsuccored children would eventually cause. And until the end of the century, with few exceptions, these children did not seem to register on the consciousness of the elite. For them, over the course of the century the children ceased to be a nuisance and simply became a tool for personal salvation. In essence, the foundlings suffered yet another abandonment.

In colonial Havana, efforts to ameliorate the experiences of children, especially foundlings, were often confined to theoretical exercises and frequently did not find any positive expression in the lives of those for whom the efforts were made. The deep affection held for some children as individual member of families was not extended to the vulnerable population of children without families. Clearly this failing was partly due to the indifference and occasional hostility of the adults who were agents of the institutions that were responsible for the care of foundling children.

And what do these children tell us? They tell us that they lived in a world where survival was dependent on adults who had vested interests in the success of those children. As a group, the young had no economic or political power with which to claim the rights declared to be theirs by various institutions and royal decrees. Nine hundred and thirty-eight children in Casa Joseph show us that the promises of love and care were honored more in the breech than in the keeping. The history of the house itself reveals that the primary concern of the secular and clerical leaders of Havana was not in assuring that the children were cared for but in wrangling over the financial investment required for the upbringing of children unwanted even by their own parents.

Young children had access to rights only when adults or institutions acted on their behalf. In the best of situations, the adults' interest took the form of love, as in a family. Abandoned children, however, depended on the social conscience of astute and tender, if not politically savvy, adults willing to battle for them. As an institution, Casa Joseph provides evidence that, while in colonial Spanish America there were moral and religious principles that attempted to regulate individual behavior by tying salvation to acts of charity, there were none that regulated corporate behavior. This fact proved devastating to Casa Joseph and its charges, as in the early years of the eighteenth century corporate and personal interests did not leave room for support of foundlings. The powerful communities of the city were unwilling, or perhaps unable, to respond to the predicament of the abandoned children, so consumed were these groups with self-interest.

The actions of the key players in the drama surrounding Havana's foundlings in the early part of the century exemplify Reinhold Niebuhr's description of corporate moral behavior: "The social impulses, with which men are endowed by nature are not powerful enough . . . to apply with equal force toward all members of a large community."[73] Consequently, groups, whether they exist within a given society or across national boundaries, are incapable of acting outside of their collective self-interest even though their individual members may be selfless. Neither the bishops in Havana nor the commercial and governmental interests of the city intentionally abused the children of Casa Joseph. Nevertheless, in the power struggles that consumed everyone involved, high child mortality rates were the results. Unfortunately, for those 938 children abandoned at Casa Joseph during the first half of the eighteenth century, the social structures and institutions created to guarantee their ongoing care were impotent in the face of competing forces. And by the end of the century, it was simply too little too late.

✦ NOTES ✦

1. Archivo General de Indias (hereafter, AGI), Santo Domingo 336.

2. *Libro en que se asientan las partidas de los niños expósitos que se echan en el torno de la Cuna de esta ciudad.* Book 1:1711–56. Havana: Archivo Arzobispal (hereafter, AA).

3. Leví Marrero, *Cuba: Economía y sociedad*, vol. 8, *Del monopolio hacia la libertad comercial (1701–1763) (III)* (Madrid: Editorial Playor, S. A., 1980), 113. The *Recopilación de leyes de los reynos de la Indias* stipulated that royal approval was required for the founding of religious institutions. See bk. 1, tít. 6, ley 2, among others.

4. AGI, Santo Domingo 512. In AGI, Santo Domingo 324 (29 February 1712) the bishop is quoted as having written, "that carried away by their needs or by their own frailness, they [women] commit some mistakes in secret."

5. Ibid.

6. Ibid.

7. AGI, Santo Domingo 512; AGI, Santo Domingo 384.

8. AGI, Santo Domingo 512, n. 20. The house was located "in a lot on Oficios Street that makes a corner along . . . Ricla Street . . . in a block delimited by these two streets as well as Mercaderes Street and Teninet Rey" (Luis F. le Roy y Gálvez, *Fray Gerónimo Valdés, obispo de Cuba: Su vida y su obra* [Havana: 1963], 7). It would cost an additional sixteen thousand pesos, according to the bishop, "to put it in the perfect order," an expense he was willing to assume "in obedience and obsequiousness to Your Majesty and the special need of this city" (AGI, Santo Domingo 512).

9. AGI, Santo Domingo 512.

10. AGI, Santo Domingo 384, fol. 104.

11. AA.

12. For children abandoned in later years (1766–75), the survival rate improved (n=223, 35.9 percent) (AGI, Santo Domingo 1881).

13. The fate of the remaining twenty-six children left at Casa Joseph is a mystery.

14. AGI, Santo Domingo 380. The return of children by the house to their parents raises one perplexing question: Did not the deposit of children occur

in anonymity? Obviously children could not be returned if their parentage were unknown. Yet in the case of Casa Joseph, over its first forty-one years at least fifteen children were returned. Of those fifteen, six were returned because they were mulatto (n=3), black (n=2), or Indian (n=1), clearly in keeping with the bishop's stated policy of not accepting nonwhite children; whenever possible, those without "pure blood" were removed from the home's care. In the one instance in which both the name of the mother and her race (white) appear in the records, the child was not returned (AA).

15. AA. The paucity of information about age at abandonment precludes any conclusion being drawn about the age at which children were typically left at Casa Joseph.

16. AA.

17. We have information only on 401 of the amas employed by Casa Joseph from 1711 to 1752.

18. Some women (n=87) took care of more than one child but not simultaneously. We know of only forty-four women who at some point in their employment by Casa Joseph had at least two children, sometimes with both nursing, from the house at the same time. We know nothing about any other children who might have been in the ama's home, but it would be safe to assume that some of the amas had recently given birth.

19. AA.

20. AA.

21. This practice was unlike that of the Inclusa, Madrid's foundling home on which the operations of Casa Joseph were to be patterned. The Inclusa kept children in its care until they were eight years old. Upon reaching that age, boys were sent to a home for deserted children and girls to a beaterio. They stayed in their new homes until they learned a trade, married, or took religious vows. Isabel dos Guimarães Sá writes, "The age at which children left nurse care varied across Europe. In some areas they stayed with their nurses only during breast-feeding, while elsewhere they stayed from five to sixteen years, commonly returning to the foundling home after seven. . . . After their return to the hospital, the children were redistributed in a variety of ways. They might be returned again to their wet nurses, this time with the status of informally adopted children. They could be given to other people who would foster them in return for their labor or even integrate them as family members. Finally, they might remain in the hospital and be put to work for the hospital's benefit" (Isabel dos Guimarães Sá, "Circulation of Children in Eighteenth-Century Portugal," in *Abandoned Children*, ed. Catherine

Panter-Brick and Malcolm T. Smith [Cambridge: Cambridge University Press, 2000], 31).

22. AGI, Santo Domingo 336. A similar arrangement already existed in Lima. In 1680 Charles II gave royal backing to an arrangement made by Viceroy Conde de Lemus whereby two hundred fifty pesos per month, drawn from a tax on meat, were to be given to the foundling hospital (*hospital de niños expósitos*). In 1718, Philip V confirmed that another thousand pesos were to be given annually, also drawn from the meat tax, to the Lima foundling home (AGI, Indiferente 1543, n. 1, fols. 24 B 24v and 32 B 33v). In 1779 Viceroy Juan José Vertiz y Salcedo designated income from Buenos Aires's first press for the city's new foundling home, although, according to historian Vicente Quesada, "the grant was . . . illusory" (Vicente G. Quesada, "Fundación de la casa de niños expósitos en Buenos Aires," *La Revista de Buenos Aires* 1 [1862]: 340, 341).

23. Margaret E. Crahan, "Civil-Ecclesiastical Relations in Hapsburg Peru," *Journal of Church and State* 20, no. 1 (winter 1978): 101.

24. AGI, Santo Domingo 336.

25. AGI, Santo Domingo 512.

26. Ibid.

27. AGI, Santo Domingo 338. The tax was one real per head of livestock, large and small, for consumption in Havana and four reales per box of soap that came from New Spain for use in Cuba (AGI, Santo Domingo 380). During the course of the casa's first two administrations (1711–59), other than the tax for the waterway no governmental source of support was found.

28. For example, much in line with Philip's actions in the eighteenth century were those of his predecessor, Queen Isabella—monarch of Castile at the time of Columbus's voyages—who two hundred years before Philip V's reign declared the newly encountered Indians to be her children and under her protection.

29. AGI, Santo Domingo 380, as quoted in Marrero, *Cuba*, 8:114.

30. AGI, Santo Domingo 325; AGI, Santo Domingo 512. The foundling home in Lima fared no better. In 1722 the administrator of the casa cuna in Lima asked the king to order the payment of all subsidies in arrears (AGI, Indiferente1543, n. 1, fol. 24 B 24v). Apparently by 1733 the situation remained unresolved for the administrator wrote the king and complained again (ibid., fol. 32 B 33v).

31. AGI, Contaduría 1161A; AGI, Contaduría 1167.

32. AGI, Contaduría 1161A.

33. AGI, Santo Domingo 405. Similar petitions were made twice in 1729. The enclosing of the waterway was seen as the best method to ensure a clean water supply, a long-standing concern of the cabildo.

34. AGI, Santo Domingo 380. Notaries Blas de León and Dionicio Pancorbo recounted stories of children being passed from one care giver to another as well as the apocryphal stories of children being left to die in the plazas. In their versions, pieces of meat were tied around the children's necks to encourage attacks by dogs (AGI, Santo Domingo 380).

35. Ibid.

36. Ibid.

37. AGI, Santo Domingo 513A. *Lara de anniversariis* is an early seventeenth-century canonical law code. *Avendano de exequendiis mandatis* is a sixteenth-century law code.

38. AGI, Santo Domingo 405.

39. Ibid.

40. Concentration of wealth and power in the merchant elite is evident in that the first four titles of nobility granted to residents of Havana were given to men involved in tobacco (Marrero, *Cuba*, 8:140). It was these same men who held sway in the secular cabildo. Marrero writes that "the resistance of the oligarchic council to approve taxes among the citizens for specific works . . . [was] because the aldermen resisted paying taxes, generally being the richest and having bought their offices," (Marrero, *Cuba*, 8:62).

41. AGI, Santo Domingo 534.

42. Ibid.

43. AGI, Santo Domingo 483.

44. AGI, Santo Domingo 1315, as cited in Marrero, *Cuba*, 8:121.

45. In this case each solar measured 12.5 meters by 20.8 meters.

46. AGI, Santo Domingo 384.

47. AGI, Santo Domingo 1577.

48. This money came from ten plots of land over which the bishop had control as well as two ecclesiastical fines (AGI, Santo Domingo 1157). While the money that the bishop left Casa Joseph represented a sizable gift relative to the house's total income, the majority of Valdez's estate was left to the University of Havana (Marreo, *Cuba*, 8:114).

49. AGI, Indiferente 1543, fol. 70 B 70v. In 1763 the king directed that the bequeathed house, in Campeche, a neighborhood in the middle of the parish Espíritu Santo, valued at ten thousand pesos should become the new home

of Casa Joseph. The king further ordered that the old location, "being in the middle of the commercial area," would be "in great demand" so it should be sold for a similar amount. One wonders if the prime location of the house could have been the root cause of many of the casa cuna's problems. Did the commercial interests in Havana want the property? Were they willing to "starve" the house out of its current location by withholding support, both governmental and private?

50. AGI, Santo Domingo 427, n. 4. The records give no indication of any alms being given to Casa Joseph or specifically collected for it.

51. AGI, Santo Domingo 343; AGI, Santo Domingo 427, n. 4.

52. AGI, Contaduría 1167.

53. AGI, Santo Domingo 343.

54. AGI, Santo Domingo 427, n. 4.

55. Ibid.

56. Ibid.

57. AGI, Santo Domingo 344.

58. AGI, Santo Domingo 1577, n. 4.

59. AGI, Santo Domingo 1134. The vacante was that of Bishop Juan Lasso de la Vega who served in Cuba from 1731 to 1752.

60. Evaristo Zenea, *Historia de La Real Casa de Maternidad de esta ciudad, en la cual se comprende la antigua casa cuna, refiriéndose sus fundaciones, deplorable estado y felices progresos que después ha tenido hasta el presente* (Havana: D. José Serverino Boloña, Impresor de la Real Marina, 1838), 27.

61. Ibid.

62. César A. Mena and Armando F. Cobelo, *Historia de la medicina en Cuba*, vol. 1, *Hospitales y centros benéficos in Cuba colonial* (Miami: Ediciones Universal, 1992), 217.

63. Ibid., 271, 226.

64. René Salinas Meza, "Orphans and Family Disintegration in Chile: The Mortality of Abandoned Children, 1750–1930," *Journal of Family History* 16, no. 3 (1991): 323–24.

65. Quesada, "Fundación de la casa de niños expósitos en Buenos Aires," 342.

66. Ibid., 343.

67. Ibid., 348.

68. Pilar Gonzalbo Aizpuru, "La casa de niños expósitos de la ciudad de México: Una fundación del siglo XVIII," *Historia Mexicana* 31, no. 3 (1982): 426.

69. AGI, Santo Domingo 1881, fol. 70. A beaterio was a home for religious women, beatas, who did not live under the rules of a particular order. As late as the 1820s the beaterio had not been built. Fortunately in 1792 the Royal Beneficence House was opened to shelter young girls (Mena and Cobelo, *Historia de la medicina en Cuba*, 217).

70. AGI, Santo Domingo 1577, n. 4.

71. Silvia Arrom, *Containing the Poor: The Mexico City Poor House, 1774–1871* (Durham, NC: Duke University Press, 2000), 4.

72. Between 1764 and 1790 annual slave imports averaged two thousand persons (Louis A. Pérez Jr., *Cuba: Between Reform and Revolution* [Oxford: Oxford University Press, 1988], 60).

73. Reinhold Niebuhr, *Moral Man and Immoral Society: A Study in Ethics and Politics* (New York: Charles Scribner's Sons, 1932), 13.

CHAPTER SIX

The Church, the State, and the Abandoned

Expósitos in Late Eighteenth-Century Havana

Ann Twinam

❧

Introduction

✦ In 1801, an *expósito* returned to the Casa de Expósitos, or foundling home, in Havana to seek his roots. He asked the priest in charge to take out the book of entries and look up the date and time that he had been placed as an infant in the torno, or revolving door, and deposited as abandoned.[1] When the priest found the entry, he appended his own note to the original details: he observed that there was a difference between the race of the foundling as an infant and as an adult. Since the Casa de Expósitos traditionally gave entering infants the racial benefit of the doubt, the abandoned baby had originally been listed as "apparently white." However, decades later, the cleric added, "The [person] listed in this entry presented himself to ask me for it, and he turned out to be a *pardo*, as he himself confessed."

Embedded in this incident is the essence of why the place of expósitos in society became contested ground at the end of the eighteenth century. Expósitos were ambiguous terrain: in a colonial world where genealogy and race marked social place, expósitos often had neither. In Havana,

infants abandoned at the Casa were automatically granted fictitious parentage as they were assigned the surname of Valdés, in honor of the institution's founder.[2] In race as well, even through each entering baby was
described as "apparently white," substantial if unknown numbers were
mulattoes or pardos.

By the late eighteenth century, such natal and racial ambiguities
became a focus of conflict among the church, the monarch, imperial
bureaucrats, and local elite. The church and monarch worked on behalf
of expósitos. When clergy baptized infants unrecognized by their parents often due to their illegitimate status, they blurred evidence of illicit
liaisons. When priests accepted infants in the institution of the Casa and
entered them as "apparently white," they also obscured evidence of racial
mixture. In 1794, Spanish monarch Charles IV intervened on behalf of
expósitos with a royal *cédula*, or order, that proved to be among the most
radical of the Spanish Bourbon's social reforms. It declared the abandoned to be children of the king, ordered that they be given the natal and
racial benefit of the doubt, and be treated as legitimate and as white.[3] In
contrast, imperial bureaucrats who served on the Cámara, the subgroup
of the Council of the Indies, stalled implementation of expósito reform.
They cooperated with local elite who feared that any legislation that gave
expósitos the natal and racial benefit of the doubt might open up dangerous potentials for upward social and racial mobility.

As this expósito returned to the Havana Casa his birth and racial status
may have been unclear, but one variable was not—his age. Deposited in the
torno as a newborn, he revisited the foundling home as an adult. Such an
obvious observation is not so obvious, for it introduces the often-ignored
variable of life-course analysis, or exploration of changes in an individual
life or of individual lives "in the context of historical time."[4] While life-
course analysis is intrinsic to the methodology of historians of infancy and
of childhood, it has not been much considered in the study of adults.[5] Yet
the personal encounter between the expósito and priest over his variable
status as white infant on paper and an adult with a dark complexion sig-
nals how life course might influence the formulation and the execution of
imperial policy. It may not have seemed immediately threatening, nor was
it particularly controversial, when the Spanish monarchy issued a decree
that privileged helpless infants or abandoned children. Yet the cleric's
insistence that the returning expósito's status as pardo be officially noted

in the records illustrates that such indulgence might not be forthcoming when the same law awarded expósito privileges to adults.

This exploration of the attitudes of church, state, and local elite toward expósitos as children and as adults divides into three approaches. The first section considers who was an expósito, for this is a much misunderstood designation. Then analysis centers on the shift in royal policy toward expósitos that culminated in the benchmark 1794 decree. The conclusion explores how bureaucrats in the Cámara of the Indies put the brakes on reform, ceding control to local elite. Essential to this analysis are two sets of archival sources. First are the records of the Havana Casa de Expósitos, detailing the entry and disposition of abandoned infants throughout the eighteenth century.[6] Second are a series of petitions from adult expósitos directed to the Council and Cámara of the Indies, asking that the state intervene to overcome the discrimination against them, followed by internal Cámara discussion as to any ultimate action.[7]

Expósitos

There has been much confusion concerning the expósito, especially since there could be substantial disparity between an infant's official listing on a baptismal certificate and his or her actual circumstance. The fate of expósitos varied widely: many were not abandoned, and some were informally acknowledged and raised by their parents. Others, especially those entered in the Havana Casa de Expósitos, might be true orphans, in fatal peril. Understanding the context in which infants received the expósito designation provides a necessary background to the late eighteenth-century debate over their ultimate fate.

Technically, the Catholic Church controlled the expósito designation, for this was a category assigned to newborns at baptism.[8] When both parents of an infant refused to be listed on the baptismal record and thereby acknowledge the child, the baby officially became an expósito, or was given the alternative but functionally equivalent designation of unknown parents (*padres no conocidos*). Illegitimacy was the usual reason that mothers and fathers refused to acknowledge their parentage. Yet sometimes mothers and fathers of illegitimate children had other options: for example, if the parents were unmarried, but single, they might acknowledge their infant with the alternative designation of *hijo natural*. This was a much more favorable listing, given that the subsequent marriage of the couple would totally and automatically legitimate any offspring conceived prior to the ceremony. However to designate an infant as a *natural*, at least one parent had to come forward, swear that both were single, and admit the sexual relationship that led to pregnancy. If they did not, their child was categorized as an expósito. In every other case of illegitimacy—be it the technical incest of a sexual relationship between cousins, or adultery, or sacrilege (usually in which the father was a priest)—the parental origins of such illegitimate infants were hidden with the expósito or padres no conocidos designations.

It is essential to underline that even though the baptismal listing of expósito was interchangeable with that of illegitimate, it was not always interchangeable with that of orphan. Many expósitos who were not recognized by their parents at the baptismal fount were nonetheless taken in and cared for by their families. It was not uncommon for parents to orchestrate private ceremonies where they first "abandoned" infants and then "found" and "adopted" them.

The outlines of such a process emerge in Santiago de Cuba where Regidor Don Joseph Antonio Echavarría's clandestine affair with widow Doña Rosalia Ramos led to the births of two daughters, Doña María and Doña Caridad.[9] When each daughter was born, the infant was secretly carried from the house of her mother and deposited at the door of her father, who then "discovered" her, took her in, and had her baptized, in the case of Doña María as an expósita, and that of Doña Caridad as of padres no conocidos. The regidor then raised his daughters with the help of his sister. Although Doña María and Doña Caridad were expósitas, they grew up with their kin in easy circumstances, were informally recognized by their father, and officially provided for in his will. After his death, the two purchased official civil legitimations through a crown procedure known as *gracias al sacar*, which is why their story can be traced.[10]

The situation of Doña María Josepha de Acosta Riaza provides another classic example of a Havana woman who, even though technically abandoned as a child, was lovingly cared for by her family.[11] Since her father, Don Félix, was married when he had a sexual relationship with her mother, Doña María was born in adultery and therefore received the traditional listing of "unknown parentage" on her 1753 baptismal certificate. Yet from infancy her social status was unambiguous: everyone knew that she was Don Félix's illegitimate daughter, and her birth was, as one family friend later recalled, a "notorious public fact in this city." Since Don Félix was a regidor, serving in one of the most prestigious positions on Havana's city council, his status enhanced that of his illegitimate daughter.

Doña María herself emphasized that she was fully accepted into her father's family: "my father throughout his life not only recognized me always in private as his daughter, but in public. He carried me to his own home after my infancy and maintained me there until he established me in a state which was equal with the children of his marriage." Dr. Don Francisco, one of Doña María's half-brothers, also emphasized the totality of her recognition, testifying that the family treated her as a sister "in domestic and public acts." Doña María's informal recognition by her family enhanced her social rank to the extent that she was able to marry Don Antonio de la Paz, treasurer of the Royal Rents in Havana. Like the sisters from Santiago, she eventually purchased civil legitimation. Designation as an expósito, therefore, did not necessarily mean abandonment. Spanish American elite, including those in Cuba, used this listing to blur the origins of their illegitimate offspring, many of whom were raised by their kin.

Elite expósitos found themselves in a special position. Although they were linked by blood to their powerful families, their illegitimate birth still deprived them of honor, which meant they suffered substantial prejudice in the public sphere, and their inheritance rights—if they had any—were limited.[12] Illegitimate males were prejudiced in holding political office, either in the imperial bureaucracy or local civil posts; they could not graduate from universities, practice as lawyers, doctors, or notaries; they faced dual prejudice from church and state if they hoped to enter the priesthood. Both male and female illegitimate children were considered less than acceptable marriage partners, for their lack of honor meant that they could not pass this distinction on to their children, thus perpetuating their social and civil inferiority.

The surest remedy for elite expósitos to end discrimination was to purchase civil legitimation through gracias al sacar. However, starting in the 1780s, the Council and Cámara of the Indies began to discriminate against expósitos and refused to legitimate them if they could not prove that their parents had been single and that they were hijos naturales, not bastards. One Indies official summarized this antibastard policy in the 1790s, remarking that the state should discourage such legitimations to "keep men to their duty so they might cease from committing such excesses so prejudicial to religion and to society."[13] Bureaucrats argued that one way to discourage elite sexual promiscuity was to punish lovers by condemning their illegitimate sons and daughters to a permanent inferior status. The ultimate goal of this policy was to buttress the elite family thereby maintaining the social hierarchy, although at the expense of illegitimate relatives.[14]

In vivid contrast to the world of expósitos adopted and incorporated into their families was the world of the truly abandoned. The most common fate of these infants was to be placed in the turning door of the Havana Casa de Expósitos—the same institution that is the subject of Ondina González's chapter in this volume. Unfortunately, the records of the Casa are not complete: available data exists only from 1711–53 and from 1790–1806, thus providing a snapshot of the first half of the eighteenth century and of the decades at the turn of the nineteenth century. During these years 4,313 infants—fairly evenly divided between boys and girls—were deposited at the Casa: 938 arrived before 1753; 3,375 from the 1790s to 1806. (See Tables 6.1 and 6.2, below.) The information recorded by the priests in charge of the institution was uneven. The priests always noted the date the baby arrived at the Casa; sometimes they marked the time, described the baby's clothes or other identifying items, or summarized the contents of any letter that had been attached. Such notes usually informed if the baby had been baptized, the parish where this occurred, and the name given at the ceremony. No doubt such markers were especially important if parents returned for infants or when adult expósitos arrived years later to seek information concerning their origin.

As time passed an infant's original Casa entry might be overlaid with additional information, although Havana's priests were eclectic with such notations. Sometimes a cleric might add details for only a few months or a single year. Even so, such entries permit sporadic exploration of other patterns attached to the history of early childhood, including when babies were brought to the Casa, their immediate survival rates, and any later relationships with their kin.

One stereotypical image—that illegitimate infants were born in secret and promptly carried to the turning door—is not born out by the Casa statistics. In the 1790s, one scrupulous cleric provided a brief run of entries that noted when the infant was born and when the baby was turned over to the Casa. Of the fifty-three babies with such information, only two were deposited the day of their birth and less than one-fourth (n=12, 22.6 percent) were carried to the Casa in their first week. Rather, the majority—more than one-third—of these infants (n=19, 35.9 percent) were deposited the second week; while another fourth (n=13, 24.5 percent) arrived during week three. The large majority of mothers who gave up their children—83 percent—delivered their babies to the Casa within three weeks of the baby's birth. (See Table 6.3, below.) Such a time frame suggests that mothers had some emotional investment in the babies they abandoned—they apparently chose to suckle their babies in the difficult first days, improving their chances for survival, even though this must have made the later parting even more difficult.

Not surprisingly, when babies were brought to the Casa they were deposited in the darker hours, after the sun had set and when street traffic was at the minimum. (See Table 6.4, below.) By the end of the century depositors left babies during the dawn hours. It takes very little imagination to think of those thousands of mothers who must have held their babies throughout the night, knowing that at dawn that they, their lover, a relative, or a servant, would take their infant and place it in the revolving door.

For a rare few, the separation of mother and child may not have been too long, for there seems to have been a custom of depositing infants on one side of the door and retrieving them on the other. This tradition resembled the ceremonies already described in which elite expósitos were "deposited" in private residences. In the case of the Casa, the real mother might volunteer to be the wet nurse and raise the infant as a foster mother, thereby preserving her reputation until later arrangements, possibly even marriage with the father, might be worked out.[15] Yet such happy outcomes were rare. Of the 1,801 expósitos deposited in the Casa from 1790–99, only fourteen entries bear the comment that the baby was later legitimated due the parents' subsequent marriage. In nine other cases, the entries noted that one or the other parent had returned to recognize the infant.

Five infants listed in the books of the Casa had a special fate: years later they appeared in applications either to be legitimated or to receive favored treatment because they were expósitos. Their life histories provide special insight into those combinations of variables that produced happier outcomes for infants deposited at the turning door. An immediate conclusion is that gender mattered—no baby boys who entered the Havana Casa were ever legitimated through gracias al sacar. Rather, five baby girls benefited when, years later, the legitimate men in their lives—a husband, a son, and two fathers—eventually submitted petitions on their behalf.

Of these five lucky infants, the baby girl most at risk was María Manuela, deposited at the Casa de Expósitos in 1752.[16] Her parents never returned for her, and so she assumed the surname of the orphanage founder, Valdés, which meant that she was permanently marked in Havana society as figuring among the abandoned. Little is known of her early life, except that she married well to Don Juan Luis Marqueta, who held a city council office (*mayordomo de propios*) and thus belonged to the local elite. It was Don Juan Luis who appealed to the Cámara of the Indies on her behalf in 1796, complaining that even though she was "white and free of all bad race" she was looked down upon as being "born of a [sexual] liaison condemned and punished by the laws." Royal officials agreed that her special status as a child of the Casa meant that she should be given the benefit of the doubt in such matters.

A second baby girl abandoned at the turning door also took the surname of Valdés, although there remains an intriguing mystery as to whether her real mother might have returned for her. This was because after infant Francisca Sales y Valdés was placed in the turning door in 1734 she was given to María de Flores—a single mother who had presumably been pregnant since she was paid to breast-feed the baby.[17] María cared for Francisca long after the typical two years of suckling, for she kept and loved the baby girl until Francisca's marriage—at age twelve—to Don Andrés Lezama, a royal notary. María wrote a will that declared that Doña Francisca was her "daughter." It was this testament that years later provoked a petition from Doña Francisca's son, Don Joseph Lezama, who served as a royal official in the Tobacco Administration in Havana. He begged that the Cámara rule that "even if the said María Flores really had been the mother of Doña Francisca Sale" that his mother still be considered an orphan and a child of the Casa. Why would Don Joseph make such an appeal? There is strong evidence that María was racially mixed, and so Don Joseph preferred that his mother be officially considered abandoned and an orphan rather than that his mother's, and therefore his own, whiteness—essential for holding office—be questioned. The Cámara agreed that both Doña Francisca and her son should continue to enjoy the traditional benefit of doubt as to birth and race that attached to every infant that entered the Casa.

The three remaining baby girls abandoned at the turning doors of the Casa did not assume the surname Valdés because their fathers eventually claimed them. Don Francisco Garro Zayas was a priest living in Havana who must have kept track of his daughter, for she took his name and he applied for her legitimation in 1779.[18] He admitted that he had "found himself with the desire to contract marriage with Doña Francisca de la Cruz," but that the marriage had not taken place and so they had deposited their infant daughter in the Casa, "hiding their names." However the Cámara rejected his petition, complaining that he had neither proven that he was single when he fathered the infant María, nor had he provided a notarized copy of her deposit in the Casa.

The final two abandoned infants must have known the identity of their father early in their lives, for habanero Don Juan Antonio Morejón confessed that "the natural love he had toward them" had made it impossible "to hide he was their father."[19] Even so, he had deposited baby Rita Josepha in the turning door one night in 1779 and sister María de Jesús one dawn in 1782. The administrator of the Casa had sent both infants to wet nurses, the first to Juana Rita who lived "outside the [Havana city] wall" and her sister to a María Montecinos. No doubt Don Juan Antonio had tracked these women down, for he later admitted that everyone knew he was the father, given "the care with which he has attended to their assistance and education." When he applied for the legitimation of his eleven- and fourteen-year-old daughters in 1793 he still protected the name of their mother, for she was married to someone else, although she had long ago been abandoned by her husband. He pleaded that his daughters be legitimated both to inherit his properties and so "the ugly note" of their birth would not subject them to the "lack of charity" of local society.

The fate of these five orphaned infant girls left at the Casa—to be married well, recognized, loved, and even legitimated—were the rare exceptions. As González underscores in her chapter on church-state struggles over the institution early in the century, for most babies, abandonment at the Casa proved a virtual death sentence.[20] In the early nineteenth century, Cuban historian Evaristo Zenea suggested that the Havana Casa had become a veritable "tomb for infants," located in a "few badly ventilated rooms." He envisioned the resident nurse "with breasts exhausted at the time with three or four babies and pregnant, perhaps with spoiled milk."[21] Apparently, the problem was less finance than bad management, since the institution had an endowment of some ninety-five thousand pesos by the 1780s.

Even though the infant death rate of the Havana Casa was shocking, this institution did not compare badly with counterparts elsewhere. The

Mexico Casa de Expósitos registered a 67 percent rate of infant mortality from 1767 to 1774.[22] One historian calculated there was a 75 to 80 percent mortality rate in the eighteenth-century Seville Casa, concluding, "practically every expósito is a dead child."[23] Indeed, it was the dire state of expósitos in peninsular Spain as well as in the Americas that produced that most radical Bourbon social reform, the royal cédula of 1794 that legitimized expósitos.

The State and Expósitos

The eighteenth century marked a major shift in the Spanish crown's legislation and attitudes concerning the young, particularly toward expósitos. In the seventeenth century, expósitos had been consigned as cannon fodder for the Spanish navy: a 1623 Pragmatic directed Casa administrators to forgo teaching them to read or write and instead to funnel them into artisan crafts or into the navy. A 1677 edict ordered that Andalusian and Granadan expósitos be sent to Cádiz to be trained as sailors, gunners, and pilots. At the same time the fate of female expósitos was totally ignored.[24]

By the late eighteenth century, expósitos had been transformed into fictive offspring of the monarch who were to be protected and valued. One insight into this altered viewpoint emerged vividly in an incident from Spain in 1788 when a group of local reformers belonging to the Sociedad Económica de Amigos del País intervened to rescue two expósitos who had been taken up by a group of traveling acrobats.[25] The performers had obtained their presumably unwilling charges from the Valencia Casa de Expósitos. Word of this unacceptable adoption reached royal officials, who took the children from the acrobats, noting that training in "violent contortions of [the] body" was not considered a satisfactory occupation for orphans.[26]

In the Americas, Havana was one of the first colonies to experience the changed policy. In 1772, the Council of the Indies ruled that infants deposited in the Havana Casa de Expósitos should henceforth enjoy the privileges of legitimates, a concession later extended to orphans in selected other colonial cities.[27] The culmination of such reform was Charles IV's 1794 royal cédula, which extended legitimation to every expósito throughout the empire.

Contained in the introduction to the 1794 decree was the rationale for the reform.[28] It described the plight of expósitos in Spain; an evaluation that would no doubt have been familiar to habaneros who knew of conditions in their own city and its Casa de Expósitos as well. The decree deplored the "miserable situation" whereby thousands of Spanish infants died due to delays in depositing them in institutions prepared to accept them. Even when babies arrived at the turning doors, they were at the mercy of wet nurses employed by the institution who sometimes had to be coerced to suckle them along with their own infants. Such situations, the king lamented in the decree, could only produce "continuous infanticides." Even if infants were able to overcome these hazards, they faced prejudice as adults, given that they were "treated with the greatest contempt and held as bastards, *espúreos* [sacrilegious], incestuous, and adulterous."

The 1794 decree added a novel shift, suggesting that it was not only illegitimacy but also disadvantageous social conditions that led to infant abandonment. Challenging the popular understanding that most expósitos were illegitimate, it stated that indigent parents also abandoned babies "when they see no other way of preserving their life." Charles IV henceforth demanded that expósitos receive the benefit of the doubt and be "held as legitimated by my royal authority and legitimated for all the general civil effects." Such generosity extended not only to expósitos placed in institutions but also to everyone baptized with the designation of unknown parentage (expósito and padres no conocidos). The decree went on to charge peninsular and American royal officials to fine anyone who denigrated expósitos, or who called them "illegitimate, bastard, *espúreo*, incestuous or adulterous."

Now what was radical about this decree? From one perspective, the decree simply appeared to widen the scope of previous practice to the level of the empire—after all the same concession had already been given to the Havana Casa in 1772. Yet in both process and scope, this Bourbon reform posed an extreme challenge to the social and racial status quo. After all, in the last decades of the eighteenth century the officials of the Council and Cámara of the Indies had actively worked to restrict the categories of illegitimates eligible to purchase gracias al sacar and obtain a civil legitimation. Their goal was to send the message that sexual promiscuity would not be tolerated, nor would illegitimacy be ameliorated for offspring who were expósitos, especially if they were the product of adulterous and sacrilegious liaisons.[29] The 1794 cédula wiped away that policy and those distinctions—from now on all expósitos were to be given the benefit of the doubt and were to be considered legitimate. Furthermore, the decree was extended universally to all expósitos, and expósitos ran a wide gamut from the offspring of the elite, to the poor, to the racially mixed.[30]

Although providing such concessions to expósitos might not have been as socially controversial in the comparative homogeneity of peninsular Spain, in the complex world of the castas of colonial America, such a program was explosive. The effect was to give expósitos not only the natal but also the racial benefit of the doubt. Nor was expósito legislation limited to the earliest stage of the life course: although the law targeted infants, it had its greatest impact when these infants survived to become adults and eligible for the privileges of legitimacy and status promised by the 1794 decree. To trace how such expósito legislation came to a fast and early end is to explore how the Council and Cámara officials combined with the local elite to override the legislation and put the brakes on the 1794 reform.

Council and Cámara Response to the 1794 Expósito Decree

Perhaps it is not surprising that it was a case from Cuba that crystallized the attitudes of the bureaucrats of Council of the Indies and precipitated their decision not to enforce the 1794 expósito decree. As the eighteenth century drew to a close, Spanish American elite everywhere felt increasingly challenged by social and racial pressure from below. This was particularly manifest in Cuba where the opening of trade and the dynamics of the sugar boom created an upwardly mobile, sometimes darker-skinned cohort of nouveau riche eager for entrance into elite circles. The response of local elite, especially in Havana, was to close ranks and discriminate viciously against anyone not meeting their traditional standards of honor, including legitimacy and racial purity.[31] In that sense the added notation of the Havana priest that the adult expósito who returned to the foundling home in 1801 was a pardo, and not white, was consonant with late colonial attempts to identify social place and to curtail mobility.

Since infants and children were confined to the private sphere of home and family, adult expósitos were usually at the heart of contests over altered status.[32] Even after the legislation was proclaimed, these illegitimate sons and daughters of the elite—presumably the most likely to benefit from such legislation—continued to complain to the Cámara that they faced discrimination. Understanding why they continued to appeal and how Cámara officials responded to their claims illuminates why and how bureaucrats brought this most radical of Bourbon social measures to a decisive halt.

The disinclination of Cámara officials to enforce the 1794 decree became manifest as they confronted the shocking, if totally engaging, application of Cuban matron Doña María Jardines.[33] Her 1797 petition encapsulated many of the inherent contradictions of the new expósito policy, for only in colonial Latin America might a mother who acknowledged and raised her children at home apply so that her offspring might enjoy the benefits attached to orphans! Doña María wrote a chatty and confiding letter that provided telling details of her life that must have horrified *camaristas* who had worked for decades to discourage promiscuity and who now saw their efforts threatened by the new legislation.

Doña María began her letter with a short description of her own difficult early years, for she had been baptized as an expósito and given to an adopted mother who had left her at a hacienda in the countryside. When she grew up the "human fragility that so combats the strongest spirits" had overcome her, and she "had the disgrace to lose her virginity with a certain man who, even though distinguished, had an impediment to marrying me." Doña María never clarified if her lover had been a relative, married, or a priest, but the relationship was long-lasting, given that she gave birth to "twelve children . . . including seven sons." As was customary, all twelve had been baptized as expósitos and raised by their mother with the "greatest decency," so that they were of "good inclinations, pacific, fearful of God and of justice, [and] obedient to all superiors." Doña María assured royal officials of her own superior status: she was "white," and possessed "some fortune," including "houses, slaves, animals, and ten haciendas."

Her problem was that although the expósito decree of 1794 had given her and her offspring "innumerable privileges," she was not convinced that these would be sufficient to ensure their future. There were too many "abuses, [and] contrary interpretations" concerning the law, and "vulgar [and] indiscreet perturbations of peace and of civil and political society." She offered to cede one her best haciendas to the crown in exchange for a decree that threatened the "most severe and restrictive penalties" if anyone dared to challenge the qualifications of her sons to enter the church, or to hold positions in the military, positions usually reserved for those who were white and legitimate. Doña María's request no doubt reinforced the

Cámara's growing perception that the 1794 decree would not be sufficient by itself to overcome prejudice against expósitos.

Besides the vibrant personality that shines through her letter to the Cámara, Doña María's petition revealed a significant shift in the strategy of expósitos at the edge of elite acceptance. She no longer appealed to officials to guarantee her personal rights as an expósita, as this was presumably assured by the 1794 legislation. Nor did she simply ask for a royal decree specifically confirming both her and her offspring's right to enjoy the benefits of royal legislation. Instead, she asked Cámara officials to join her in a preemptive strike—to issue a decree that anticipated that the 1794 legislation would not eliminate prejudice and that would threaten penalties in advance to anyone who dared to question her or her family's status.

The Cámara lawyer who reviewed Doña María's letter went to the heart of the matter and questioned how Doña María's sons and daughters could be abandoned when she admitted that she was their mother! Noting that the 1794 decree specified that the parents of expósitos had to be unknown, he decided "that it is not so that the referred are expósitos, nor can it be believed that they do not have known parents." Consequently, he refused on technical grounds to recommend that the Cámara support the protection that Doña María sought for her offspring. However, the lawyer also recognized that even though Doña María was known as the mother, baptismal certificates officially established expósito status, so he left Doña María a dubious opening. He suggested that if someone discriminated against her children and called them "illegitimate for some civil effect," that she might "use her right as it applies, with the corresponding justification of the quality of expósitos." The Cámara agreed.

This cryptic decision was the turning point in the Council and Cámara's enforcement—or more accurately—their decision not to require compliance concerning the 1794 decree. The ultimate effect was that royal officials withdrew from any active enforcement of the expósito decree and simply left petitioners to resolve their own fates at the local level. Bureaucrats essentially told Doña María that if her offspring faced prejudice, she first had to convince the local elite who discriminated that her children should be counted as expósitos. If she were successful, she might then resort to the 1794 decree to ensure their privileges, although the Cámara would not intervene to guarantee their rights. The Cámara therefore ceded to the local elite the right to decide whether Doña María's offspring would be treated as legitimated offspring of the king or as bastards.

Given the refusal of the Cámara to enforce the expósito legislation for white adults who faced discrimination, it should come as no surprise that it was even less willing to support those who were racially mixed. As early as 1772 bureaucrats had proclaimed that "neither in Spain nor in the Indies have [expósitos] enjoyed nor ought they enjoy all the qualities of the truly legitimate."[34] Rather, officials suggested that it would "poison the Republic to classify them as noble and of pure birth, in equality with those who are certain of their true parents." They had added a special stricture about American expósitos, given the "mixture of Negroes, mulattoes and other castes that are accustomed to spring from such bad disposition." Even though the monarch might have originally ordered that expósitos be given the natal and racial benefit of doubt with the 1794 decree, camaristas shared the popular prejudice against those of unknown origin and possible racial mixture.

The refusal of Cámara officials to intervene on behalf of expósitos threw the decision-making process back to informal, but traditional pathways. The Cámara yielded the ground to local elite who could decide on their usual person-by-person basis whether they chose to recognize a person as an expósito, and if so, what benefits that might or might not bring. In the short term, such a reversion dampened the extremely explosive issue of race, as it limited any mobility of expósitos to those who had personally passed elite scrutiny. Yet given the rising prejudice of the late eighteenth century, elite judgments concerning expósito mobility were more likely to be in the negative.

And so, this most radical Bourbon social reform measure died a quick death. Why was the Cámara able to obstruct implementation of the 1794 expósito decree? At its core, the legislation foundered because it contradicted essential Hispanic precepts as to how social and racial mobility should operate. Even Cámara officials were reluctant to accept the expósito legislation because it challenged prevailing beliefs about how evidence was to be assessed. It violated the predominant Hispanic presumption of guilt, that missing information hid the negative—in this case that expósitos were bastards or racially mixed.[35] Nor was there any particular consensus in Spain, much less in the Americas that expósitos—especially adult expósitos—merited the privileges attached to legitimation.

An even more radical aspect of the 1794 expósito decree was its universal coverage, for it bypassed the traditional mobility processes and tried to legislate for a category of individuals, rather than for the individual.

Throughout the colonial era, both the state and the local elite had abetted a modicum of social and racial mobility on a person-by-person basis. It was not unknown for local elite to overlook the racial mixture or the illegitimacy of a particularly talented or wealthy adult and informally permit him or her to pass as a person of honor in the public sphere. The state formalized such mobility through the gracias al sacar when it permitted qualified illegitimate petitioners to purchase their legitimation, or even individual pardos to buy their whiteness. The 1794 decree contradicted this traditional pattern whereby mobility—whether given informally by local elite who sanctioned passing, or formally by the state through gracias al sacar decrees—was awarded on a person-by-person basis. Indeed it was precisely because no established process existed to enforce such a blanket decree that the Cámara, by choosing inaction, was able to thwart its execution.

The 1794 legislation also ultimately failed because it ignored the differential social prices attached to the legitimation of infants compared to that of adults. Stages of the life course made all the difference. Although it may have been appealing to privilege helpless infants abandoned on doorsteps or left on roadways, it was quite another matter to concede social benefits when those infants became adults. Social dislocation occurred when elite Cubans observed, for example, the marriage of Doña María Josepha de Acosta Riaza, born of adultery, to a local royal official, or when they were asked to support similar matrimonial mobility for the five expósita daughters of expósita Doña María Jardines. Even more threatening was the desire of Doña María's seven expósito sons to become militia officers or priests, or to hold public office. Most dangerous of all was the social threat posed by a "white" expósito infant who grew up to be a pardo now eligible for the perquisites of expósito adults. Legitimizing an infant exacted a relatively small social price; privileging an adult proved a much more costly matter.

For all these reasons the bureaucrats in the Council and Cámara of the Indies joined with local elites to thwart reform, refusing to concede any generalized benefit of the doubt or to condone mobility for adults with natal and racial defects. It would be left to succeeding generations, the next generation on the American continent and several more after that for Cuba, to provide alternative solutions to the social and racial hierarchies resulting from centuries of the Spanish American colonial heritage.

Table 6.1: Entry of Babies to the Havana Casa de Expósitos by Decade

Decade	# Expósitos
1710	258
1720	224
1730	141
1740	193
1750–53	122
Subtotal	**938**
1790	1801
1800–1806	1574
Subtotal	**3375**
Total	**4313**

Source: AA-Havana, Books 1, 4–7.

Table 6.2: Selected Data on Gender of Infants Deposited at the Casa de Expósitos

Year	Male	Female	% Male	% Female
1711	11	13	45.8	54.2
1712	14	9	60.9	39.1
1721	11	15	42.3	57.7
1731	9	4	69.2	30.8
1733	6	4	60.0	40.0
1741	1	3	25.0	75.5
1751	26	14	65.0	35.0
1791	79	81	49.4	50.6
1801	96	97	49.7	50.3

Source: AA-Havana, Books 1, 4–7.

Table 6.3: Age of Newborns Deposited at the Havana Casa de Expósitos

Time Period	Number		Time Period	Number	
Week 1			Week 3		
Day of Birth	2		Day 1	1	
Day 2	4		Day 2	2	
Day 3	1		Day 3	2	
Day 4	2		Day 4	2	
Day 5	2		Day 5	2	
Day 6	0		Day 6	3	
Day 7	1		Day 7	1	
Subtotal	**12**	**22.6%**	**Subtotal**	**13**	**24.5%**
Week 2			Week 4	2	
Day 1	5		Week 5	3	
Day 2	1		Week 6	2	
Day 3	2		Later	2	
Day 4	5		**Subtotal**	**9**	**17.0 %**
Day 5	0		**Total**	**53**	**100.0%**
Day 6	6				
Day 7	0				
Subtotal	**19**	**35.9 %**			

Source: AA-Havana, Books 4–7.

Table 6.4: Time of Deposit of Infants at the Havana Casa de Expósitos

Time	1711		1712		1721	
	#	%	#	%	#	%
12–4 a.m.	0	0.0	2	7.7	4	16.0
4–8 a.m.	2	15.4	7	26.9	5	20.0
8 a.m.–12 p.m.	1	7.7	1	3.8	0	0.0
12–4 p.m.	0	0.0	0	0.0	0	0.0
4–8 p.m.	2	15.4	2	7.7	2	8.0
8–12 p.m.	8	61.5	14	3.9	14	56.0
Total	**13**	**100.0**	**26**	**100.0**	**25**	**100.0**
Time	1751		1791		1801	
	#	%	#	%	#	%
12–4 a.m.	0	0.0	0	0.0	0	0.0
4–8 a.m.	0	0.0	114	71.2	54	28.7
8 a.m.–12 p.m.	3	7.9	4	2.5	0.47	25.0
12–4 p.m.	1	2.6	8	5.0	24	12.8
4–8 p.m.	5	13.2	12	75.0	41	21.8
8–12 p.m.	29	76.3	22	13.8	22	11.7
Total	**38**	**100.0**	**160**	**100.0**	**188**	**100.0**

Source: AA-Havana, Books 1, 4–7.

✦ NOTES ✦

1. Archivo Arzobispal (Havana, Cuba), Casa de Beneficiencia y Maternidad (hereafter, AA-Havana), Book 6, 1801. A version of this paper was delivered in April 1999 at the Association of Caribbean Historians. Havana, Cuba.

2. AA-Havana, leg. 36, exp. 46, 1874. María Emma Mannarelli remarks on a similar custom in Lima where expósitos took the name Atocha, in her *Pecados públicos: La ilegitimidad en Lima, siglo XVII* (Lima: Ediciones Flora Tristán, 1994), 299.

3. Nara Milanich, "Historical Perspectives on Illegitimacy and Illegitimates in Latin America" in *Minor Omissions: Children in Latin American History and Society*, ed. Tobias Hecht (Madison: University of Wisconsin Press, 2002), 72–101. See especially the discussion of illegitimacy and "filiation" as a "socially constructed designation," 93.

4. Tamara Hareven, "Family History at the Crossroads," *Journal of Family History* 12 (1987): x.

5. Cynthia Milton focuses on caste and class differences in infants and children in colonial Quito, noting contradictory policies that both criminalized and protected them (Cynthia Milton, "Wandering Waifs and Abandoned Babes: The Limits and Uses of Juvenile Warfare in Eighteenth-Century Audiencia of Quito," *Colonial Latin American Review* 13, no. 1 [June 2004]: 103–28). Bianca Premo carries life-course analysis a step further by exploring how the courts, perpetrators, and parents in criminal cases of "minors" under the age of twenty-five manipulated the category of age, especially attempting to increase or mitigate punishment if offenders fell near adult status (Bianca Premo, "Minor Offenses: Youth, Crime, and the Law in Eighteenth-Century Lima," in Hecht, *Minor Omissions*, 117, 122–25).

6. The records of the Havana Casa de Expósitos are contained in AA-Havana, Book 1 (1711–56), Book 4 (1790–96), Book 5 (1796–99), Book 6 (1799–1803), and Book 7 (1803–6). Also see Ondina González, "Down and Out in Havana: Foundlings in Eighteenth-Century Havana," in Hecht, *Minor Omissions*, 102–14, for analysis of the early years.

7. Analysis of expósito legislation and of 244 petitions for legitimation directed to the Council and Cámara of the Indies forms the basis of my *Public Lives, Private Secrets: Gender, Honor, Sexuality and Illegitimacy in Colonial Spanish America* (Stanford: Stanford University Press, 1999).

8. See Twinam, *Public Lives*, 130–39.

9. Archivo General de Indies Seville, Spain (hereafter, AGI), Santo Domingo 1488, n. 15, 1796. I will cite documents at first mention and will not cite them again unless there is an intervening reference.

10. Since the fifteenth century the Spanish monarchs had legitimized illegitimate children after their birth. By the eighteenth century this was an institutionalized process in which petitioners submitted information on their birth and circumstances to the Cámara, a subgroup of the Council of the Indies, and officials decided whether to grant the favor (*gracias*) for a specified sum. See Twinam, *Public Lives*, 50–55.

11. AGI, Santo Domingo 1470, n. 14, 1786.

12. Twinam, *Public Lives*, 41–50, 218–28. Issues of inheritance were complicated depending on the category of illegitimacy, whether there was recognition of the illegitimate and/or a will, and if the property descended from the mother or the father. Technically, since expósitos had no known parents, inheritance should not have been an issue, but in reality many expósitos received property from parents.

13. AGI, Santo Domingo 1481, n. 23, 1791.

14. Twinam, *Public Lives*, 84–86.

15. León Carlos Alvarez Santalo found that approximately 5.4 percent of parents returned for a baby left in the Sevilla Casa de Expósitos in the seventeenth century, 4.1 percent in the eighteenth century, and 2.6 percent in the nineteenth century, *Marginación social y mentalidad en Andalucía occidental: Expósitos en Sevilla (1613–1910)* (Seville: Grafitálica, 1980), 103. Mannarelli, *Pecados públicos*, 290, recounts an example in which a mother reclaimed an infant in the Lima Casa de Expósitos.

16. AGI, Santo Domingo 1488, n. 20, 1796.

17. AGI, Santo Domingo 1474, n. 11, 1789.

18. AGI, Santo Domingo 1466, n. 3, 1779.

19. AGI, Santo Domingo 1484, n. 14, 1793.

20. See Ondina E. González's contribution to this volume, "Consuming Interests: The Response to Abandoned Children in Colonial Havana" (see Chapter 5).

21. Evaristo Zenea, *Historia de la Real Casa de Maternidad de esta ciudad en la cual se comprende la antigua casa cuna, refiriendose sus fundaciones, delorable estado y felices progresos que después ha tenido hasta el presente* (Havana: D. Jose Severino Boloña, Impresos de la Real Marina, 1838), 26–27. González, "Down and

Out," 107, provides data suggesting that in the early eighteenth century most
wet nurses took but one infant to suckle from the Casa.

22. Felipe Arturo Avila Espinosa, "Los niños abandonados de la casa de niños
expósitos de la ciudad de México, 1767–1821," in *La familia en el mundo
Iberoamericano*, ed. Pilar Gonzalbo Aizpuro and Cecilia Rabell (Mexico City:
Universidad Nacional Autónoma de México, 1994), 302.

23. Alvarez Santalo estimates that approximately 10 percent of annual births in
Seville were deposited in the Casa (*Marginación social y mentalidad*, 43–44,
193). Guiomar Dueñas-Vargas notes a 41 percent mortality rate for babies
deposited in the Bogotá Casa in 1810, "Gender, Race and Class: Illegitimacy
and Family Life in Santafé Nuevo Reino de Granada, 1770–1810" (PhD diss.,
University of Texas at Austin, 1995), 268. As in Havana, the death rates of
some European foundlings bettered as the eighteenth century progressed,
although conditions varied widely from country to country and city to city.
Foundling mortality in mid-eighteenth-century Paris was around 68 percent,
while 90 percent of abandoned infants in late eighteenth-century Rouen died
before they reached a year (Jane Ruth Potash, "The Foundling Problem in
France, 1800–1869: Child Abandonment in Lille and Lyon" [PhD diss., Yale
University, 1979], 13). By the late nineteenth century the mortality rate in
Paris foundling homes hovered around 32 percent, while death still claimed
72 percent of infants in St. Petersburg, 80 percent in Naples, and 86 percent
in Moscow institutions. See Louise A. Tilly, Rachael G. Fuchs, and David
Kertzner, "Child Abandonment in European History: A Symposium," *Journal
of Family History* 17 (1992): 12; David I. Kertzer, "Gender Ideology and
Infant Abandonment in Nineteenth-Century Italy," *Journal of Interdisciplinary
History* 22 (summer 1991): 8–10. George Sussman notes the difficulties of
calculating infant mortality rates (George Sussman, "Parisian Infants and
Norman Wet Nurses in the Early Nineteenth Century: A Statistical Study,"
Journal of Interdisciplinary History 7 [spring 1977]: 639). Ann R. Higginbotham
estimated that illegitimate children had "at least" double the crude death
rate of legitimate babies in Victorian London (Ann R. Higginbotham, "'Sin
of the Age': Infanticide and Illegitimacy in Victorian London," in *Victorian
Scandals: Representations of Gender and Class*, ed. Kristine Ottensen Garrigan
[Athens: Ohio University Press, 1992], 260; Kertzer, "Gender Ideology," 8–
10, suggested that mortality of children born illegitimately in nineteenth-
century Italy was double to triple that of legitimate children. Such calculations
are complicated by the unknown number of infant deaths that occurred
before babies were brought to institutions as well as the lack of subsequent
recordkeeping after the first infant months or years.

24. *Novísima recopilación de las leyes de España* (hereafter, *NR*) (Madrid: Boletín Oficial del Estado, 1805), bk. VII, tít. XXXVII, leyes I–II, contains the seventeenth-century expósito legislation.

25. Richard Herr notes that one of the mandates of these Bourbon-inspired societies was to supervise vocational training, which may be why they became involved in this case (Richard Herr, *The Eighteenth-Century Revolution in Spain* [Princeton, NJ: Princeton University Press, 1958], 156).

26. The eighteenth-century laws are in *NR*, bk. VII, tít. XXXVII, leyes III–V.

27. Richard Konetzke reprints the 1772 royal decree, which orders that expósitos of the Havana casa be treated as legitimates (Richard Konetzke, *Colección de documentos para la historia de la formación social de hispanoamérica, 1493–1810*, 5 vols. [Madrid: Consejo Superior de Investigaciones Científicas, 1958–62], 3:1, n. 224. Archivo Histórico Nacional [Madrid, Spain, Consejos Libros 1497], n. 33, 1794) mentions the privileges of the Cartagena expósitos. See Guillermo F. Margadant, "La familia en el derecho novohispano," in *Familias novohispanas, siglo XVI al XIX*, ed. Pilar Gonzalbo Aizpuru (Mexico City: El Colegio de México, 1991), 51, for a 1772 decree that gave the presumption of innocence to expósitos although its consequences were not as extensive in the Indies because so many expósitos were racially mixed. In a 1786 case royal officials noted that expósitos not only enjoyed the "state of legitimates" but that they were eligible for "offices of honor that require clean blood" even though the laws demanded that candidates had to prove their "quality" and "purity," which orphans clearly could not (Konetzke, *Colección de documentos*, 3:2, n. 295, 1786).

28. The decree is contained in *NR*, bk. VII, tít. XXXVII, ley IV.

29. See Twinam, *Public Lives*, 275–86, 298–306.

30. See Milton, "Wandering Waifs and Abandoned Babes," 117–18, on the diversity in Quito.

31. Ibid., 204–15, on geographical variations in discrimination throughout the Spanish empire and on its increase in the late eighteenth century.

32. However, see Milton's recent case study of the impact of expósito legislation in colonial Quito, although even here the greatest concern—that native expósitos might be free from tribute—applied to adult privileges.

33. AGI, Santo Domingo 1492, n. 42, 1797.

34. Konetzke, *Colección de documentos*, 3:1, n. 225, 1772.

35. Royal officials declared that when there was doubt concerning someone's "quality" that "one ought to presume the most favorable," but documents make clear that this was not the popular attitude (Konetzke, *Colección*

de documentos, 3:2, n. 296, 1786). In Konetzke, *Colección de documentos*, 3:1, n. 225, 1772 officials commented that "neither in Spain nor in the Indies [have expósitos] enjoyed nor ought they enjoy all the qualities of the truly legitimate." The 1794 decree also pointed out that expósitos were treated with the "greatest contempt and held as bastards" (Konetzke, *Colección de documentos*, 3:2, n. 338, 1794).

CHAPTER SEVEN

Slavery and Childhood in Brazil (1550–1888)

Elizabeth Anne Kuznesof

∾

✦ Doña Nininha, the granddaughter of a Brazilian slave on a rural *fazenda* in Rio de Janeiro, gave this testimony to historian Hebe Castro in 1994, conveying the pain and fragility of the infancy of a slave child: "My mother was the youngest daughter. I never knew the others. My grandmother's first children were sold away to other plantations. . . . My mother said the older children were fathered by the *Senhor* [master]. My grandmother nursed the legitimate children of the Senhor; she said that her own children cried to nurse and she could not nurse them. She worked in the kitchen then and when she had time off that she could nurse a child, she was forced to nurse the child of the Master. This drove her own baby wild, to see her nurse the baby of the Senhor."[1]

Doña Nininha's recollections underscore how extraordinarily vulnerable the slave condition was. Brazilian slavery resulted in continuous violence for slave women, threatened the integrity of families, and challenged the relationship between babies and their mothers. In fact, precisely for these reasons, prior to the 1980s historians generally doubted that significant numbers of slaves in the Atlantic world were able to develop families.

For Brazil the existence of a slave family, not to mention a "slave child-hood," seemed completely impossible, even less believable than for the United States or the Caribbean.

Yet, by deducing or filtering out information on children from both old and new sources, this chapter presents an overview of slave childhood in Brazil during the years of Portuguese colonial rule and the Brazilian empire. This research, which covers a series of distinct topics ranging from the pervasiveness of African culture in child rearing, to the reproductive history of slave women, to the nature of the rural and urban slave family in Brazil, has led to a few preliminary conclusions. The first is that African culture and religion held clear importance for the solidarity and sense of common identity of the slave community and the slave family and children in Brazil. The one important factor that distinguished Brazilian slavery from slavery in other regions in Latin America was that people born in Africa were the majority populations in all significant regional centers during the country's most dynamic phases of development. Throughout the time of slavery, which lasted until 1889, the predominance of African-born slaves among Brazil's slave population was much more pronounced than elsewhere in the Americas. Some scholars have even referred to colonial Brazil as an "African country."[2] This was overwhelmingly true in the Northeast and in Rio de Janeiro and somewhat less true in more interior provinces.

The second finding in this study is the unexpectedly strong participation of slave fathers in the birth and childhood of their children, a phenomenon that essentially undermines most prior studies on slave families. Although the strong significance of the single mother has been recognized (and is highlighted here as a major aspect of slave society), the emergence of the slave father as a dimension of slave childhood is new. This finding suggests that bonds between fathers and their children, and fathers' involvement in the education of their children, may have been much greater than previous scholarship has concluded.

A third observation is that the rural context indisputably facilitated stable two-parent slave families in comparison to urban areas or mining areas, particularly after the end of the eighteenth century when the slave trade slowed. This is surprising since many previous studies have concluded that slaves retained more autonomy in the urban context and thus would be more likely to marry. A slave child, however, was more likely to grow up with two parents on a large plantation in a rural area.

In addition, this chapter tackles the question of what made slave childhood different from childhood among Brazil's free population. It reinforces a strong conclusion already reached by a number of scholars.[3] In many ways it can be said that slave children experienced similar levels of poverty, unhygienic surroundings, and material deprivation as other poor Brazilian children in the late eighteenth and early nineteenth centuries. But because slave children had little control over their own lives (and since slave parents likewise had little authority in the lives of their children), the influence of context (rural or urban location, for example) on many aspects of their lives was even greater than for free children. The most important factor that made slave childhood distinct from other kinds of childhood was the impact of the slave condition itself, which precluded legal recognition of kinship or marriage among slaves. This fact greatly increased the fragility of the slave family, since the slave child was vulnerable to being separated from family members at any point.

African Societies, Religion, and Childbirth

The fact that slave populations were predominantly African well into the nineteenth century in most of Brazil, including São Paulo and Rio de Janeiro, seriously challenges the strong historiographical tendency to ignore the importance of African cultural traditions and family structures in Brazilian slave society. The "São Paulo School of Sociology" in particular argued that the slave system destroyed African culture and values, creating a promiscuous society without morals.[4] Yet several nineteenth-century slave communities were known to have more than 70 percent African-born slaves in their populations. This background clearly had a strong influence on culture and forms of solidarity in slave communities. It is likely that a slave woman—whether Brazilian born (*creole*) and partnered with an African man or herself African—would have done her best to socialize her children with African values. As Robert Slenes argued about the study of the slave family, "historians will have to pay more attention to the norms, the practices, and the 'memories' of Africa than they have done until now."[5]

Although a great number and variety of African societies fed into the Brazilian population through the slave trade, the vast majority of slaves came from West Central Africa, including the Congo and Angola, with smaller numbers originating from the Mina Coast. Several anthropologists and historians have convincingly argued the existence of a common West Central African culture with specific constellations of basic symbols, beliefs, values, and rituals that had overriding importance for all the tribal societies in the region.[6] Among common aspects of this culture was a belief system that included charms and rituals to protect the community from disease and death.[7]

West Central Africans focused their religious lives on the cult of spirits of recently deceased ancestors—the *shades*. The shades were "the source of social values and order, and through the ritual of Kumina, or 'the African dance,' the Central Africans communed with them and thus ensured their beneficence to the group."[8] Practices that survive today in the form of musical rituals culminate in possession by the shades. An eighteenth-century native of the Niger, Ibo Olaudah Equiano, similarly described a society of villages united by religious beliefs with an emphasis on ancestor cults and a myth of patrilineal descent from a common founder or founders.[9]

Marriages in West Central Africa often resulted from an agreement between parents when their children were seven or eight years old. The exchange of women between tribal societies through marriage was highly significant. Since women were the primary nurturers and educators of children, the marriage system provided a means for the spread of culture and beliefs. The flexibility of West Central African culture and its propensity to accept new rituals, symbols, beliefs, and myths also facilitated communication and acceptance between different African traditions in Brazil.[10]

Childbirth in West Central Africa ordinarily occurred with the company and assistance of women relatives and members of the neighborhood, who delivered the child and knotted the umbilical cord. For six days after birth the mother lay on her mat with her child and washed neither herself nor the child. On the seventh day the room was cleaned from top to bottom. Even the cinders of the hearth were taken and thrown into the river. An *alase*, or priest, then rubbed palm oil on the head of the child and bathed him in the container from which the cinders were thrown away. The priest dissolved a few grains of salt in his own mouth and, blowing a few drops of saline saliva on the forehead of the child, called aloud the name the child's father had told him in advance.[11]

Although the mother gave birth to the body of the child, the father also secluded himself to meditate and commune with the spirits so he could receive an appropriate name for the child, often through a dream.[12] The wrong name could lead to "spirit sickness" and bad luck. The giving of the name by the father was conceptualized as a kind of spiritual birth of the child. The mother gave birth to the body, but the father gave birth to the spirit. We will see this vision of birth continued within slavery in colonial Brazil.

In Central Africa babies were nursed for at least one year, and usually for three years. Often the infant was tied to the mother's back with a knotted cloth while she worked in the fields. The child had no separate cradle but slept near the mother, covered with cloths. Male infants were circumcised in West Central African culture in a religious ceremony at age six or seven. Children of both sexes also were scarified at that time, being incised with knife markings that identified particular tribes.[13] Children of both sexes younger than fifteen often went without clothes.[14] Among the Niger Ibo, residence was patrilocal, and families lived in either nuclear or extended family groups. Authority was based on age grading for both sexes. Corporal punishment for children was rare.[15]

Children in the Slave Trade

Although scholarship on the proportion of children in the slave trade has been based on partial and often contradictory data, scholars substantially agree in a few areas. Children under three years of age probably constituted no more than 5 percent of all slaves imported to Brazil in the eighteenth and nineteenth centuries. While ages were not given, young children were distinguished in records by the terms *"cria do peito"* (children who are nursing) and *"cria de pe"* (toddlers).[16] However, children ages ten to fourteen were clearly one of the largest groups of all slaves imported, and the mortality of children on the Middle Passage was no greater than for adults.[17] From 1822–33, 20.4 percent of slaves imported to Rio de Janeiro were aged infant to fourteen, according to tax records.[18] Children were often not counted as part of cargo, which implies that the proportion of children on the ships may have been even higher than available numbers suggest.[19]

Mary Karasch examined travelers' accounts, which reported that, although most slaves were over age five, the majority of slaves being sold in Rio were between the ages of eight to ten or twelve to fourteen. Based on records of slave ships into Rio (1838–52), Karasch argued that 83 percent of imported slaves were between the ages of ten and twenty-two and that "almost two-thirds of those imported on such ships were under the age of 14 or 15."[20] With the clear preponderance of males (between 2:1 and 3:1) among slaves at market, Karasch hypothesized that almost 43 percent of those arriving on slave ships were boys under fourteen.[21] All scholars agree on the prevalence of boys ten to fourteen among imported slaves. Adult women, by contrast, formed only 7 percent of slave cargoes.

The most recently arrived slaves to Rio were confined in enclosed warehouses in the Valongo slave market. The newspaper, *Aurora Fluminense*, published in the 1820s, inveighed against the Valongo as an "inhumanity of the Middle Ages," and many protested the mass burials of dead slaves in the Valongo cemetery.[22] The traveler Charles Brand visited the Valongo in a busy period in 1827 and described the scene.

> The first flesh-shop we entered contained about three hundred children, male and female: the eldest might have been twelve or thirteen years old, and the youngest not more than six or seven.

7.1. Jean Baptiste Debret, *Mercado Valongo* (Valongo slave market).
Source: Luiz Felipe de Alencastro, Serge Gruzinski, Tierno Mónenembo,
Patrick Straumann, and Jean Baptiste Debret, *Rio de Janeiro:
La ville métisse* (Paris: Changdeigne, 2001), 69.

The poor little things were all squatted down in an immense wareroom, girls on one side, and boys on the other, for the better inspection of the purchasers: all their dress consisted of a blue-and-white checked apron tied round the waist. . . . The smell and heat of the room was very oppressive and offensive . . . in this one room they live and sleep, on the floor, like cattle in all respects.[23]

Whatever the proportion of children imported to Brazil in the slave trade, it is clear that those imported as slaves were mostly older than age seven, which according to Portuguese law was the age at which children were qualified to work.[24]

Fertility Among Slave Women

Until the 1980s there was a virtual consensus among scholars that the birth rate of slaves in Brazil was extremely low, primarily because of the harsh conditions of slavery.[25] One theory held that the very high infant and child mortality rates among slaves made fertility rates based on the child/mother ratio appear low. This possibility will be considered below. Another theory is that the low incidence of slave marriages lowered slave fertility, yet fertility rates probably had little to do with church-sanctioned marriages. In fact, even most slave women who married had given birth at least once before marriage.

In 1976 the historian Robert Slenes argued that the idea of low slave fertility was a myth. Since then other scholars have concurred.[26] Slenes held that the fact that the crude birth rate was lower than the crude death rate did not necessarily mean that intrinsic fertility was low. Over time in most of Brazil the slave population born in Brazil began to resemble the profile of statistically "normal" populations, with a similar age pyramid, particularly after 1850 when the slave trade ended. Thus, Slenes concluded that even though "fertility rates of Brazilian bondsmen were far below those of American slaves, and probably substantially less than those of free Brazilians. . . . [i]t is not true that slave fertility rates were low in Brazil."[27]

What did exist for much of the history of Brazilian slavery was a highly distorted sex ratio.[28] When the sex ratio is combined with the fact that many slave owners did not permit slaves to marry nonslaves or slaves owned by other slave masters, we see that the possibility for sexual partnership and family stability was unlikely. In the late eighteenth and nineteenth centuries, however, it appears that a number of slave owners on large plantations utilized slave reproduction as a strategy for stability and good order, and on smaller plantations they used slave reproduction precisely to increase the slave population.

Infant and Child Mortality Among Slaves

High levels of child and infant mortality were characteristic of both free and slave populations in Brazil from the sixteenth to the end of the nineteenth century. In Rio de Janeiro during the period 1845–47, infants in both free and slave populations accounted for 30.2 percent of total mortality. If deaths of children aged one to ten are included in mortality calculations (and most deaths occurred under age three), the percent of total deaths increases to 52 percent.[29] Until the end of the nineteenth century, contemporary authors commonly remarked that half of all the children born in Brazil died before their fifth birthday. As a result life expectancy for Brazilian male slaves was roughly half that of life expectancy of U.S. male slaves in the nineteenth century.[30]

Alarming levels of infant mortality in Brazil provoked several studies by physicians in the nineteenth century. They found that among significant causes for infant mortality, for both free and slave children, were lack of sufficient clothing (because of the custom of allowing children to go naked), the "dampness of dwellings," improper diet, lack of medical care, hunger, and the neglect of childhood diseases.[31] Beriberi was one of the major causes of infant slave deaths in nineteenth-century Brazil, since slave diets—heavy in manioc flour and dried beef—lacked niacin, and most also lacked thiamin, known to prevent the disease.[32] Undoubtedly, mortality was an important and constant dimension of everyday life for both the free and slave populations. Not only was mortality very high among infants (primarily from dysentery, malnutrition, and starvation as well as from infectious diseases), but approximately one in five births in Brazil reportedly resulted in the death of the mother.[33] Maria Luiza Marcilio calculated all maternal deaths in childbirth during the period 1799–1809 in São Paulo at 154.4 in 1,000.[34] Registered deaths of infants under one year were in the vicinity of 239 to 288 per 1,000 births in São Paulo at the turn of the nineteenth century.[35] Although precise data is lacking, we can assume that the rate for the slave population would have been still higher.

The very high mortality among all children created a peculiar mindset in colonial Brazil that some have called "indifference." Parents often said that "the death of children is a blessing." Children who died soon after birth were called "angels." Deceased children of the poor were usually wrapped in cloth and buried close to the house, unbaptized and pagan. Many children died before being named because of the expectation of their early death. Others were given the same name as a sibling who died earlier. Many slaves and members of the popular classes believed that babies were spiritually akin to wild animals or forest demons, that babies were born without souls, and that the babies themselves might decide not to live.[36] Even elite parents did not follow the body of a child to the cemetery because they believed it was "bad luck" and might attract death to the other children in the family.[37] These attitudes undoubtedly constituted a kind of psychological protection for parents, which became widespread in the face of frequent loss of children through death.

Early Childhood and Adolescence in Slavery

The official policy of the Portuguese government was always to eradicate as much as possible any and all African cultural traits that might challenge Portuguese norms. These would include aspects of language, family organization, dance, and music as well as religion. This policy was influenced by a paranoia concerning the possibility of conspiracy among persons of African descent and the fact that beginning in the seventeenth century the white population was numerically inferior to that of the slave and mixed-race populations. These policies were also continued in nineteenth-century Brazil after independence from Portugal.

The policy centered on two major areas: (1) the creation and maintenance of kinship and family ties, and (2) festivals or events in which persons of African descent would congregate, speak in their own languages, sing songs that whites could not understand, and perform dances considered by the Portuguese to be immoral. In the case of kinship, for example, colonial laws were drawn up stating that only whites could be selected as ritual kin or godparents of slaves in an effort to prevent links between freed slaves or free Afro-Brazilians and the slave population.

Yet remnants of African culture, beliefs, languages, and behaviors persisted in Brazil for three key reasons. First, the constant influx of slaves from West Central Africa continually revitalized African traditions.

Second, indifference, laziness, and insufficient personnel meant that edicts against African practices and contacts were not enforced. And third, the African custom of maintaining oral traditions through the constant telling and retelling of stories that epitomized their beliefs and culture—stories passed from father to son and from community leaders to the community—limited the effectiveness of these repressive efforts.[38]

The predominance of young males among arriving African slaves probably meant that African initiation rituals for adolescent boys were important in Brazilian slave communities, particularly in rural areas. These rituals constituted a significant form of public ceremony that would also have served to create bonds between the boys and their new communities. The bonds would be particularly meaningful between adult male slaves and the new adolescent boy slaves.[39] In the city, adolescent initiation might include the introduction of *capoeira*—a Rio-centered training regimen for male discipline and bonding for mutual defense.[40]

Popular religion in colonial and nineteenth-century Brazil combined elements from indigenous, Portuguese, and African sources, all characterized by extreme levels of religiosity and belief in diverse supernatural beings, both benign and malicious. Portuguese votive images proliferated in the Brazilian countryside, many of them different representations of the Virgin Mary. Practitioners viewed these saintly images as mediums or miracle-makers appropriate to solve particular problems.[41] Devils and evil spirits were part of this belief system as well, even within Catholicism, including belief in witches, vampires, fairies, the Evil Eye, omens, fortune tellers, incantations, demons, spells, love potions, and the like.[42] These beliefs were commonly incorporated into children's games and popular medicine.

Popular culture, witchcraft, and sorcery emphasized love and fecundity. African and Portuguese traditions included charms and spells for fertility as well as to protect the lives of the pregnant woman and the child. Altar stones, herbs, toads, crayfish, bats, snakes, doves, rabbits, and hoot owls also were thought to be useful for sexual magic, including the attraction of a lover or husband, the consummation of a marriage, the impregnation of a woman, and the successful birth and survival of a child. These ideas influenced slave culture as well as colonial Brazilian culture in general.[43]

João Imbert, traveling in Brazil in the early nineteenth century, described birthing practices among slaves as involving a community of slave women and midwives. The women moved the mother's limbs into

7.2. Jean Baptiste Debret, *Coleta para a manutencão da igreja do Rosário* (Collection for the Church of the Rosary). Debret, a French traveler in early nineteenth-century Brazil, captured the kind of mixing of traditional African rituals with European Catholicism into which slave children would be socialized early. In this illustration he features the regalia worn by what appear to be leaders—or kings and queens—of the brotherhood of the Rosary, which collected alms for the maintenance of its church. Source: Luiz Felipe de Alencastro, Serge Gruzinski, Tierno Mónenembo, Patrick Straumann, and Jean Baptiste Debret, *Rio de Janeiro: La ville métisse* (Paris: Changdeigne, 2001), 116.

different positions, exhorted her to "*pucha, pucha*" (push, push), offered her relics and rosaries to kiss, and insisted she pray to her name saint. After the birth, the head of the child was massaged to give it better form, and the umbilical cord was cut far from the body and smeared with oil and pepper.[44] After birth, the father sought chickens, wine, onions, and other preferred foods for the mother and her baby with considerable insistence, threatening to run away if the overseer refused to provide what the slave wanted. Clearly the slave fathers took their paternal roles seriously, in spite of the structural limitations of slavery.[45] In general the slave populations prized rituals that focused on community and family and quickly adapted Christian rituals to their own culture. This was especially clear in the case of baptism.

According to colonial Portuguese law, new slaves arriving in Brazil had to be baptized within a year, and most slaves were baptized on arrival and before being sold. In addition, Africans and Afro-Brazilians in Brazil were very anxious to be baptized and for their children to be baptized. In Africa, the large volume of water used in baptisms by black priests may have signified purification to the slaves.[46] Slaves also believed that baptism provided the protection of a powerful spirit.[47] According to Karasch, baptism "had the character of an initiation ceremony in the sense of integration into a black community."[48] João Rugendas observed that baptized slaves in Brazil treated unbaptized Africans as "savages" until they had undergone the ritual.[49] Likewise Englishman Henry Koster reported that Brazilian slaves felt they could be seen as inferior if they were not baptized.[50] Undoubtedly this feeling would also have encouraged slaves to seek the baptism of their children.

The Catholic institution of ritual kinship (godparenthood or *padrinazgo*, and coparenthood or *compadrazgo*) was a part of the required Christianization process. These relationships were established especially at baptism, christening, and marriage ceremonies, creating vertical relationships between the person being baptized and the godparents, as well as horizontal relationships between the godparents and all of the extended family of the baptized. Godparenthood was intended to be a relationship with a spiritual sponsor who provided guidance to the newly baptized Catholic.[51] Brazilian slaves avidly adopted the institution of ritual kinship. Although scholars have tried to identify an African counterpart to this institution, none has been found.[52]

Slave babies were provided with godparents as a part of baptism. The baptism ritual and the creation of a supportive network of ritual kin certainly reinforce the idea that children among slaves were cared for by adults. This mechanism allowed slaves essentially to create an extended family network within the slave community, sometimes utilizing ritual kinship as a means to acknowledge a relationship originating in Africa. Although Portuguese law mandated white godparents for slaves, this requirement was often ignored. If the child to be baptized lived with both slave parents, the most common practice was for a slave couple of a similar African background to be chosen as godparents. Slave children of single mothers, however, usually had godparents from the free population, and their godparents were more likely to be white.[53] All those who have investigated the topic agree that the slave owner virtually never became the godfather of his own slave.[54] Instead it was common for free whites or mulattoes outside the household or plantation of the baptized to be named as godfathers of the slave children of single mothers, either because the godfathers chosen were actually the natural fathers or as a means of seeking protection from powerful patrons. The godfather was frequently called upon later for support or protection of both the baptized and his or her family.

The infancy of a slave child was very much influenced by whether the owner wished to take advantage of the opportunity to use, rent, or sell the mother as a wet nurse, or *ama-de-leite*. Ironically, the birth of a baby provided incentive for the slave mother to be sold or rented to a third party. Infants were generally nursed for three years in both Brazilian and African culture. Nineteenth-century Brazilian newspapers include many advertisements to rent or sell lactating slaves with or without their young children. Some ads specified that the child would accompany the mother while other ads gave this option. Some stated clearly that her child would not come with her. It is apparent from this literature that a wet nurse sold without child brought a better price.[55]

Related anecdotal evidence refers to the practice of slave women leaving their newborn children at Rio's foundling home, the Santa Casa de Misericordia, at the insistence of the master. Other slave mothers may have left their babies behind with ritual kin or a member of their community who could nurse. Those slave children whose mothers served as wet nurses, however, may have actually had a better life, healthier living conditions, and better nutrition as a result of their mothers' work. Additionally, the slave children in those circumstances frequently grew up as the companions of the white children who shared their mother's milk, playing together in the master's house.[56]

Slave women who worked in the fields often carried their babies strapped to their backs in cloth slings. In some cases babies might be left in a field shack during the day, suspended in hammocks, or left on floor mats. The babies may have been left untended or, one imagines, with a slave no longer able to work. It was generally said that a Brazilian baby's feet never touched the ground in its first two years of life. Although this mainly describes the elite, the practice of constant nursing and carrying infants was also practiced in West Central Africa and was continued among the slaves.[57]

In urban areas the slave child spent less time in the master's household and with the master's children than on the streets chasing after his or her mother. City streets often "swarmed with so many black children that municipal councils threatened to impose sanctions on masters who let the children [of their slaves] grow up in the streets."[58] Urban authorities had enormous difficulties controlling the activities of slaves in urban areas. Slaves were required to carry a pass from their master, which essentially allowed the slaves to go anywhere they wished. Donald Ramos reported that authorities in colonial Minas Gerais essentially lumped slaves and freedmen together for purposes of legislation since there was little difference in their lives. There, urban female slaves often worked for wages as washerwomen, midwives, cooks, or bakers; men worked as artisans, barbers, or porters. They were required to give a fixed sum to their owners and could usually keep the rest. Children over the age of seven often worked alongside their mothers.[59]

When the slave child was considered able to work, usually between the ages of seven and ten, he or she was taken out of the domestic arena and introduced to some kind of light task.[60] While no formal education of the kind white children received was offered to the slave child, it was not unusual for a slave boy to be put into an apprenticeship, or for a slave girl to become a domestic laborer on the same plantation or even be rented out to another household.[61] According to an 1831 census for Minas Gerais, at ten years of age 20 percent of all children (including free, freed, and slaves) listed occupations; for ages thirteen and fourteen those percentages rose to 44 percent. For boys agricultural work was the most common occupation, while the girls worked mostly as domestic servants or in textiles.[62] Fairly young children might even be sold away from parents and kinfolk to work.

The Slave Family

Most important to a consideration of childhood among slaves is the question of the existence of the slave family. In general scholars seem agreed that slaves' living situations were largely determined by the family into which they were born or which purchased them.[63] Contemporary nineteenth-century paintings by Debret and Rugendas illustrate the domestic lives of slaves and their integration into the families of their owners. The structure of Brazilian society and the position of slaves within the slaveholding family are also clearly demonstrated in the censuses of the eighteenth and nineteenth centuries. Whenever possible, the censuses expressed the relations of authority and subordination within the household through the idiom of legitimate kinship and family ties. In those censuses it was often the case that occupation was provided only for the head of household, while in lieu of other members' "occupations," the census taker decided to list their relationship to the head of household, for example "wife," "son," "slave," or person added to the household as a dependent and subordinate "*agregado*."

Slaves were generally listed in censuses as a group, often alphabetically by first name or divided only by sex, with no indication of kinship or occupation.[64] An effort seems to have been made to obscure the kinship, which we know existed among many slaves. In fact, "kinlessness," or the idea that whatever family ties slaves may have established carried no legal significance, was a central tenet of slaveholding ideology worldwide.[65] As Sonia Giacomini observed, "This expression—'slave family'—never appeared even once in the sources, not even in the legislation referring to slaves and their children."[66] The reason clearly was the inherent contradiction between the slave as property and the slave as a father or mother, given that kinship obligations and rights were ordinarily conferred in the family sphere only for free populations within Brazilian law.

Compared to families in the free population, the family lives of slaves developed not only in conjunction with events in their own lives, such as marriages, births of children, and deaths, but also with events in the lives of their masters. As property, slaves were subject to the Portuguese inheritance law that divided assets equally among heirs. Slaves effectively lived within two family cycles, with the survival of their own families subject to events in both families. This made even apparently stable slave families inherently vulnerable.[67]

Although the scholarly literature emphasizes ways in which the slave family was restrained or made insecure by its slave condition, some plantation studies suggest that owners favored slave marriage (formal or consensual) and the organization of slaves in family units. For example, Stuart Schwartz showed that in 1731 and 1752 the Engenho Santana of Bahia was organized in nuclear family units, 61 percent and 79.8 percent respectively.[68] This pattern may have been associated with the fact that Jesuit priests managed the plantation, but other evidence suggests the nuclear family may have been more widespread. For example, in eighteenth-century Parnaiba, "nuclear families constituted the most common slave family type" after the creole population expanded.[69] The São Paulo census of 1801 also indicates a pattern of slave families, with some formalized marital relationships noted, although adult slaves were predominantly male and African in origin.[70] In large part the ability of slaves to construct families was dependent on there being a substantial presence of available females. In 1798 the sex ratio of the captaincy of São Paulo slave population was 117.27 males per 100 females, while in the city of São Paulo itself, the ratio was nearly equal, allowing significant numbers of slaves to establish families.[71]

The socioeconomic context in which the slave lived was extremely significant in terms of family formation. In Brazil slaves were found in every possible context—in urban areas, in mining towns, in rural areas with mixed farming, and on plantations focused on individual crops such as sugar or coffee. In urban São Paulo 43.6 percent of households had one or more slaves in 1836, with five to seven slaves most common.[72] An average 3.6 slaves populated each of Rio de Janeiro's households in the 1830s. In the rural *bairros* of São Paulo in 1836 only an estimated 28 percent of households owned slaves, and most of these slaves lived on plantations with more than fifteen slaves.[73] It is also important to note the significance of the freed and free-born population with African background in Brazil, which reached about 30 percent of the total population by 1800.[74] With such a high percentage of the black population being free, slaves living in populated areas could not easily be distinguished as slaves because of their race. Many households, both with and without slaves, included free African or mixed-race members. In addition, some slave women and men appeared in the census as spouses of free Africans or mulattoes.[75]

Urban areas (including about 7 percent of Brazilian population in 1800) were characterized by a substantially higher number of women than men, smaller households, fewer children, many fewer slaves, and often fewer economic opportunities for slave men than in rural areas. Female-headed households were common, and women headed slave households as well as free households.[76] Slave children had fewer opportunities to know their fathers in urban environments than in rural areas. Slaves were also less likely to have a reasonable physical space for family life in the urban context even though they had more freedom from the whims of their masters.

In spite of the belief that there existed no slave family in Brazil the evidence suggests that individual planters and their families often recognized slave families in practice.[77] In particular, slaves living on larger plantations (from ten to three hundred slaves) had better prospects for a stable family life. In Campinas in 1872, 82 percent of slave children (ages one to nine)

7.3. Jean Baptiste Debret, *Uma senhora brasileira em seu lar* (A Brazilian lady at her hearth). Debret here depicts a tranquil domestic scene among a Brazilian slave mistress, her female slaves, and their children, in which learning to read, sewing, serving, and playing all occur simultaneously. Source: Luiz Felipe de Alencastro, Serge Gruzinski, Tierno Mónenembo, Patrick Straumann, and Jean Baptiste Debret, *Rio de Janeiro: La ville métisse* (Paris: Changdeigne, 2001), 61.

who lived on plantations with ten or more slaves lived with both parents. Only 7 percent of children had neither parent present. For those living on small plantations (fewer than ten slaves), 27 percent lived with two parents; 36 percent had neither father nor mother living with them.[78] One theory holds that by the eighteenth and nineteenth centuries masters had begun to encourage slave marriage to "control them." Sandra Lauderdale Graham, however, offers the more nuanced argument that "Brazilians generally found family a useful way of ordering society, their own slaves included." Planters found "marriage for their slaves convenient both because it meshed with the Catholic culture that permeated all of Brazilian social life, . . . and because married slaves were measurably more content."[79]

Alida Metcalf and other historians agree that slaves who belonged to masters with many slaves found it easier to form nuclear families.[80] The data she examined indicates that slaves on large plantations were more likely to marry than those who lived among fewer slaves although always in slightly lower proportions than the general population. The insistence of planters that slaves choose marriage partners from the same plantation may have actually assisted in developing more stable slave families, at least on large plantations. Metcalf emphasized the relative helplessness of the slave family with respect to its own stability. A family that lived on a large plantation was more secure, but the death of the master could result in the family being split apart by sale or inheritance.[81] Masters also always had the option to split families apart through sale for business reasons.

Owners of plantations with fewer than fifteen slaves also followed reproductive strategies in eighteenth- and nineteenth-century Minas Gerais. Historian Tarciscio Botelho studied plantations in this region devoted to mixed farming and livestock economies and demonstrated that as the creole slave population increased, the median age fell, and the sex ratio improved substantially among slaves, indicating trends toward increased child birth and family stability.[82] João Luis R. Fragoso and Manolo G. Florentino found that by the nineteenth century plantation owners used positive strategies to reinforce the slave family and to encourage reproduction.[83] Based on property *inventarios* for 1872, Fragoso and Florentino found ten plantations with a total of seventy-nine extended slave families, comprising 505 individuals or 39.4 percent of total slaves in all ten plantations. Owners consciously encouraged large slave families and may have avoided splitting them up. Again, the requirement that slaves marry or form their families only within the plantation would have encouraged a strong network of kinship relations within the slave community on large plantations.

The above evidence of the structural existence of slave families in eighteenth- and nineteenth-century Brazil should not obscure the fact that slave children were nevertheless slaves and subject to the physical control of their masters. To what degree did slave parents actually have a voice in the nurturing of their children? Did slave families have a common domestic economy that allowed for the development of family bonds, and did slave parents have the chance to educate and care for their children? Although slave testimony is rare, testimonies from two long-lived ex-slaves interviewed in the 1980s provide some clues and indicate that the stability of the slave family was far from secure.[84]

Mariano Pereira dos Santos was a slave on a large agricultural fazenda in Parana from 1870 to 1880. Maria Chatinha worked on a fazenda in Tremembe, São Paulo. Mariano testified that slave children stayed with their parents while young but were often taken away by the owners while the former were still children; the slave parents had no further rights over their offspring. They were put to work at an early age.[85] Maria Chatinha testified that children were baptized and received first communion and that the children of the master usually played together with the slave children on the fazenda.[86] Both Mariano and Maria Chatinha confirmed the essential absence of formal marriages among slaves on the fazendas. These testimonies illustrate both the existence of a family life for slave children and its precarious nature as an economic and social entity.

Slave Children's Housing, Diet, and Provision Grounds

Clearly the living space of the child slave was important to his or her welfare, in terms of health, hygiene, and even survival as well as for emotional support and education. The existence of some privacy and/or opportunity to share experiences with family members would also be important. Contemporary physicians cited dank, dark, nonhygienic housing as a reason for high levels of child mortality in nineteenth-century Brazil. Slave housing in urban Rio de Janeiro in the mid-nineteenth century varied according to the circumstances of the slave master or mistress and whether the slave was used for domestic labor or production.

One doctor observed that even slaves in rich houses in Rio frequently slept in humid, dark, and unventilated quarters or in the corridors outside their owners' bedroom. Other slaves slept in dark, humid quarters with iron bars on the windows under the owner's veranda, or on mats on wet ground among household goods and animals. Often slaves, animals, and stored goods occupied the lower level of a two-story house. In other houses, slaves lived in "dark cubicles" divided by thin partitions in the kitchen area.[87] These domestic slaves—in contrast to other urban slaves who were hired out and had their own residences—ordinarily lived with constant supervision and little independence.

Rio's industrial and commercial slaves worked in warehouses, shops, stores, sweatshops, and factories, often in windowless buildings. Slaves aged seven and older were included in these workforces. At night all the slaves were locked up to sleep in these same buildings, often in chains.[88] Slaves who were allowed to rent space in the *corticos*, or tenement houses, lived in cramped quarters with whole families in a single room, often sharing cooking with other tenants.[89] In Rio de Janeiro and in Ouro Preto, Minas Gerais, more fortunate slaves built wattle-and-daub huts on found land and reported to their owners in the morning. Many of these were slaves who arranged their own work and brought an agreed upon income to their owner.[90]

In rural Brazil, slave quarters, or *senzalas*, were separate mud-walled and grass-thatched huts or row houses divided into rooms, each occupied by a family or family-like unit.[91] Children lived with parents, most often with two parents, at least by the eighteenth century. For example, a rare 1791 inventory was made of the 1,347 slaves living on the Fazenda Santa Cruz near Rio de Janeiro. Slaves were enumerated by household in their huts, which stretched in two rows on one side of the church square. The male, if one was present, was listed as head of household followed by his wife and children or grandchildren. Most single slaves up to age twenty-four lived with their parents, and three-generation households were not uncommon. Underscoring the unexpectedly important role of slave fathers, twenty-three households consisted of single fathers and their children.[92] Such living circumstances may well have created a sense of family stability and a shared fate.

The history of provision grounds, like that of slave living conditions, has a substantial bearing on the history of Brazilian slave childhood, for the existence of property affected family work routines, property ownership, and nutrition. Several scholars argue that slave masters strategically allowed slave families to have their own *roças*, or provision grounds, to grow subsistence crops that could be sold for cash or utilized by the family.[93] Some contemporary planters viewed provision grounds as a way to make the slaves happier and more productive. For example, Miguel Calmon in 1834 argued, "A master should give his slave some property . . . [to] inspire in him a desire to work and even . . . to form a family."[94] Provision grounds opened the possibility of communal activities and a family economy in which family members worked together on the provision grounds. Stanley Stein reported that slaves raised coffee, corn, and beans, working on Sundays or Saints' Days. Often children accompanied their fathers to the roças and worked beside them, while the women stayed behind to cook, wash, and sew. Later the women carried the noon meal to their families in the field.[95]

An improved diet and quality of life for children may have been facilitated by slave provision grounds. According to B. J. Barickman, on most plantations with sugar mills (*engenhos*) and cane farms in the Northeast owners distributed rations in addition to permitting the slaves provision grounds. Since slave rations typically included only cassava flour and jerked beef, or *angu*, made from corn, those slave communities that received only rations may have experienced endemic beriberi, a cause of infant mortality.[96] The vegetables, corn, and beans grown in garden plots and the small livestock or chickens raised around slave quarters could have substantially improved the diet of nursing mothers and small children and led to better chances of survival. In addition slaves with provision grounds were able to sell excess produce to purchase other goods and possibly save to purchase their own or their children's freedom.

Prospects for Manumission

The possibility of freedom was an important and essential aspect of Brazilian slavery, described often as a "shared dream" of slaves. The constant growth of the free black and mulatto population throughout Brazil provided a visible example of this possibility. This was true though only a small percentage of slaves were manumitted.[97]

The prospect of freedom may have functioned as a form of social control of slaves, causing them to be more cooperative and to work harder.[98] In addition, masters who freed slaves often made that freedom contingent on continued good service. One study of *cartas de alforria*, or letters of freedom, for slave women demonstrated that owners repaid women's contribution of children to the plantation by setting their children free.[99] In 1848 statesman Jose Bonifacio succeeded in having a law enacted that incorporated the principle of particularly manumitting fertile women who had given birth to five live slave children.[100] Nonetheless, freed slaves accounted for no more than 0.5 percent to 2 percent of the population of the cities of Rio de Janeiro, Salvador, and Paraty.[101]

Slave children were always favored when it came to manumission. Although there were fewer slave children than adults in Brazil (and therefore in total fewer children manumitted), children as a group were the most likely to be freed. Brazilian-born and mixed-blood slaves were also freed more often than African slave children. According to a study of Bahia from the late seventeenth until the middle of the eighteenth century, 80 percent of slaves freed were creoles, slaves of mixed ancestry, women, and children. The high proportion of children among the freed was in part attributable to the simple fact that children under age seven or even ten had less economic value than adults and thus represented little loss to owners.

It is also possible that slave children may have been freed because of masters' affection. In Bahia, 71 percent of manumission cases involved masters who claimed to be motivated to grant freedom because they had raised the slave in their home or because the slave was born in the master's house and out of gratitude for the good services of the mother.[102] Some added that they "loved the slave as if s/he were a son [or daughter]" and that the slave "was brought up as if s/he were the master's child."[103] Although some slaves received "deathbed manumissions" to discharge the conscience of the master, most owners managed somehow to describe these deeds as redemptive while still requiring service or payment from the slave.[104] In some cases masters knew they were the fathers of slave children and may have freed children for that reason, especially if the owner was single and needed an heir.[105] Kathleen Higgins found that in cases in which European male owners granted manumissions as gifts to mulatto children, more than one-third (36.2 percent) of those children received the grants from their self-proclaimed fathers.[106] There also was a strong likelihood that slave children with free and/or white godparents (or only a godfather) would be manumitted.[107]

About half of manumissions in colonial Brazil occurred through charity. The other half occurred through purchase, usually by the slaves themselves or their family members.[108] While manumission was entirely in the power of the master and beyond the slave's control, accepting payments for manumission provided masters quick and easy cash and was less trouble than putting slaves on the market, where prices depended on fluctuations in the economy and the physical conditions of slaves. In addition, the master might wish to free himself of a troublesome slave or a slave who was sick, elderly, or too young to work, and thus would accept an offer of self-purchase.

What is more, the freedom of children could be purchased at a lower price than that paid for adults. Slave mothers were especially likely to buy the freedom of their children before they bought their own. Since slave women were more likely to be involved in street selling or urban occupations, they had more opportunities to accumulate funds for this purpose, and many slave women succeeded in putting together the funds for such purchases.

In some cases it was actually the slave father who bought the child's freedom, but those records are harder to trace since the identity of the father was often unclear. The situation of Quiteria, a slave woman in Paraiba, is an exception. She had five children by as many "unknown fathers" and nevertheless convinced each father to pay for his child's freedom while he or she was still young. She later bought her own freedom and maintained ties with all her children.[109] In Sabara, Minas Gerais in 1790 a slave mistress freed a child named Faustino in exchange for forty drams of gold paid to her by the slave father. There is no record that the mother was ever freed.[110]

Yet, even if a child was manumitted at a young age, whether at baptism because of a slave master's affection or because a family member managed to purchase him or her, it is unlikely that his or her childhood would have been substantially different than had freedom not been achieved.[111] It is very likely the child would stay with slave parents, and parents might even have had to pay to keep the child with them. Sometimes the owner failed to sign a letter of manumission for some years, and the danger of being enslaved again was substantial. In one crucial respect, however, being a free child of slave parents did hold a significant advantage: the child would not be sold away from his or her family.

Conclusion

In some ways Brazilian slave children had lives very like the lives of other poor Brazilian children. Mortality was extremely high, and many did not survive to celebrate their first birthday, causing parents to see their children as "angels" or as "spirits" who might not want to stay on the earth. Slave fathers actively participated in early childhood rituals of many children, although many slave children grew up with a single mother, particularly in urban areas. In rural areas, slave children often lived in separate huts with their parents and worked alongside their parents on the family provision grounds. The introduction to godparents and other ritual kinfolk through baptism made children aware of a larger community of slaves and free blacks of similar ethnic backgrounds. Many were introduced to a combination of African, indigenous, and Portuguese folk and religious beliefs during their childhood. Music and rituals kept them aware of their background and close to the slave community. The occupations of young slaves after the age of seven were similar to those of other poor children.

Still, life for slave children was far from easy. This was true not only or even principally because of difficult living conditions, but rather because the slave family had little control over their lives. Most rural Brazilian slave children were brought up knowing both parents, or at least their mothers, but there was little security concerning the structure of their lives. Anything that might happen to the slave owners could destroy a slave family and result in the separation of a child from parents and siblings. Inheritance, sale, or economic decline could easily have devastating results for a slave family. For that reason many slaves were determined to obtain their own freedom and that of their family members. Usually the children's freedom was the first purchased because children were the least expensive to liberate. In a real sense, however, slave children remained intrinsically enslaved until their family members were liberated as well.

✤ NOTES ✤

1. D. Nininha, RJ, 59 years, 9/19/1994, in Ana Lugão Rios and Hebe Mattos, *Memorias do Cativeiro: Familia, trabalho e cidadania no Pos-Abolicão* (Rio de Janeiro: Civilizacão Brasileira, 2005), 101. Translation of quoted material by Elizabeth Kuznesof.

2. Joseph C. Miller, "Retention, Reinvention, and Remembering: Restoring Identities Through Enslavement in Africa and Under Slavery in Brazil," in *Enslaving Connections: Changing Cultures of Africa and Brazil During the Era of Slavery*, ed. Jose C. Curto and Paul E. Lovejoy (Amherst, MA: Humanity Books, 2004), 85.

3. See Christine Húnefeldt, *Las manuelos, vida cotidiana de una familia negra en la Lima del S. XIX* (Lima: Instituto de Estudios Peruanos, 1992), 1–17, for a discussion of the impact of racial mixture on urban populations in Latin America.

4. Florestan Fernandes, *A integracão do negro na sociedade de classes* (São Paulo: Dominuis EDUSP, 1965), 1:34–38, 71–102, 110–18, 152–90; Roger Bastide, *As religioes africanas no Brasil* (São Paulo: Pioneira EDUSP, 1971), 1:104–5.

5. Robert W. Slenes, "A formacão da familia escrava nas regioes de grande lavoura do Sudeste: Campinas, um caso paradigmatico no seculo XIX," *Populacão e familia* I, no. 1 (January/June 1998): 21–22. Translation by the author.

6. Willy de Craemer, Jan Vansina, and Renee C. Fox, "Religious Movements in Central Africa: A Theoretical Study," *Comparative Studies in Society and History* 18, no. 4 (October 1976): 458–75, 463; Mary Karasch, "Central African Religious Tradition in Rio de Janeiro," *Journal of Latin American Lore* 5, no. 2 (1979): 233–53. Miller argues that ethnicity in Africa involved a "creative fluid series of identities," which involved a whole range of connections and identifications rather than a particular allegiance ("Retention, Reinvention," 86–87).

7. Craemer, Vansina, and Fox, "Religious Movements," 469.

8. Monica Shuler, *"Alas, Alas, Kongo": A Social History of Indentured African Immigration into Jamaica, 1841–1865* (Baltimore, MD: Johns Hopkins University Press, 1980), 71–72.

9. G. I. Jones, "Olaudah Equiano of the Niger Ibo," in *Africa Remembered*, ed. Philip Curtin (Madison: University of Wisconsin Press, 1967), 63.

10. Karasch, "Central African Religious Tradition," 235.

11. D'Avezac, "Notice sur le pays," 255; and Ayuba Suleiman, "Capture and Travels of Ayuba Suleiman," 50, both in *Africa Remembered*, ed. Philip Curtin (Madison: University of Wisconsin Press, 1967).

12. Shuler, *"Alas, Alas, Kongo,"* 79.

13. D'Avezac, "Notice sur le pays," 256; Suleiman, "Capture and Travels," 50.

14. D'Avezac, "Notice sur le pays," 155.

15. Jones, "Olaudah Equiano," 60–69.

16. Herbert S. Klein, *The Middle Passage: Comparative Studies in the Atlantic Slave Trade* (Princeton, NJ: Princeton University Press, 1978), 57–58, 68; Manuel dos Anjos da Silva Rebelo, *Relacoes entre Angola e Brasil 1808–1830* (Lisbon: Agencia Geral do Ultra Mar, 1970), 82–87.

17. Klein, *Middle Passage*, 242.

18. Manolo Garcia Florentino, *Em costas negras: Uma história do trafico atlantico de escravos entre a Africa e o Rio de Janeiro (séculos XVIII e XIX)* (Rio de Janeiro: Arquivo Nacional, 1995), appendix 41, 299, also see 67.

19. Katia M. de Queirós Mattoso, *To Be a Slave in Brazil: 1550–1888* (New Brunswick, NJ: Rutgers University Press, 1994), 37–38.

20. Mary C. Karasch, *Slave Life in Rio de Janeiro, 1808–1850* (Princeton, NJ: Princeton University Press, 1987), 32. This was a total of 3,270 slaves for ships in 1830–41. See table 2.2 in Karasch's work.

21. Ibid., 33. Florentino disagrees with this estimate. Based on an estimate from 393 slaves to Rio in 1822–33, Florentino finds 20.4 percent were ages fourteen or younger, most of those ages ten to fourteen; 79.1 percent were adults, ages fifteen to forty. Seventy-five percent were male. See *Em costas negras*, 67, 299.

22. Karasch, *Slave Life*, 38.

23. Charles Brand, *Journal of a Voyage to Peru* . . . (London, 1828), 13, as cited in Karasch, *Slave Life*, 38.

24. Elizabeth Kuznesof, "Legal and Religious Rights and Responsibilities of Brazilian Childhood: A History (1500–1937)," *Revista Populacão e Família Ibero-Americana* 5 (2003): 258; Katia M. de Queirós Mattoso, "O filho da escrava," in *Historia da crianza no Brasil*, comp. Mary del Priore (São Paulo: Historia Contexto, 1991), 78.

25. Robert W. Slenes, "The Demography and Economics of Brazilian Slavery 1850–1888" (PhD diss., Stanford University, 1976), I:271.

26. Horacio Gutierrez, "Crioulos e Africanos no Parana, 1798–1830," *Revista Brasileira de Historia* 8, no. 16 (March 1988/August 1988): 163–66; Robert W. Slenes, "Escravidão e familia: Padrões de casamento e estabilidade familiar numa comunidade escrava (Campinas, Seculo XIX)," *Estudos Economicos* 17, no. 2 (1987): 223–24; Alida C. Metcalf, "Searching for the Slave Family in Colonial Brazil: A Reconstruction from São Paulo," *Journal of Family History* 16, no. 3 (1991): 284, 288–89. Also see Laird W. Bergad, *Slavery and the Demographic and Economic History of Minas Gerais, Brazil, 1720–1888* (Cambridge: Cambridge University Press, 1999), 107, 142.

27. Slenes, *Demography*, 316–17.

28. Ibid., 273.

29. Kenneth F. Kiple, "The Nutritional Link with Slave Infant and Child Mortality in Brazil," *Hispanic American Historical Review* 69, no. 4 (1989): 689.

30. Thomas W. Merrick and Douglas H. Graham, *Population and Economic Development in Brazil: 1800 to the Present* (Baltimore, MD: Johns Hopkins University Press, 1979), 56–57.

31. Jose Maria Teixeira, *Causes of the Mortality of Children in Rio* (Rio de Janeiro: Baron de Lavradio, 1887). "Some Considerations of the Causes of Mortality in the Children of Rio de Janeiro and the Diseases most Frequent in the First Six or Seven Months of Life," a series of articles in the *Jornal de Academia Imperioal*, 1847.

32. Kiple, "Nutritional Link," 688. Beriberi is characterized by partial paralysis of the extremities, emaciation, and anemia. While beriberi had not been associated with infant deaths in scholarship on Brazil, Kenneth Kiple argues it could have been important in cases of prolonged nursing by niacin-deficient mothers. Furthermore, a natural increase in the slave population appears to have been higher in Minas Gerais, an area in which fresh pork, maize, and beans (good sources of niacin) were common in the slave diet.

33. Gilberto Freyre, *The Masters and the Slaves* (New York: Alfred A. Knopf, 1966), 366, 378–79; Maria Luiza Marcilio, *La ville de São Paulo* (Rouen: Rouen Nizet, 1968), 205.

34. Marcilio, *La ville*, 205.

35. Elizabeth Kuznesof, *Household Composition and Urban Development: São Paulo 1765 to 1836* (Boulder, CO: Westview Press, 1986), 61–62.

36. Freyre, *Masters*, 147, 151–53.

37. Mme. Toussaint-Samson, *A Parisian in Brazil* (Boston: James H. Earle Publisher, 1891), 130–31; Freyre, *Masters*, 388; Jose Lins do Rego, *Plantation Boy* (New York: Alfred A. Knopf, 1966), 350.

38. A. J. R. Russell-Wood, *The Black Man in Slavery and Freedom in Colonial Brazil* (New York: St. Martin's Press, 1982), 95–98.

39. Miller, "Retention, Reinvention," 90.

40. Ibid., 100.

41. Laura de Mello e Souza, *The Devil and the Land of the Holy Cross: Witchcraft, Slavery, and Popular Religion in Colonial Brazil* (Austin: University of Texas Press, 1986), 64.

42. A. H. de Oliveira Marques, *Daily Life in Portugal in the Late Middle Ages*, trans. S. S. Wyatt (Madison: University of Wisconsin Press, 1971), 206–8, 226, 276; Padre Jose de Anchieta, *Carta fazenda a descripcão das innumeras coisas naturaes* (São Paulo: Typ da Casa Eclectica, 1900), 47–48.

43. Charles Wagley, *Amazon Town: A Study of Man in the Tropics* (New York: Macmillan, 1953), 246; Marvin Harris, *Town and Country in Brazil* (New York: Columbia University Press, 1956), 165.

44. João Imbert, *Manual do fazendeiro ou tratado domestico sobre as enfermidades dos negros* (Rio de Janeiro: n.p., 1832), 249–50, as cited in Stuart B. Schwartz, *Sugar Plantations in the Formation of Brazilian Society: Bahia, 1550–1835* (Cambridge: Cambridge University Press, 1985), 404.

45. Schwartz, *Sugar Plantations*, 404–5.

46. Karasch, *Slave Life*, 255–57.

47. Shuler, *"Alas, Alas, Kongo,"* 36.

48. Karasch, *Slave Life*, 257.

49. João M. Rugendas, *Viagem pitoresca atraves do Brasil*, trans. Sergio Millet (São Paulo: Editora Martins, 1967), 134–35.

50. Henry Koster, *Travels in Brazil*, 2 vols. (Philadelphia: n.p., 1817), 198–99.

51. See the discussion in Kathleen J. Higgins, *"Licentious Liberty" in a Brazilian Gold-Mining Region: Slavery, Gender and Social Control in Eighteenth-Century Sabara, Minas Gerais* (University Park: Pennsylvania State University Press, 1999), 121–44.

52. Russell-Wood, *Black Man*, 187–90.

53. Alida C. Metcalf, *Family and Frontier in Colonial Brazil: Santana de Parnaiba, 1580–1822* (Berkeley: University of California Press, 1992), 189.

54. Stuart Schwartz, *Slaves, Peasants, and Rebels: Reconsidering Brazilian Slavery* (Urbana: University of Illinois Press, 1992), 142; Donald Ramos, *A Social History of Ouro Preto: Stresses of Dynamic Urbanization in Colonial Brazil, 1695–1725* (Ann Arbor, MI: University Microfilms, 1972), 242–58; Metcalf, *Family and Frontier*, 189.

55. Sonia Maria Giacomini, *Mulher e escrava: Uma introdução historica ao estudo da mulher negra no Brasil* (Petropolis: Vozes, 1988), 51–54.

56. Mario Jose Maestri Filho, *Depoimentos de escravos Brasileiros* (São Paulo: Icone Editora Ltda., 1988), 33, 45.

57. Nancy Scheper-Hughes, *Death Without Weeping: The Violence of Everyday Life in Brazil* (Berkeley: University of California Press, 1992), 276–77.

58. Mattoso, *To Be a Slave in Brazil*, 113.

59. Ramos, *Social History*, 231–32.

60. Maestri Filho, *Depoimentos de escravos*, 33; Mattoso, "O filho da escrava," 78.

61. Horacio Gutierrez and Ida Lewkowicz, "Trabalho infantile em Minas Gerais na primeira metade do seculo XIX," *Locus: Revista de Historia* 5, no. 2 (1999): 14–16.

62. Ibid., 20–21.

63. Karasch, *Slave Life*, 68; Metcalf, "Searching for Slave Family," 294.

64. This was true in the São Paulo censuses I worked with as well as the Vila Rica census of 1804 and the Iguape census of Bahia for 1835.

65. See the discussion in B. J. Barickman, "Reading the 1835 Parish Censuses from Bahia: Citizenship, Kinship, Slavery, and Household in Early Nineteenth-Century Brazil," *The Americas* 59, no. 3 (2003): 309–10.

66. Giacomini, *Mulher e escrava*, 29. Also see Schwartz, *Slaves, Peasants, and Rebels*, in which he chides historians focusing on slave life or culture as possibly engaging in "ethnographic fantasy" (Schwartz, *Slaves, Peasants, and Rebels*, 39).

67. See the discussion in Metcalf, "Searching for the Slave Family," 292–93.

68. Schwartz, *Sugar Plantations*, 395–96, table 14–4.

69. Metcalf, *Family and Frontier*, 163.

70. Archivo do Estado de São Paulo, Macos de populacão, 1802 (based on analysis by Elizabeth Kuznesof).

71. Kuznesof, *Household Economy*, 82, table IV:5.

72. Ibid., 108.

73. Ibid., 108, 144.

74. Ibid., 83–84.

75. See Sandra Lauderdale Graham, *Caetana Says No: Women's Stories from a Brazilian Slave Society* (Cambridge: Cambridge University Press, 2002), 34, for a discussion of how nonslaves are introduced into slave families as part of a network of kin.

76. Francisco Vidal Luna and Herbert S. Klein, *Slavery and the Economy of São Paulo 1750–1850* (Stanford: Stanford University Press, 2003), 150; Donald Ramos, "City and Country: The Family in Minas Gerais, 1804–1838," *Journal of Family History* 3, no. 4 (1978): 375.

77. Evidence that slave owners in Spanish America also made efforts to keep children together with their mother or parents can be found in various sources. For Peru, see Frederick P. Bowser, *The African Slave in Colonial Peru: 1524–1650* (Stanford: Stanford University Press, 1974), 268–71.

78. Slenes, *Escravidão e família*, table 4, 227.

79. Lauderdale Graham, *Caetana*, 32.

80. Metcalf, "Searching for the Slave Family," 289. See also Iraci Del Nero da Costa, Robert W. Slenes, and Stuart B. Schwartz, "A família escrava em Lorena (1801)," *Estudos Economicos* 17, no. 2: 246–48; Richard Graham, "Slave Families on a Rural Estate in Colonial Brazil," *Journal of Social History* 9, no. 3 (spring 1976): 386, 390.

81. Alida C. Metcalf, "Vida familiar dos escravos em São Paulo no seculo dezoito: O caso de Santana de Parnaiba," *Estudos Economicos* 17, no. 2 (May/August 1987): 229–43.

82. Tarcisio Rodrigues Botelho, "Familias e escravarias: Demografia e familia escrava no norte de Minas Gerais no seculo XIX," *Populacão e Familia* 1, no. 1 (January/June 1998): 216–17, 222–33.

83. João Luis R. Fragoso and Manolo G. Florentino, "Marcelino, filho de Inocencia Ciroula, neto de Joana Cabinda: Um estudo sobre familias escravas em Paraiba do Sul (1835–1872)," *Estudos Economicos* 17, no. 2 (May/August 1987): 151–73.

84. Maestri Filho, *Depoimentos de escravos*, 33.

85. Ibid., 33.

86. Ibid., 5.

87. Karasch, *Slave Life*, and sources cited therein, 126–27.

88. Ibid., 59.

89. Sandra Lauderdale Graham, *House and Street: The Domestic World of Servants and Masters in Nineteenth-Century Rio de Janeiro* (Austin: University of Texas Press, 1988), 16.

90. Ibid., 60. Also see Ramos, *Social History*, 231.

91. Stanley Stein, *Vassouras: A Brazilian Coffee Country, 1850–1900* (New York: Atheneum, 1970), 22, 43–44. Schwartz, *Sugar Plantations*, 136.

92. Graham, "Slave Families," 390.

93. For an interesting discussion of the roça as a factor in slave autonomy, see Ciro Cardoso, "A brecha camponesa no sistema escravista," *Agricultura, escravidão e capitalismo* (Petropolis: n.p., 1979). See Fragoso and Florentino, "Marcelino," 151–73; Schwartz, *Sugar Plantations*, 156–57; Stein, *Vassouras*, 170–71.

94. Miguel Calmon du Pin e Almeida, *Ensaio sobre o fabrico do assucar* (Bahia: n.p., 1834), 60. Also see B. J. Barickman, "'A Bit of Land, Which They Call *Roça*': Slave Provision Grounds in the Bahian Reconcavo, 1780–1860," *Hispanic American Historical Review* 74, no. 4 (1994): 653.

95. Stein, *Vassouras*, 170. Stein does not specify if this meant both boys and girls or only boys.

96. Kiple, "Nutritional Link," 677–90.

97. Freedom as a constant possibility has been emphasized by several authors: Mattoso, *To Be a Slave in Brazil*, 145–49; Hebe Maria Mattos de Castro, *Das cores do silêncio: Os significados da liberdade no sudeste escravista, Brasil século XIX* (Rio de Janeiro: Arquivo Nacional, 1995); and Carl Degler, *Neither Black nor White: Slavery and Race Relations in Brazil and the United States* (New York: Macmillan, 1971).

98. Slenes, *Demography and Economics*, II:484–85.

99. Ibid., 228.

100. Representacão de Jose Bonifacio de Andrada e Silva a Assembleia Geral Constituinete, O Americano, 22/1/1848, as cited in Giacomini, *Mulher e escrava*, 33–34.

101. Mattoso, *To Be a Slave in Brazil*, 147. The figure might have been higher in Minas Gerais.

102. Ligia Bellini, "Por amor e por interese: A relacão senhor-escravo em cartas de alforria," in *Escravidão e invencão da liberdade: Estudos sobre o negro no Brasil*, comp. João Jose Reis (São Paulo: Editora brasiliense, 1988), 79–80.

103. Ibid.

104. See Kris Lane, "Captivity and Redemption: Aspects of Slave Life in Early Colonial Quito and Papayan," *The Americas* 57, no. 2 (2000): 225–46, for a discussion of the material capital/spiritual capital continuum.

105. See example in Graham, *Caetana*, 112.

106. Higgins, *"Licentious Liberty,"* 161. These were cases in Sabara from 1710–59.

107. Ramos, *Social History*, 248; Bellini, "Por amor," 81.

108. Schwartz, *Slaves, Peasants, and Rebels*, 46.

109. Metcalf, *Family and Frontier*, 171–72.

110. Higgins, *"Licentious Liberty,"* 145.

111. Ramos, *Social History*, 235.

CHAPTER EIGHT

Like a Servant or Like a Son?

Circulating Children in Northwestern Mexico (1790–1850)

LAURA SHELTON

MARTÍN, A YOUNG BOY OF EIGHT OR NINE YEARS WHO LIVED IN THE northwestern Mexican state of Sonora, could call many places home. He was the illegitimate son of Don José María Carlueyo, and his mother, a wet nurse, gave Martín to her sister when he was an infant. Martín's aunt in turn sent him to live with a man named Don Carlos Rivera, who had no biological connection to Martín's family. Martín's history of movement and "adoption" was recorded in the civil courts of Sonora, Mexico, because his father, Carlueyo, eventually tried to reclaim him in a custody battle against Rivera in 1843.[1]

While Martín's father accused Rivera of treating the boy as a common servant, or *criado*, Rivera argued that he alone had provided Martín with sustenance and education, as if Martín was his own son (*como hijo*). Martín's circulation from household to household and his ambiguous status as both an "adopted son" and servant reflect the lives of other children growing up outside the households of their biological parents in nineteenth-century Sonora.[2] The dispute over Martín, a boy who was a servant or perhaps an "adopted child," reveals a region in transition during a time when relationships of reciprocity and obligation between servant and *patrón*, and between child and elder, changed character in the context of nineteenth-century liberal expansion.

Politically, liberal expansion at this time translated into an emphasis on individual liberties, such as freedom of press, freedom of speech, and privileging individual property rights. In the particular case of Sonora, however, business leaders and politicians stressed privatization of property and laissez-faire economic policies. Sonorans who embraced liberalism did so largely hoping it would stimulate the mining industry and encourage exports, such as beef, wheat, and corn. Among the greatest challenges these Sonoran landowners and miners in the nineteenth century faced, however, was chronic labor shortages. In this context, employers tried many strategies to "recruit" and keep workers, including using the labor of children such as Martín.[3]

This essay focuses on custody battles as well as censuses, wills, assault charges, law codes, and accusations of flight from employment to explore how the informal practice of children circulation reflected the changing nature of childhood and parental obligation in early nineteenth-century northwestern Mexico. State authority, manifest in the form of the judiciary, enforced a form of patriarchy that granted ultimate authority over children to guardians rather than biological kin. Patriarchy, as a set of practices in which male household heads exerted economic, political, legal, and physical authority over female relatives and younger male kin, also extended to employers and their power over servants.[4] By the end of the colonial period in Sonora, custody disputes, wills, charges of flight, and law codes reveal the growing authority of the employer/guardian over servants, an authority that overshadowed even fathers' claims to custody. These cases suggest that during Sonora's liberal transition from a colonial outpost to republican statehood, local judges began to undermine *patria potestad*, a father's legally sanctioned right to exercise authority over his children, in favor of guardians who provided material support to the children they "adopted."[5]

Throughout Sonora's colonial and early republican history, taking in unrelated children was not part of a formal legal process of adoption. Rather, it was an informal social practice through which people provided care for young children with the expectation that the children would, in return, provide labor to the household as they grew older. During the course of the nineteenth century, however, guardians laid greater claim to the custody of the children they had raised, and, critically, they enjoyed legal support from local judges. Exchanging and circulating children among relatives and acquaintances became the nexus between an informal social practice with roots in the colonial era and the more systematic experimentation with convict labor, child labor, and other kinds of coerced labor systems in independent Mexico.

Martín's case, among others, provides a glimpse into the lives of abandoned children and orphans destined for an ambiguous form of servitude. His experience suggests that, in some contexts, the history of childhood can provide vital clues about how state governments' efforts to promote commercial expansion in nineteenth-century Latin America affected the daily lives of even the region's youngest residents.

In addition, the final ruling in Martín's case has a bearing on our understanding of the nature of patriarchy and its relationship to parental rights in Latin America during the region's "long nineteenth century." Ultimately, local judges in Sonora were willing to privilege the guardian's claims to Martín over Carlueyo's rights as the boy's father. Though Martín's father regained custody of his son, it was only on the condition that he agree to pay Martín's guardian for his expenditures, including food, clothing, lodging, and education.

Martín's case also reveals what made Sonora's patterns of child circulation and patronage unique. Scholars of Spanish America's urban centers have demonstrated how changes in the late colonial period—a growing emphasis on the practice of child rearing, parental responsibility, education, and financial support—generally benefited mothers as the patriarchal influence of the father waned.[6] Although custody disputes in Sonora echo these scholars' arguments about the larger pattern of decline in patria potestad, they also show that, in contrast to Latin America's colonial urban centers such as Mexico City and Lima, custody battles in the periphery mostly strengthened the authority of nonparental patrons or guardians over their servant/children. In Sonora, custody disputes in civil courts during the nineteenth century more often involved a parent and an unrelated guardian rather than two parents. In the eyes of the judges, whoever raised a child and bore the expenses of food, clothing, and education was entitled to custody, and therefore, the child's labor and loyalty later in life.

While Sonora's civil court archives contain only sixteen complete custody disputes—a relatively small number—these suits nonetheless reveal considerable detail about the daily lives of young children and the attitudes of their guardians in nineteenth-century Sonora.[7] Guardian and parent testimonies, although clearly influenced by the desire to maintain or gain custody, give glimpses into the ways people thought about child rearing and both moral and practical education. Over a period of several decades, guardians appealed to the same rhetoric of reciprocity and obligation between old and young to convince judges of their right to keep their young charges. During these custody cases and sometimes even in criminal suits, the children themselves also provided accounts of their living conditions and treatment. And neighbors, relatives, and other witnesses weighed in on the daily existence and care of these children. Thus the value of these sources is not strictly in their numbers but rather in their content and the extent to which they corroborate broader patterns in child circulation evident in wills, censuses, law codes, and criminal suits.

Although custody disputes were relatively uncommon, the practice of circulating children was more widespread than custody cases alone suggest. Children who lived with extended kin and unrelated guardians appeared in wills and censuses. Census takers, for example, generally referred to unrelated children as *criados*, *domésticos*, or *sirvientes*, recording the ages of everyone living in a household.[8] The ambiguous status of these dependant children is also evident in where they were listed in local censuses. Census takers sometimes placed them in two separate columns as both servants and as family members alongside children and spouses.

While censuses confirm the presence of children living with extended kin and unrelated guardians, wills and custody suits point to the larger importance of reciprocity in everyday social relations in Sonora. During the course of the century, ideals of reciprocity took on economic as well as sentimental significance. Credit and aid from neighbors and relatives often depended on personal reputation. Furthermore, reciprocity, whether in the form of labor, loans, or the promise to raise a child, involved relationships at all levels of local society. Most Sonoran communities were rural, and the presence of the state and the church was comparatively weak. In contrast, in urban centers in Latin America during this period, the elite embarked on the task of building orphanages and foundling hospitals. They enlisted the resources of a growing state and employed private charities and alliances with the church to create institutions that would eventually play a primary role in the lives of orphans and abandoned children. Sonora had no orphanages and no convents, the two institutions that typically took in abandoned children in urban settings.

In Sonora, the act of raising a child had priority over the fact of paternity, which, by tradition and law, was a basic feature of patriarchal right. A father's claim to his children was deemed less than that of a guardian's, particularly in terms of access to labor and reciprocity from children the latter had raised as dependents. A guardian/master's right held sway in Sonora's civil courts as the region embarked on an era of commercial growth and liberal reform by the second half of the nineteenth century.

Finally, custody disputes and other historical records reveal more than continuity and change in social custom and law in postcolonial northern Mexico. They shed light on how a social practice with roots in the region's colonial period—that of young children growing up among unrelated guardians and extended kin—played a part in facilitating nineteenth-century commercial expansion. In Sonora, where ambitious cattle ranchers and wheat growers complained constantly about needing more workers, taking in other people's children became one of several strategies for relieving chronic labor shortages.

The Diverse Origins of Circulating Children in Sonora

Although it is impossible to calculate exactly how many children in nineteenth-century Sonora shared Martín's experience of being raised outside of his natal home, several types of documentation suggest that the practice was as commonplace as it was informal. Orphans and illegitimate children were especially likely to circulate among extended kin, acquaintances, or strangers, but some children with surviving parents faced a similar fate. Collectively, the documents underscore the importance of extended family in raising and caring for children as well as displaced children's vulnerability to various kinds of abuses, particularly labor exploitation.

Guardians, however, understood child labor as a relationship based on reciprocity, obligation, and charity. In wills, guardians sometimes described their decision to take in a young criado as an act of personal piety, especially in light of the region's lack of orphanages and convents. But they also expected their young charges to show gratitude. If guardians provided food, clothing, and education, they expected children to reciprocate with their labor once they grew older, usually around age eight or nine. Thus, it is no coincidence that Sonora's custody battles involved children between the ages of eight and eleven.[9]

Labor patterns—including the use of young criados—changed dramatically as people in the region came to grips with their new political and
economic situation after the end of Spanish colonialism. With independence in 1821, northwestern Mexico faced the subsequent loss of Spanish
subsidies for defense against indigenous mobilization from Apaches on the
northern periphery and Yaquis to the south. In addition to armed rebellions
in 1825–27 and 1832–33 by the Yaquis, Apaches raided ranches, farms, and
small towns, causing residents to flee to neighboring settlements or to
leave the region entirely. By the 1830s, Apaches posed a serious challenge
to Mexican colonization and hopes for expanding commercial mining
and agriculture in the northern part of the state. Protracted civil warfare
among the region's leading families over issues such as regional autonomy
and the location of the state capital exacerbated indigenous rebellions.[10]

Because of the nearly constant warfare that Sonorans endured, some
historians have looked to raiding to explain the practice of guardians taking in young dependants for labor. High levels of adult mortality, warfare,
and kidnapping certainly contributed to children living apart from biological kin. In northern New Spain as well as other peripheral regions of
the Spanish empire in the colonial period, the Spanish and some indigenous groups engaged in systematic kidnapping of children during raids.[11]
Persistent warfare between Mexican and indigenous communities, particularly Apaches, increased the number of orphans living on Sonora's
northern periphery in Spanish, mestizo, and indigenous households.
Thus, the movement of children was, in part, rooted in the region's history of raiding and kidnapping, a violent practice that lasted well into the
nineteenth century.

Still, raiding and kidnapping among warring communities did
not account for all the children in Sonora raised away from their biological parents during the region's colonial era. Child circulation in late
eighteenth-century Sonora was especially prevalent when children were of
working age. Circulation crossed ethnic lines among groups that traditionally had more intimate contact with Spanish colonizers, including Opata
and Pima families.[12] This practice created social bonds between families of
diverse ethnic status during times of peace, and not all children growing
up among unrelated guardians were products of interethnic warfare.

Some districts of northwestern Mexico expanded as the region's economic orientation shifted from the Sonoran highlands to lowland urban
centers closer to the coast, particularly the district of Hermosillo. Here,

the rural economy took on an increasingly commercial character as agriculture shifted steadily from that of subsistence to market-oriented production. For notables, particularly *hacendados* and mine owners, devising sustainable and lucrative strategies for labor recruitment became a growing priority. Older, often ad hoc measures of circulating children among kin and neighbors to meet labor needs intersected with regional commercial expansion.[13]

Yet, although the region's "frontier" setting influenced how children circulated among kin and strangers, it is also clear that the practice was part of a broader trend evident throughout Latin America and Europe. Some historians of northern Mexico, like scholars of other peripheral regions, have argued that Sonora's isolation from "the center," the constant ethnic warfare, and its harsh environment created an exceptional regional identity with unique social practices. Yet similarities with the rest of Latin America and Europe suggest that some historical processes in northwestern Mexico are best understood in the context of political and economic changes occurring on a global scale.[14]

Students of the history of childhood in Europe have generally portrayed growing abandonment and illegitimacy as a result of population growth and industrialization in the nineteenth century. But these accounts fail to explain the prevalence of the practice in northern Mexico, where population grew only slowly and industrialization would not occur until the twentieth century.[15] Furthermore, as other chapters in this volume show, cultural practices of abandonment and the exchange of children date long before the eighteenth and nineteenth centuries in Iberian colonial regions.

Nonetheless, patterns of circulation certainly intensified in Sonora during the nineteenth century. Scholarship on the history of childhood in Latin America has pointed to the dramatic effects of commercialization, migration, and urbanization on child circulation during the postcolonial period. In cities, these children were vital links in the relationship between people across social status.[16] In more rural settings of Latin America, such as northeastern Brazil—a region that perhaps holds more in common with northern Mexico than does Mexico City—local elite turned to orphans for labor after the abolition of slavery in the late nineteenth century.[17] In northwestern Mexico, efforts to expand cattle ranching, mining, and wheat growing certainly drove Sonoran entrepreneurs to seek out much-needed labor in a variety of ways by looking to the region's indigenous communities, its jails, its debtors, and the children of less fortunate neighbors. By turning to these strategies, including the circulation of children, employers drew on social relationships and informal practices that had roots in the region's colonial past.

Finally, custody disputes, along with wills and civil proceedings over inheritance, underscore that the age-old issue of illegitimacy continued to be a reason why children were sent to live with extended kin and unrelated guardians, figuring prominently alongside warfare, poverty, and a parent's death. Census records reveal that plebeian men and women in consensual unions were more likely to raise their illegitimate children than were elites. But in cases where they could not afford to care for their offspring, these parents sometimes sent their children away with the hope that a guardian might provide a better future or, at the very least, relieve their own material woes.

The illegitimate children of notable families were sometimes sent away in order to protect the mother's public reputation.[18] These children of more privileged origin usually remained among extended kin, including aunts, uncles, and grandparents, but as some custody cases suggest, illegitimate children from more prominent families sometimes lived under conditions of servitude as well. Elites' attempts to hide illegitimate births met with limited success in these small rural communities. For notables, illegitimate births likely brought shame and dishonor to families. Indeed, communities on the periphery of northern Mexico shared social attitudes regarding female honor and legitimacy with Latin America's urban centers as well as Mediterranean Europe during the eighteenth and nineteenth centuries.[19] At the very least, unmarried women and their families in each of these regions turned to secrecy and abandonment as a strategy for dealing with their illegitimate offspring.

In spite of clear attempts to hide the identity of illegitimate children, court testimonies indicate that neighbors and friends often knew the true origins of offspring living among notable families. For example, in 1832, Ignacio Salazar, the illegitimate son of Josefa Salazar, filed a civil suit in Santa Ana to claim a share of his maternal grandfather's inheritance. Witnesses in the case testified that most people in the community knew Ignacio was actually the illegitimate son of Salazar, even though his grandfather had raised him as an "adopted son" in his own household.[20] But although a child's true identity was public knowledge (meaning most acquaintances and neighbors were aware of the child's origins), the offspring of these relationships still often faced displacement, living among extended kin or strangers.[21]

Custody and Patriarchy

Sonora's custody battles between parents and extended kin or unrelated guardians highlight an emerging uncertainty among court officials over whether guardians had a more legitimate claim to custody than did biological parents. Judges weighed patriarchal right against the guardians' claims to the labor of children they raised. While fathers often appealed to their rights of patria potestad, mothers, by law, had a more ambiguous legal claim to their offspring. Women could not, for example, manage their minor children's financial affairs without explicit permission of a husband or a judge and could never legally employ patria potestad in their attempts to establish guardianship of their offspring.[22] Nonparental guardians could only appeal to a sense of obligation and reciprocity to maintain custody of their young dependants, but they did so to great effect.

Court officials were decidedly sympathetic to claims of unrelated guardians and extended kin who could prove that they had cared for, fed, clothed, and educated a child. Among the twelve custody disputes that involved a contest between a parent and an unrelated guardian, only two parents, both fathers, gained custody of their children, and then only on the condition that they agree to repay the expenses the guardian had incurred while raising their children. Ties of reciprocity and obligation between children and their caregivers took precedence over biology for judges, who resolved that guardians had a more legitimate claim to their young charges' labor and loyalty.

Arguably, the judges' emphasis on child rearing and the costs of care and education of young dependants reflects the influence of Bourbon-era rhetoric, which stressed the practice of raising and educating children for the betterment of the state and society. As Sonya Lipsett-Rivera has argued, this shift in Bourbon policy could diminish a father's patriarchal authority over children while increasing the importance of motherhood, giving women stronger claims to the guardianship of their children.[23] In the case of Sonora, however, emphasis on rearing children also benefited guardians over all parents, both mothers and fathers, in legal contests. The impact of Bourbon policy varied depending on cultural context, and in northwestern Mexico, the informal practice of circulating children among extended kin and wealthier neighbors came to play a role in how Sonoran judges understood who was entitled to the custody of young dependants.

One of the earliest custody cases in the Sonoran judicial records was a 1792 dispute that proved typical of later custody battles because reciprocity and obligation between the child and the guardian figured prominently in the outcome. It involved a widow, Doña Isabel Pullol, and Jacinta Morena, the mother of a young boy named José Antonio.[24] Years before the legal battle, Doña Isabel's brother had an illicit relationship with Jacinta Morena, who gave birth to their illegitimate son, José Antonio. Since he was an infant, the child had lived with his aunt, who had received the boy from her brother, Don Francisco. At the time of the lawsuit, José Antonio was seven or eight. In her testimony, Doña Isabel complained repeatedly that she had made considerable sacrifices to raise and care for her nephew from the time he was a baby, and now that she was growing older, she depended on him to take care of her errands and other obligations. Doña Isabel also requested the testimony of a local mission priest, whom she had enlisted to teach José Antonio to read and to learn a trade. The case reached the Intendiente Gobernador, Don Enrique de Gumarest, who concluded that José Antonio should remain in the custody of his aunt, unless his mother paid for the costs Doña Isabel incurred while raising the boy. Doña Isabel ultimately maintained custody of her nephew in large part because she was able to convince Gumarest that she, and not his biological mother, was deserving of José Antonio's companionship and assistance now that she was an aging widow, precisely because she had raised the boy and provided him with an education.[25]

Just over fifty years later in the town of Rayón, a father, Don José María Varela, sued a widow, Gertrudis Contreras, for custody of his illegitimate daughter, María del Rosario Varela, who was around seven years old. Although Don José María could not claim his daughter as his legitimate heir, he did argue that under patria potestad he had the right to have custody of his daughter, especially since she had reached an age at which the law prescribed a child's education falls to the father. Gertrudis, however, called Don José María's claim to patria potestad into question, since María del Rosario was a product of an adulterous relationship as Don José María was married to another woman when he had an illicit relationship with María del Rosario's mother. In addition to questioning the father's appeals to patria potestad, Gertrudis argued that she had made considerable sacrifices to raise José María's daughter, expecting that the girl would care for her in old age.

Her pleas mirrored the invocation of reciprocity made fifty years earlier by the widow and aunt, Isabel Pollul, but Gertrudis's appeals to reciprocity were less effective. This time, the court sided with the father, but largely because Don José María could prove he had provided money for his daughter's care throughout her childhood. Neighbors who testified on Don José María's behalf stressed again and again that he had fulfilled his parental obligations to María del Rosario by paying for a wet nurse after her mother died in childbirth and by giving Contreras money for clothing and food. Gertrudis tried to appeal the decision, also stressing her own sacrifices in providing María del Rosario with food, clothing, and a decent moral education, but, unfortunately, the final outcome of her case is lost.[26]

These two cases, although occurring more than fifty years apart, demonstrate how court officials privileged those who could prove that they had paid for the care and education of a child, sometimes over biology. Complete custody disputes are scarce, but the cases consistently reflect a long pattern of guardians and extended kin using similar language and rhetoric, arguing that guardians who cared for and educated children deserved loyalty and devotion later in life. Rulings in these cases implicitly diminished the rights of biological parents, including fathers, who could not prove they provided material support for their children. Moreover, they legitimated the role of the state in mediating disputes over patriarchal authority.

In addition to custody battles, Sonora's servant laws from the early nineteenth century provide further insight into the fact that lawmakers in the region understood the relationship between employers and their young servants as similar to that between a father and his child. This legislation, passed in 1831 and again in 1843, bestowed employers with tremendous power over the physical mobility and day-to-day conduct of their workers and permitted corporal punishment. Workers had to receive formal permission to leave their employer's property, and employers could punish them if they disobeyed the law. The 1843 law explicitly gave employers responsibility for the religious and moral education of their servants, and for the first time, it emphasized the importance of this parent-like obligation in the cases of young male and female workers and all domestic servants. These laws certainly buttressed the image of the employer as a kind of "father figure" to his workers by codifying the employer/guardian's authority over the moral and religious conduct of his youngest workers. Thus, their relationship was not simply a contractual arrangement limited to the exchange of labor for wages. Although these laws were designed for all workers regardless of their age, the articles emphasized their applicability to young servants, enshrining the ambiguous status between young dependants as servants and "adopted" children in mid-nineteenth-century state law.[27]

The Question of Treatment

Displaced children were in an unequivocally subordinate position in relationship to their guardians, and the term criado more accurately described the status of most of these children than does "adopted child."[28] Final wills and testaments provide some insight into the fate of indigenous servant children raised in mestizo and Spanish households in colonial Sonora, demonstrating how living and working conditions among them varied from those of extreme violence and depravation to relatively benign paternalism. In 1798, for example, in the city of Arizpe, Antonia Ana de Murrieta left one of her criados, Gabriel Padilla, a house in her will. Gertrudis Corella, also from Arizpe, left an Apache servant named José Corella fifty pesos, while another servant received an orchard. Both Corella and Murrieta mentioned in their wills that these servants had lived with them from childhood.[29]

Murrieta and Corella, like others who raised indigenous children as dependants, often recognized those who obeyed them and remained in their service with property and explicitly chastised and "disinherited" others who proved less reliable. Murrieta, for instance, withdrew sixty pesos from a child she had raised because he had been "ungrateful" for her care and education. The money instead went to another, a criado of Apache descent, whom she had also raised.[30] These criados—some favored, others "disowned"— were mostly captured indigenous children who had lived with their guardian/employers (*amos*) from a very young age. In their wills, women such as Corella and Murrieta often wrote about their relationship with these servants in familial terms, describing how they had raised them from early childhood (*infancia*). These gestures of largesse and censure demonstrate the ambiguous position of criados, and, on occasion, they reveal a sense of paternalistic responsibility and genuine affection. But while sentiments of filial bonds are evident in some wills, by their nature, these documents tell us more about the guardian's viewpoint, and we have little idea whether the affection conveyed by the adults was reciprocated by the criados.

What is more, other kinds of evidence, largely from penal records, demonstrate that violence could as easily dominate relationships between children and their guardians as could affection. In addition to using their labor, guardians, like biological parents, some abused their dependants. It is impossible to know if children who circulated among extended kin and acquaintances were treated worse than children raised in their natal households, since only extreme mistreatment of any child concerned court officials. A case involving Florentina Reina of Hermosillo, who regularly beat and mistreated her "adopted son," Juan Martínez Encinas, suggests that other family members and neighbors intervened in only the direst situations, as was often true too with *mal trato* cases in marriage.[31] In Martínez's case, neighbors had long disapproved of how Reina dealt with Juan, in large part because he was only five to seven years old. Still, they intervened only after Reina burned the child's feet, impairing his ability to walk normally for the rest of his life.

As Nara Milanich has suggested in her study of child circulation in nineteenth-century Chile, the violence children such as Juan Martínez endured was part of the subordination inherent in their ambiguous status as "adopted children" and criados. In addition to the imbalance in the relationship brought on by their comparative youth, many children also confronted a class and ethnic order in which guardians held a privileged status.[32] Among female criadas, prevailing gender norms tolerated a certain degree of sexual assault, especially among the young. For example, in the city of Hermosillo in 1832, a thirteen-year-old girl identified only as María Josefa accused her guardians, Miguel Cruz and his wife, Luz Salazar, of forcing her to have sex with a neighbor. María Josefa claimed that Miguel forcibly placed her in a room with an older man who raped her and paid Miguel one hundred pesos. On another evening, Miguel's wife, Luz, tried to bring another man to have sex with María Josefa, but she escaped. According to María Josefa, she had lived with Miguel and Luz for about three weeks at the time of the accusation, and she told the judge that she had been poorly treated during her stay with them, charging Luz in particular of trying to turn her into a prostitute.[33]

Thus, while under the best of circumstances, relationships with guardians could encompass acts of charity and sometimes even bequests of property, corporal punishment and abuse of power also characterized relationships between guardian and child. Moreover, while some emerging orphanages in Latin America's urban centers made attempts to ensure the safety of abandoned children by requiring contracts promising good treatment from guardians, Sonora had no comparable requirements. Only the willingness of neighbors, local priests, and the courts to intervene for a child offered some recourse.[34]

A case of fourteen-year-old Manuel Moreno from San Felipe reveals that under the worst conditions some children, especially older ones, took matters in their own hands and fled mistreatment. When Manuel's uncle, Rafael Quijada, went before the judge in Arizpe to complain that Manuel had escaped his custody to live with another uncle, he referred to Manuel interchangeably as a "servant" (sirviente) and as his "nephew" (sobrino). According to the uncle's testimony, Manuel Moreno fled multiple times, and, on one occasion, Rafael Quijada had his sons and other servants hunt for the youth and bring him back, where he was whipped publicly as punishment for leaving his employment. Rafael paid Manuel for his labor, and, in his initial suit, he also complained that Manuel owed him around three pesos for a monthly salary he had advanced the youth before his flight.[35] In daily practice, the relationship between Rafael and Manuel was one of employment more than a filial bond between elder and youth.

Conclusion

The case of Manuel Moreno again highlights an important pattern in the relationships between children and guardians in the nineteenth century: the ambiguity children experienced when raised outside their natal households. Far from new, the practice of sending children to live with and work for extended family, neighbors, and even strangers had colonial precedents. Kidnappings and raids of rebellious indigenous neighbors, along with abandonment, illegitimacy, poverty, and migration, contributed to the circulation of children in Sonora. But these social practices changed in character during the region's postcolonial era, when Sonoran landowners and entrepreneurs tried various strategies to recruit the labor they needed to fulfill their goals of commercial expansion on Mexico's northern periphery. Although the emphasis on child rearing over biology may have weakened patriarchal authority within families, evidence from custody battles, legal disputes between criados and their guardian/masters, and state servant laws suggest that another kind of patriarchy—that which bound workers to their *patrones*—grew stronger. Significantly, local notables did not create a new ideology and rhetoric to justify the power they enjoyed in these arrangements. Rather, they drew on "traditional" visions of filial loyalty, obligation, reciprocity, and respect to move them into a new period of commercial expansion by the end of the nineteenth century.

✦ NOTES ✦

The author would like to thank the editors of this volume, Ondina González and Bianca Premo, and Meghan Winchell for comments on drafts of this essay.

1. Archivo Histórico del Gobierno del Estado de Sonora (hereafter, AHGES), Fondo Poder Judicial, Civil (hereafter, FJC), Hermosillo, vol. 1244, "Promovido por Don José María Carlueyo reclamando un hijo bastardo á Gertrudis Miranda," 1843.

2. In this essay, I use Nara Milanich's expression, "circulation of children," which is how she characterizes the widespread movement of children raised outside their natal households in nineteenth-century Chile. This concept aptly describes similar processes occurring in Sonora during the same period. See Nara Milanich, "The Children of Fate: Families, Class, and the State in Chile, 1857–1930" (PhD diss., Yale University, 2002), 197–206.

3. I also identify the emergence of liberal ideology through the language plaintiffs used to describe themselves, particularly their increasing use of the term *ciudadano*, or citizen, as opposed to the colonial term vecino, or resident, with specific legal privileges. See Charles Hale, *Mexican Liberalism in the Age of Mora, 1821–1853* (New Haven, CT: Yale University Press, 1968), 39. For a systematic examination of changes in land reform in Sonora, see Saúl Jerónimo Romero, *De las misiones a los ranchos y haciendas: La privatización de la tenencia de la tierra en Sonora, 1740–1860* (Hermosillo, Mexico: Gobierno del Estado de Sonora, Secretaría de Educación y Cultura, 1995).

4. See Bradford E. Burns, *Patriarch and Folk: The Emergence of Nicaragua, 1798–1858* (Cambridge, MA: Harvard University Press, 1991); Elizabeth Dore, "The Holy Family: Imagined Households in Latin American History," in *Gender Politics in Latin America: Debates in Theory and Practice* (New York: Monthly Review Press, 1997), 101–17; Gerda Lerner, *The Creation of Patriarchy* (New York and Oxford: Oxford University Press, 1986).

5. Patriarchal authority of the father in colonial and nineteenth-century Latin America was encoded in law, a concept known as patria potestad. Patria potestad refers to a father's legal authority over his legitimate offspring. See Joaquín Escriche, *Diccionario razonado de legislación civil, penal, comercial y forense, 1837* (Mexico City: Universidad Nacional Autónoma de México, 1996), 515–16. For discussions of how laws related to patria potestad changed

over time in Mexico, see Silvia M. Arrom, "Changes in Mexican Family Law in the Nineteenth Century: The Civil Codes of 1870 and 1884," *Journal of Family History* 10, no. 3 (1985): 307–10.

6. Sonya Lipsett-Rivera provides an excellent analysis of Bourbon-era ideologies on child rearing and family law and explains the meaning of *educación* in the context of eighteenth-century Mexico, which referred not only to formal training but also proper upbringing (Sonya Lipsett-Rivera, "Marriage and Family Relations in Mexico During the Transition from Colony to Nation," in *State and Society in Spanish America During the Age of Revolution*, ed. Victor M. Uribe-Uran [Wilmington, DE: Scholarly Resources, 2001], 138–41). For late colonial Lima, Bianca Premo also uncovers a growing emphasis on education, material support, and good treatment in custody disputes before royal judges, who were generally receptive to these arguments from litigants, whether fathers, mothers, or unrelated guardians (Bianca Premo, *Children of the Father King: Youth, Authority, and Legal Minority in Colonial Lima* [Chapel Hill: University of North Carolina Press, 2005], 181–201).

7. Among sixteen complete custody disputes, only four involved estranged spouses. In the other twelve cases, either a mother or a father reclaimed a child or children from an extended relative, such as an aunt, or from an unrelated guardian.

8. For census records, see AHGES, Fondo Poder Ejecutivo (hereafter, FE), Aconchi, Banámichi, Cumpas, Huepac, vol. 258, 1848; AHGES, FE, Hermosillo, vol. 1088, 1840; AHGES, FE, Hermosillo, vol. 258, 1853.

9. The fact that biological parents initiated these suits when their children were between ages eight and eleven suggests that perhaps they too were moved by a desire for labor as well as by feelings of attachment.

10. For discussion of these regional conflicts, see Biblioteca Central de la Universidad de Sonora, Colección Pesqueria (BCUSCP), José Francisco Velasco, *Noticias estadísticas del Estado de Sonora*, 172–73; Stuart Voss, *On the Periphery of Nineteenth-Century Mexico: Sonora and Sinaloa, 1810–1877* (Tucson: University of Arizona Press, 1982).

11. For studies of violence, kidnapping, and "adoption" in other peripheral regions of northern Mexico as well as Latin America, see Ana María Alonso, *Thread of Blood: Colonialism, Revolution, and Gender on Mexico's Northern Frontier* (Tucson: University of Arizona Press, 1995), 44–45; James Brooks, *Captives & Cousins: Slavery, Kinship, and Community in the Southwest Borderlands* (Chapel Hill: University of North Carolina Press, 2002); José Mateo, "Bastardos y concubinas: La ilegitimidad conyugal y filial en la frontera pampeana bonaerense (Lobos 1810–1869)," *Boletín del Insituto de historia*

Argentina y Americana 13, no. 3 (1996): 7–34; Gabriel Salazar, *Labradores, peones y proletarios* (Santiago: Ediciones Sur, 1984); Susan Socolow, "Spanish Captives in Indian Societies: Cultural Contact Along the Argentine Frontier, 1600–1835," *Hispanic American Historical Review* 72, no. 1 (1992): 73–99.

12. Cynthia Radding, *Wandering Peoples, Colonialism, Ethnic Spaces, and Ecological Frontiers in Northwestern Mexico: 1700–1850* (Durham, NC: Duke University Press, 1997), 126–27.

13. For analysis of nineteenth-century commercial expansion and how it affected labor relations in the second half of the century, see Miguel Tinker Salas, *In the Shadow of the Eagles: Sonora and the Transformation of the Border During the Porfiriato* (Berkeley: University of California Press, 1997), 48–57.

14. For examples and discussions of these two threads in borderland historiography, see Radding, *Wandering Peoples*, 1–5; 307–10; Voss, *On the Periphery of Nineteenth-Century Mexico*, 24–27.

15. For example, see Rachel G. Fuchs, *Abandoned Children: Foundlings and Child Welfare in Nineteenth-Century France* (Albany: State University of New York Press, 1984); Colin Heywood, *A History of Childhood: Children and Childhood in the West from Medieval to Modern Times* (Cambridge: Polity Press, 2001), 80–82. For an excellent discussion of the historiography of child abandonment in Italy, see David I. Kertzer, *Sacrificed for Honor: Italian Infant Abandonment and the Politics of Reproductive Control* (Boston: Beacon Press, 1993), 170–81.

16. Donna Guy, "Parents Before the Tribunals: The Legal Construction of Patriarchy in Argentina," in *Hidden Histories of Gender and the State in Latin America*, ed. Elizabeth Dore and Maxine Molyneux (Durham, NC: Duke University Press, 2000), 179; Linda Lewin, *Surprise Heirs I: Illegitimacy, Patrimonial Rights, and Legal Nationalism in Luso-Brazilian Inheritance, 1750–1821* (Stanford: Stanford University Press, 2003), 81–83; Milanich, "Children of Fate," 199.

17. Joan E. Meznar, "Orphans and the Transition from Slave to Free Labor in Northeast Brazil: The Case of Campina Grande, 1850–1888," *Journal of Social History* 27, no. 3 (1994): 499–515.

18. Some evidence suggests that plebian men and women in consensual unions raised their children themselves amid little or no scandal, and when property was at stake, they married later in life, as the case of Dolores Valenzuela and Pedro Muñoz illustrates. Dolores and Pedro only married when Pedro was on his deathbed, in part to ensure that Dolores and his children would inherit his estate. See AHGES, FJC, Hermosillo, vol. 1223, "Promovido por Dolores Valenzuela contra Luz Espinosa por restitución de algunos enseres," 1836.

19. Silvia M. Arrom, *The Women of Mexico City, 1790–1857* (Stanford: Stanford University Press, 1985); Ramón Gutiérrez, *When Jesus Came, the Corn Mothers Went Away: Marriage, Sexuality, and Power in New Mexico, 1500–1846* (Stanford: Stanford University Press, 1991); Kertzer, *Sacrificed for Honor*, 25–29; Linda Lewin, *Surprise Heirs II: Illegitimacy, Inheritance Rights, and Public Power in the Formation of Imperial Brazil, 1822–1889* (Stanford: Stanford University Press, 2003), 73–75; Muriel Nazzari, "An Urgent Need to Conceal: The System of Honor and Shame in Colonial Brazil," in *The Faces of Honor: Sex, Shame, and Violence in Colonial Latin America*, ed. Lyman L. Johnson and Sonya Lipsett-Rivera (Albuquerque: University of New Mexico Press, 1998), 103–26.

20. AHGES, FJC, Hermosillo, vol. 1208, "Don José Ignacio Salazar contra José Martín Salazar en que el primero reclama al segundo la herencia que le pertenence como hijo natural de la Señora Josefa Salazar," 1832.

21. Ann Twinam's treatment of public versus private knowledge in cases of illegitimacy during the colonial period is relevant to nineteenth-century Sonora because witnesses made distinctions between private and public knowledge based on levels of intimacy. They also used the expression "public and notorious" to describe knowledge that extended beyond family and intimate friendships. See Ann Twinam, *Public Lives, Private Secrets: Gender, Honor, Sexuality, and Illegitimacy in Colonial Spanish America* (Stanford: Stanford University Press, 1999), 26–29.

22. Premo, *Children of the Father King*, 24–25.

23. Lipsett-Rivera, "Marriage and Family Relations in Mexico," 138.

24. Widows were especially likely to take in orphaned and illegitimate children, and they were well represented in the custody disputes discussed above. Census data from throughout the region also suggests that widows, especially those without direct heirs, took in and raised children with the expectation that these children would reciprocate and provide them with support as they grew older.

25. "Con agravío y perjuicio notable mio, pues habiendo criado a dicho mi sobrino hasta la edad referida y estando ya viuda me servia de compañia, a ayudaba en algunas mandaditos, por lo cual a Usted suplico y pido que mande en Justicia ó que se me entregue el dicho mi sobrino pues no es razón que después de haberlo criado con mucho trabajo otro lo logré ya criados." AHGES, FJC, Hermosillo, vol. 1200, "Promovido por Isabel Pullol contra Jacinta Moreno reclamando un niño hijo de la Moreno," 1792, 3.

26. AHGES, FJC, Ures, vol. 2481, "Promovido por Don José María Varela contra Gerturdis Contreras sobre una niña que le reclama," 1846.

27. BCUSCP, *Leyes y decretos del Estado de Sonora, 1831–1850*, 26–33.

28. Witnesses in these cases used expressions such as "*hijo adoptivo*" or "*como hijo*." See AHGES, FJC, Hermosillo, vol. 654, "Criminal contra Florentina Reina por haber encendiado depravadan a su hijo adoptivo," 1842.

29. AHGES, Fondo Notarios, "Testamento cerrado de Antonia Ana De Murrieta," 1798. Cited in María del Carmen Tonella Trelles, "Las mujeres en los testamentos registrados en los distritos de Hermosillo y Arizpe, Sonora, 1786–1861: Una indagación acerca de la condición femenina en la frontera" (master's thesis, Universidad de Sonora, 2000), 58.

30. Ibid.

31. "Sabe que Florentina Reina le da mala vida al niño que tiene como hijo adoptivo." AHGES, FJC, Hermosillo, vol. 654, "Criminal contra Florentina Reina por haber encendiado depravadan a su hijo adoptivo," 1842, 7. Mal trato refers to instances when husbands abused their authority over their wives by using excessive physical punishment and/or deprived them of material support. See Richard Boyer, "Women, *La Mala Vida*, and the Politics of Marriage," in *Sexuality and Marriage in Colonial Latin America*, ed. Asunción Lavrin (Lincoln: University of Nebraska Press, 1989), 252–69.

32. Milanich, "Children of Fate," 236–38.

33. AHGES, FJP, Hermosillo, vol. 614, "Causa contra Miguel Castro y su esposa por estupro," 1832, 4.

34. Ibid., 237.

35. AHGES, Fondo Poder Judicial, Penal, Hermosillo, vol. 658, "Promovido por Rafael Quijada contra su sobrino como sirviente por fugo y como respetados su tío Marcelo Quijada," 1842.

Conclusion

"The Little Hiders" and Other Reflections on the History of Children in Imperial Iberoamerica

BIANCA PREMO

∞

✢ MEXICAN CHILDREN PLAY HIDE-AND-SEEK. OR, BETTER SAID, THEY play *escondidillas* (the little hiders), a game that looks a great deal like hide-and-seek but in which the rules are different. Each little player counts to eighteen, a number that, to my knowledge, has no magical meaning in games played in the United States. What is more, in Mexico, unlike in parts north, there is a potentially rotating designation of who is "it," and players can rely on the possibility of "salvation" from discovery.

The "little hiders" serve as a fitting metaphor for final reflections on this volume and on the craft of writing histories of children in the Spanish and Portuguese empires in general. On one level, the metaphor works for our own understanding of those histories. For readers who are familiar only with the hide-and-seek version of childhood, the histories of children in early modern Spain, Portugal, and colonial Latin America follow enough of the expected form that they lend themselves to direct translation. Thus, the chapters in this book focus on what we broadly refer to in our vernacular as "children" or "youths." They do not study, say, *primera edad*, or *puercia*—two Spanish terms employed during the era that dissected "youth" into various scientific or moral stages but also terms that appeared more often in official tracts or intellectuals' musings than in real life, much like today's child developmentalists might refer to "reflexive" and "intuitive" stages.

At the same time, the histories, like the game, demand to be expressed in their original idioms and not merely matched to modern (U.S.) equivalents. For example, rituals of community welcome following birth may have been common then as they are now, but few of us have celebrated the arrival of a new baby in a culture of death such as existed in the seventeenth century, where laboring mothers routinely risked their lives to birth children who themselves might perish within days. Or, as another example, the idea that children must be guided, and sometimes disciplined, to adhere to social norms may have existed among adults there as they do here, but it is easy to imagine a modern state agent of family social services being severely shocked by Ursula Suárez's Lenten ritual of self-flagellation.

In the arenas of historiography, theory, and historical methodology, too, "the little hiders" hold resonance. Historiographically, they evoke the elusiveness of children in scholarship on early modern Iberia and colonial Latin America—a disappearing act so visible that even recent contributions to the field adopt titles or intellectual framings that underline their topic's forgotten status.[1] Indeed, as scholarship on the history of children in the region and period has grown in recent years, it has become conventional to note that historians of the Iberoamerican empires are quite late to the game.

However, I would like to propose that these scholars are not so much trying to jump into a game already in progress as they are playing by somewhat different rules. In this conclusion to the chapters of *Raising an Empire*, I would like to offer a brief series of suggestions about how writing children into the history of the Iberoamerican empires offers alternatives to the topical and theoretical guidelines established in the history of childhood elsewhere in the world, alternatives that both raise new questions and force us to return to the classic topics of inquiry in the field.

The first alternative the essays in *Raising an Empire* provide is to unravel the traditional entwining of the history of childhood and the history of modernity. As noted in the introductory essay and as Jorge Rojas Flores also points out, a critique of modernity—of our own expectations of children and childhood—underpinned the *longue dureé*, social historical approach that Philippe Ariès advanced in his foundational *Centuries of Childhood*.[2] To recap, according to Ariès, although childhood as we know it may not have "existed" before approximately the seventeenth century, and although parents may have been "indifferent" to children, the creation of modern conceptions of childhood did not advance children's status or position in family and society. Rather, modernity ultimately regimented and disciplined children into isolation from adults.[3] In the hands of both his disciples and critics, Ariès's argument was twisted into an invective against the "abusive" parents of premodern times.[4] Yet, regardless of whether the historians of childhood who wrote in the 1970s and 1980s saw any progress in the treatment of children—regardless of whether they portrayed the dark ages as taking place in the sixteenth century or in our own era—many shared Ariès's conviction that we now live in "modern times." And modernity, as much as children, was their subject of analysis.

If childhood and children *qua* "history of childhood" in the Iberian world failed to draw scholarly attention among historians while it became a cottage industry among U.S. and European scholars, this had to do in part with the scholarly conviction that the postcolonial nations of Latin America and their mother countries were and are underdeveloped and traditional.[5] Thus, scholars of Iberoamerica felt less enticed to engage modernity, and hence childhood, as a premise for historical study. This does not mean, of course, that historians of Latin America worked in a world entirely apart from their U.S. and European counterparts since ancillary fields associated with the topic of children, particularly family and gender history, thrived. Yet historians of these regions were far more likely to be busy explaining how their poor and often politically troubled regions became poor and politically troubled (that is, failed to modernize at all) or were more preoccupied with examining the relationship between kinship, class, and state formation than in grieving modernity's effect on youthful innocence or celebrating the virtues of post-Enlightenment bourgeois child care.[6]

Many of the authors in this volume, therefore, write with different sensibilities than did those who pioneered the history of childhood in non-Iberian Europe and the United States, opening the second alternative route the history of childhood takes in Iberoamerica. In most of the essays in this volume, childhood in the past is presented not chiefly as a means to understand what modernity has won or lost for children but instead is taken more broadly, as an opportunity to better understand how the early modern Iberian political and social order, and its bequest of colonialism to

Latin Americans, was lived and reproduced. Thus the essays permit us new insights into the critical role of child rearing within the larger context of the history of colonialism rather than "modernity."

This is not to say that familiar themes in the story of Western cultural and political change (and even the rise of "modernity," if defined as enlightened, post–Old Regime republicanism) are missing here. Those who insist on viewing Iberia and its American colonies as a world apart from Europe or the United States may be surprised to see expected changes in concepts and practices associated with children occurring at the predicted times. For example, crucial transformations took place particularly during the imperial reforms of the late eighteenth century and during colonial crisis and collapse in the early nineteenth—periods covered in the essays by Isabel dos Guimarães Sá, Ann Twinam, and Laura Shelton. In this respect, we find that Latin America and Iberia share something in common with the United States, France, and Britain, where, historians have told us, the rise of the modern state and liberalism had quite a dramatic effect on traditional concepts of childhood, family order, and patriarchal power.[7]

Yet it is undeniable that the advent of rational social policy or the rise of liberalism occurred differently in a colonial context—a context that Shelton reminds us was at once intensely local and imperial. And it is this context that made Latin American childhood distinct. This uniqueness should not be sacrificed in order to force these histories into any prefabricated molds derived from the existing scholarship on children in the "West."

Put differently, the perceived difference between the "West" and the "rest" allows scholars of the history of childhood in Spain, Portugal, and Latin America to approach early modern children on their own terms, regardless of whether those terms intersect with well-developed subfields or fall outside the parameters established by Ariès. Ondina González and Valentina Tikoff are able to use understudied institutions in Seville and Havana to reconsider established tenets in the history of early modern charity, ground that has indeed been fertile in the history of childhood. But, at the same time, other authors move in historiographical circles fully apart from the literature on childhood elsewhere. Teresa Vergara firmly situates her study of immigrant Indian youths in seventeenth-century Lima within a larger corpus of scholarship on the cultural transformations the Spanish conquest brought to (or wrought on) traditional Andean identity and community ties. Meanwhile Elizabeth Kuznesof plumbs

African anthropology for homologues to Brazilian slave rituals and rites of passage.

It is worth noting that two of these chapters—Isabel dos Guimarães Sá's contribution on Portugal and Kuznesof's chapter on Brazilian slavery—draw extensively from secondary materials and preexisting literatures. Both reveal that simply reading historiographies on related fields, or consulting royal biographies or demography with an eye for the smallest individuals that inhabit their pages often yields as much information about Iberoamerican children as does an archive.

The use of secondary sources to write such chapters raises certain doubts about just how hidden our "little hiders" really are. In large part, childhood is still an undiscovered aspect of colonial lives because children have been thought to be elusive in historical documentation, even in an age when most ordinary adults left barely a written trace of their lives. Often too young to speak for themselves, even when they reached adolescence, parents, guardians, and colonial officials frequently spoke publicly for those of minority age, leaving behind records rarely reflecting children's voices.

Yet not only is there a history of childhood to be told, there is often more than one history of childhood that can be recovered from archival sources, as the two chapters by González and Twinam on Havana's Casa Joseph reveal. In one sense, these chapters can be read together, as a longer story of changing official attitudes toward abandoned children in the course of the eighteenth century. In another sense, these chapters should be considered separately, for even the history of a single institution for children can open up to reveal several broad historical phenomenon, including concepts of charity, race, social status, and notions of the "public good."

Furthermore, the histories that the authors of this volume reconstruct are not always official stories about attitudes toward children; these scholars are able to reconstruct individual lives and even the experiences of children and adolescents in surprising detail. We gain insight about the lives of real, historical children from sources that, we have been told, are too obscured by generic formula or political motives to reveal them: we see the remembered experience of an individual child from Rojas's intense reading of Ursula's *Relación*; we explore the extent and limits of parental affect and aspirations for their children from institutional records explored by Tikoff, González, and Twinam; we journey on the circuitous routes to integration in urban colonial society led by Vergara. Thus a third alternative offered in the volume is methodological.

The contributors creatively contend with the challenge in finding children in historical documentation by employing a variety of analytical tools, sometimes examining children individually or anecdotally, other times analyzing their lives in the aggregate. We find that mortality rates in Havana's foundling home or silences in the counts of human beings transported on slave ships reaching Brazil from Africa tell a story as compelling as any nun's intimate autobiography. Ultimately, the methodological lesson here is more a matter of the way we read sources than of children's historical "silence." Historians of childhood in Iberoamerica can draw not only from historical sources long ignored by political and economic historians, such as notary records or institutional records and court cases, but also reopen the pages of dog-eared sources and find the children who have been assumed lost.

As with most questions of scholarly method, this alternative also has theoretical ramifications. Some readers, particularly those following recent trends in the history of childhood, might be surprised at the number of adults that populate the pages of this volume and at the way its authors invite us to learn about how children were implicated in "traditional" historical topics of institutions, royal policy, and local politics. Indeed, as is clear from González's retracing of the historiographical development in the field in the introduction to this volume, much recent work on the theme of childhood, both about Iberoamerica and beyond, consciously eschews interpretive concerns that once dominated the field, such as those about changes in adult-child relations and whether parents loved or abused children in the past. This departure often takes the form of assertions about the importance of recognizing children's agency, or active protagonism, in historical processes as opposed to writing histories that are "really" about adults.[8]

Yet one of the most interesting aspects of the histories of children in *Raising an Empire*, I find, is the degree to which children were key colonial subjects—sometimes even objects—who were fought over, thought about, or studiously ignored by the adults around them. Here, I by no means speak for all of the authors in the volume, whose conviction that children should be viewed as significant social and economic actors in the past has borne considerable fruit in uncovering their "hidden" histories. But I would like to suggest that historians of childhood and children in

Iberoamerica are in a singularly advantageous position to move the field in a new direction, away from the "hidden history" genre. Rather than remaining content to "recover" children's past, rather than construing the belief that children and adolescents exercised agency in the past as license to isolate our subjects from their relationships and experiences with powerful individuals, groups, institutions, and transcendental phenomena, we can freely explore the connections between everyday patterns of growing up and traditional historical themes. To write a history of children that does not include in its basic narrative the adults who surrounded them (be they parents, teachers, or even judges and kings) and the concepts and ideologies that shaped their interactions with them (be they local customs or even high-minded policies and rarefied intellectual ruminations) would be to produce a story devoid of questions of power. And, ultimately and ironically, it would be to erase the possibility of children's agency.

Writing adults, institutions, and politics out of the history of childhood also risks truncating the larger context of conquest and empire-making that shaped not only the economic and political life of early modern Spain, Portugal, and the Americas but also the intimate social world through which that life was experienced. In the early seventeenth century, the indigenous Peruvian chronicler Felipe Guamán Poma de Ayala implied that the rearing and socialization of native children was a terrain on which the colonial enterprise might flounder or flourish. He admonished the Spanish crown that teaching the children of the recently "discovered" lands of the Americas the Catholic faith and "civilized" customs was a critical aspect of Spanish rule that had to be approached with care.[9] What the chronicler understood was that, in the end, Iberian colonialism in the Americas was not only a process of pulling silver from the craggy hills of Upper Peru or wringing sugar from water mills in Brazil. It was process, too, of forging sentimental ties between adults and children in ordinary, domestic settings such as slave *senzalas* and upper-class salons.

Recently, scholars of other colonial settings have insisted that the sentiment fostered through rearing children was a crucial adhesive in holding empires together.[10] Yet even though the affective ties that the Indian apprentices of Lima formed with their patrons or that which Ursula shared with her Indian maestra undoubtedly served as the social glue of colonial communities, the "sentimental" world of empire was comprised of more than affection, proximity, and dependency. This social world of child rearing was also, as the chapters on abandoned children in Havana, slave children in Brazil, and servant children in northern Mexico reveal, an ambit of violence, purposeful neglect, and labor exploitation.

Perhaps no other field of history has wrestled as long and hard with issues of love and abuse as has the history of childhood. But the historians who write in this volume, particularly those who study colonial Iberoamerica, must confront these issues not merely as necessary components in understanding what it meant to be a child before "modern times" but also as necessary components of the entire colonial enterprise.[11] Asking how everyday histories of sentiment, dependency, and familiarity balanced with the force and exploitation that made up the colonial economic and political order in Spanish America and Brazil is, therefore, a fourth alternative the region opens in the history of childhood. Future historians of childhood in colonial Latin America cannot simply assure their readers that adults in the past loved children; they must explain how that love could coexist with forms of imperial rule based on modern(izing) racial degradation, rigid hierarchy, and massive human enslavement.[12] They cannot simply assert that children were key actors in the stories of their own pasts; they must account for the larger context of violence and domination that limited even adults in the colonial setting.

The chapters collected in these pages present historical settings familiar in the history of early modern Iberia and colonial Latin America, such as charitable institutions, colonial labor systems, convents, and court tribunals. They also intersect with the classic themes in the history of childhood of sentiment, abuse, and "modernity." However, in the end, the history of childhood in Iberoamerica suggests that, within these settings and around these themes, the children who have been hidden in plain view all the while have something new to tell us: most importantly, that the adults who raised them were doing more than raising children; they were raising empires.

✦ NOTES ✦

1. Here, I am thinking of Tobias Hecht's 2002 volume, *Minor Omissions: Children in Latin American History and Society* (Madison: University of Wisconsin Press, 2002), to which I contributed an essay that began with the question of children's visibility in the historical record. Also see the comments on historiography in recent works such as Sonya Lipsett-Rivera, "Introduction: Children in the History of Latin America," *Journal of Family History* 23, no. 3 (1998): 221–24; Ann Twinam, *Public Lives, Private Secrets: Gender, Honor, Sexuality and Illegitimacy in Colonial Spanish America* (Stanford: Stanford University Press, 1999), 159; Cynthia E. Milton, "Wandering Waifs and Abandoned Babes: The Uses and Limits of Juvenile Welfare in Eighteenth-Century Audiencia of Quito," *Colonial Latin American Review* 13, no. 1 (June 2004): 103–28.

2. David Archard, *Children: Rights and Childhood* (New York: Routledge: 1993), 20–21.

3. Philippe Ariès, *Centuries of Childhood: A Social History of Family Life*, trans. Robert Baldick (New York: Vintage, 1962), 125, 413.

4. The most forceful condemnation of parents in the past was Lloyd de Mause's *The History of Childhood: The Evolution of Parent-Child Relationships as a Factor in History* (London: The Psychohistory Press, 1974). Also see Hugh Cunningham, *Children and Childhood in Western Society since 1500* (New York: Longman, 1995), 6. For the conflation of Ariès's claims about the absence of concepts of childhood with the "cruelty thesis" advanced by de Mause, see Archard, *Children*, 16–17.

5. For an overview of the stereotype of Spain as traditional and a new interpretation of the eighteenth and nineteenth centuries, see David Ringrose, *Spain, Europe and the "Spanish Miracle," 1700–1900* (Cambridge: Cambridge University Press, 1996). The discomfort with questions of Iberoamerican modernity was ready to break through as scholars and historians wrestled with, and sometimes embraced, postmodern and postcolonial theories. See, for example, Patricia Seed, "Colonial and Postcolonial Discourse," *Latin American Research Review* 23, no. 3 (1991): 181–200; Walter Mignolo, "Colonial and Postcolonial Discourse: Cultural Critique or Academic Colonialism?" *Latin American Research Review* 28, no. 3 (1993): 120–34; "The Postmodern Debate in Latin America," Thematic Issue of *boundary 2* 20, no. 3

(1993); Florencia Mallon, "The Promise and Dilemma of Subaltern Studies: Perspectives from Latin America," *American Historical Review* 99, no. 5 (1994): 1494. Also see John Beverley, "The Im/possibility of Politics: Subalternity, Modernity, Hegemony," in *The Latin American Subaltern Studies Reader*, ed. Ileana Rodríguez (Durham, NC: Duke University Press, 2001), 47–63.

6. Of course, studying "what went wrong" in Latin America is not precisely the same as forging a unique historiographical path, since it reinforces the myths and narratives of modernization, as Jeremy Adelman points out in "Latin America and World Histories: Old and New Approaches to the Pluribus and the Unum," *Hispanic American Historical Review* 84, no. 3 (2004): 403–4.

7. Notable recent contributions to this scholarship include Suzanne Desan, *The Family on Trial in Revolutionary France* (Berkeley: University of California Press, 2004); and Holly Brewer, *By Birth or Consent: Children, Law, and the Anglo-American Revolution in Authority* (Chapel Hill: University of North Carolina Press, 2005).

8. See N. Ray Hiner and Joseph M. Hawes, "Standing on Common Ground: Reflections on the History of Children and Childhood," in *Children in Historical and Comparative Perspective: An International Research Guide*, ed. N. Ray Hiner and Joseph M. Hawes (New York: Greenwood Press, 1991); Hugh Cunningham, "Histories of Childhood," *American Historical Review* 103, no. 4 (1998): 1195–96; Hecht, "Introduction," in *Minor Omissions*, especially 12.

9. Felipe Guamán Poma de Ayala, *Nueva crónica y buen gobierno*, comp. Francisco Carrillo (Lima: Editorial Horizonte, 1998), 146–47.

10. Ann Laura Stoler, *Carnal Knowledge and Imperial Power: Race and the Intimate in Colonial Rule* (Berkeley: University of California Press, 2002).

11. Although scholars of colonialism have long theorized about the role of domination in maintaining colonial order, the study of the role of affect is a relatively new, and controversial, endeavor. See Ann Laura Stoler's call to scholars of U.S. imperialism to consider intimacy and affect in "Tense and Tender Ties: The Politics of Comparison in North American History and (Post)Colonial Studies," *Journal of American History* 88, no. 3: 829–65; and the responses, particularly that written by the scholar of Spanish colonialism in northern New Spain, Ramón A. Gutiérrez, "What's Love Got to Do with It?" 866–70.

12. Indeed, the rejection of the "abuse" thesis has drawn many scholars of childhood into the historicist view that adult sentiment toward children in the past was no different than that of today, a dangerous flattening out of historical difference and the effect of historical context on sentiment that, I would argue, is especially problematic when taken up by scholars

of colonialism. For this critique leveled against the contributions in David Kertzer and Marzio Barbagli, eds., *The History of the Modern Family: Family Life in Early Modern Times, 1500–1789* (New Haven, CT: Yale University Press, 2001), see Joan Acocella, "Little People: When Did Children Become Children?" *The New Yorker* 79, no. 22 (August 18 and 25, 2003): 138–42.

Contributors

Ondina E. González, an independent scholar who holds a PhD in history from Emory University, has written on abandoned children in colonial Havana and is also coauthor of *Christianity in Latin America: A Historical Introduction* (2007).

Isabel dos Guimarães Sá is professor of history at the Universidade de Minho in Portugal. She is the author of several articles and chapters in Portuguese and English on child circulation and foundling homes in early modern Portugal, as well as the books *A circulação de crianças na Europa do Sul: O caso da Casa da Roda do Porto no século XVIII* (1995) and *Quando o rico se faz pobre: Misericórdias, caridade e poder no Império Português* (1997).

Elizabeth Anne Kuznesof is professor of Latin American history and the director of the Center of Latin American Studies at the University of Kansas. She received her PhD from the University of California at Berkeley and specializes in family history, quantitative methods, and Brazil, though her interests include all of colonial Latin America. She is the author of *Household Economy and Urban Development: São Paulo, 1765–1836* (1986), and she is presently writing a social and political history of the family in Latin America.

Bianca Premo is associate professor of Latin American history at Florida International University. She is the author of several articles and book chapters in Spanish and English on children, gender, and the law, as well as the prize-winning book *Children of the Father King: Youth, Authority and Legal Minority in Colonial Lima* (2005).

Jorge Rojas Flores is professor of history and social sciences at the Universidad de Talca and Universidad de Arte y Ciencias Sociales in Chile. A specialist on workers and childhood, his books include *Los niños cristaleros: Trabajo infantil en la industria. Chile, 1880–1950* (1996), *Moral y prácticas cívicas en los niños chilenos, 1880–1950* (2004), and *Los boy scouts en Chile: Mensajeros de nuevas auroras, 1909–1953* (2005).

Laura Shelton, assistant professor of history at Georgia Southern University, earned her doctorate at the University of Arizona. She is currently completing her first book, *Families in the Courtroom: Law, Community, and Gender in Northwestern Mexico, 1780–1850*.

Valentina Tikoff is assistant professor of history at DePaul University in Chicago, where she teaches European and Atlantic world history. Her research focuses on the history of children, the family, and charity in early modern Seville. In published work and conference papers, she also has explored issues of juvenile delinquency, education, and gender. She received her BA from Carleton College and MA and PhD from Indiana University.

Ann Twinam, professor of history at the University of Texas at Austin, received her PhD at Yale University. In addition to numerous articles and book chapters, she has authored *Miners, Merchants, and Farmers in Colonial Colombia* (1982), and *Public Lives, Private Secrets: Gender, Honor, Sexuality, and Illegitimacy in Colonial Spanish America* (1999), which was awarded the Thomas McGann Prize.

Teresa C. Vergara is completing a PhD in history at the University of Connecticut at Stors. She holds a master's degree from the Pontificia Universidad Católica in Lima, Peru, and her publications on the indigenous population of colonial Peru include "Migración y trabajo femenino: El caso de las indias en Lima," *Histórica* (1997).

Index

abandonment, 137–56, 168–71; as distinct from institutionalization, 41–62; historical studies of, 14–15; rates of, 142–43, 151; reasons for, 173. *See also* Casa de Niños Expósitos; Casa Joseph; circulation; foundling homes; foundlings; illegitimacy: as cause for abandonment

abuse, 230–32; theory of, 5, 240, 247n12. *See also* Ariès; punishment; violence

acculturation: of African slaves, 195–96; of indigenous children, 76, 77, 85–86

adoption: compared to circulation, 29, 220, 230–31. *See also* circulation; *criados*

adulterous children, 23, 173. *See also* discrimination; *gracias al sacar*; illegitimacy; *limpieza de sangre*

affection: assumed absent in premodern times, 5, 240; between masters and *criados*, 230; between masters and slave children, 208–9; physical displays of, 116–17. *See also* fathers; guardians; mothers

Africa: culture and society; 189–91; rearing traditions from, 189–91, 200

African-descent, peoples of: 187–210; as apprentices, 200; as foundlings, 141; culture, 196. *See also* slaves

age: and institutional policy, 46, 49–50, 144; at deposit, 142–43, 180; hierarchies based on, 92–93; for marriage, 22, 36n5, 37n19, 127, 134n53; for sacraments, 22; for work, 32, 78, 80, 83, 206, 223; of children in slave trade, 191–93, 212n21. *See also* illegitimacy